The Politics of Everyday Life in Vichy France

In this book, Fogg examines the effects of material distress on attitudes toward the Vichy government and on the treatment of outsiders in France during the Second World War. She contends that the period's severe material shortages and refugee situation fundamentally reshaped France's social structure. Material conditions also created alliances and divisions within the French population that undermined the Vichy regime's legitimacy. Fogg argues that shortages helped define the relationship between citizens and the state, created the very definition of who was an "insider" and an "outsider" in local communities, and shaped the manner in which native and refugee populations interacted.

Fogg's research reveals that French residents proved to be more pragmatic than ideological in their daily dealings with outsiders, with some surprising effects: Natives welcomed "quintessential" outsiders who provided an economic advantage to local communities, while French "insiders" faced discrimination.

Shannon L. Fogg received her Ph.D. from the University of Iowa in 2003. She has been an assistant professor at Missouri University of Science and Technology (formerly the University of Missouri-Rolla) since 2004. Her research has appeared in journals such as *Holocaust and Genocide Studies* and *French Historical Studies*.

The Politics of Everyday Life in Vichy France

Foreigners, Undesirables, and Strangers

SHANNON L. FOGG
Missouri University of Science and Technology

CAMBRIDGE UNIVERSITY PRESS
Cambridge, New York, Melbourne, Madrid, Cape Town, Singapore,
São Paulo, Delhi, Dubai, Tokyo, Meixco City

Cambridge University Press
32 Avenue of the Americas, New York, NY 10013-2473, USA

www.cambridge.org
Information on this title: www.cambridge.org/9780521269506

© Shannon L. Fogg 2009

This publication is in copyright. Subject to statutory exception
and to the provisions of relevant collective licensing agreements,
no reproduction of any part may take place without the written
permission of Cambridge University Press.

First published 2009
First paperback edition 2011

A catalog record for this publication is available from the British Library.

Library of Congress Cataloging in Publication Data

Fogg, Shannon Lee.
The politics of everyday life in Vichy France : foreigners,
undesirables, and strangers / Shannon L. Fogg. – 1st ed.
p. cm.
Includes bibliographical references and index.
ISBN 978-0-521-89944-4 (hardback)
1. France – Politics and government –1940–1945. 2. France – History –German occupation, 1940–1945. 3. France – Social conditions –20th century. I. Title.
DC397.F595   2008
944.081'6–dc22   2008025499

ISBN 978-0-521-89944-4 Hardback
ISBN 978-0-521-12912-1 Paperback

Cambridge University Press has no responsibility for the persistence or accuracy of URLs
for external or third-party Internet Web sites referred to in this publication and does not
guarantee that any content on such Web sites is, or will remain, accurate or appropriate.

For Mom and Tess

Table of Contents

List of Maps and Figures — page ix
List of Abbreviations — xi
Preface — xiii

Introduction — 1

1. "Life has never been so good": Shortages, Public Opinion, and Urban-Rural Interactions — 19
2. "Where we are from, that is for pigs": Alsatian Refugees in the Interior — 56
3. "They are undesirables": Gypsies during World War II — 85
4. "At any price": Housing, the Black Market, and Jewish Daily Life — 111
5. "The vast heart of mankind knows no boundaries": Refuge in Jewish Children's Homes — 151

Conclusion — 188

Bibliography — 197
Index — 219

List of Maps and Figures

MAPS

1	France (1940–44)	*page* xix
2	French departments in 1940	xx
3	Limousin region	xxi
4	Jewish children's homes in the Creuse	xxii

FIGURES

1	Loading hay, Creuse	43
2	Gypsy children	105
3	Receipt for worker's identity card stamped "JUIF"	133
4	Château de Chabannes	152
5	Jewish refugee children working at Le Masgelier	169

List of Abbreviations

ADC	Archives départementales de la Creuse (Departmental Archives of the Creuse)
ADHV	Archives départementales de la Haute-Vienne (Departmental Archives of the Haute-Vienne)
AN	Archives nationales, Paris (National Archives, Paris)
BDIC	Bibliothèque de documentation internationale contemporaine (Contemporary International Documentation Library)
CAHS	Center for Advanced Holocaust Studies
CDJC	Centre de documentation juive contemporaine (Center for Contemporary Jewish Documentation)
CGQJ	Commissariat général aux questions juives (Commissariat General for Jewish Affairs)
GTE	Groupement de travailleurs étrangers (Foreign Workers' Unit)
ORT	Organisation-reconstruction-travail (Professional Retraining and Reorientation Organization)
OSE	Oeuvre de secours aux enfants (Children's Relief Agency)
PCF	Parti Communiste Français (French Communist Party)
PQJ	Police aux questions juives (Police for Jewish Affairs)
RG	Renseignements généraux (General Bureau of Information)
SEC	Section d'enquête et de contrôle (Division of Investigations and Inspections)
SHGN	Service Historique de la Gendarmerie Nationale (Historical Service of the National Gendarmerie)
STO	Service du travail obligatoire (Compulsory Labor Service)

UGIF	Union générale des israélites de France (General Union of Israelites in France)
USHMM	United States Holocaust Memorial Museum
YIVO	Archives of the YIVO Institute for Jewish Research

Preface

This book really began in 1993 when I spent a semester studying France and World War II as part of the Normandy Scholars Program at Texas A&M University. Studying French history, politics, literature, and film introduced me to a whole new world. A month spent studying at Le Mémorial de Caen and visiting war sites throughout Normandy cemented my love for the period and for France. I learned about the Vichy government and French collaboration with the Nazis for the first time that fall. But from the beginning, it was the daily lives of individuals who experienced the war in France that grabbed my attention. Several professors at Texas A&M encouraged me to pursue graduate studies and suggested that I contact Professor Sarah Farmer at the University of Iowa. This proved to be a suggestion that would shape the direction of my future research.

When it came time to choose a dissertation topic, I still felt passionate about studying the lives of ordinary French men and women. Professor Farmer supported my interest in examining the topic of resistance from the broader, more inclusive perspective H. R. Kedward suggests in his book *In Search of the Maquis*. Kedward notes that organized Resistance relied on the support of local residents (especially women) in ways that have yet to be fully researched.[1] He also points to the continuing debate over the role food shortages played in contributing to French resistance to the Vichy regime.[2] It seemed that studying the daily material concerns of the French

---

[1] H. R. Kedward, *In Search of the Maquis: Rural Resistance in Southern France, 1942–1944* (Oxford: Clarendon Press, 1993), 88–90.
[2] Ibid., p. 7.

people would thus provide a new perspective on the resistance/collaboration debate.

Using material shortages as the prism through which to examine the infrastructure that supported Resistance requires an examination of everyday life from a local perspective. The rural Limousin region of central France became an obvious choice due to the region's agricultural production and the presence of active, guerrilla bands during the war. Research in France, however, quickly led me to realize that shortages and everyday life had political implications that went well beyond issues related to organized Resistance. Indeed, the social fabric's stability and Vichy's legitimacy rested, in large part, on daily issues surrounding provisioning.

Scholars have focused on how Vichy's political ideology shaped daily life, but they have not fully explored how daily life shaped politics. The general tendency toward strict political history throughout Europe led scholars such as Alf Lüdtke and Detlev J. K. Peukert to think about the relationship between politics and history differently by focusing on the everyday.[3] The sources revealed that there was much to be learned about the history of France during World War II by examining the quotidian – the study of the everyday attempts to explain how abstract laws and ideologies take on meaning in daily practice. It puts the emphasis on individuals rather than on abstract processes or politics broadly defined. As Alice Kaplan and Kristin Ross explain, "The Political [...] is hidden in the everyday, exactly where it is most obvious: in the contradictions of lived experience, in the most banal and repetitive gestures of everyday life."[4] The banality of daily life has meant it has been neglected as a legitimate aspect of scholarship until recently.[5] A range of newer works, however, reveals the exciting possibilities of studying the quotidian. This study follows in the footsteps of the growing number of books that examine the everyday in unusual times, such as Andrew Stuart Bergerson's *Ordinary Germans in Extraordinary Times*, Sheila Fitzpatrick's *Everyday Stalinism*, and Maureen Healy's *Vienna*

---

[3] Alf Lüdtke, editor, *The History of Everyday Life: Reconstructing Historical Experiences and Ways of Life* translated by William Templer (Princeton, New Jersey: Princeton University Press, 1995) and Detlev J. K. Peukert, *Inside Nazi Germany: Conformity, Opposition, and Racism in Everyday Life* translated by Richard Deveson (New Haven, Connecticut and London: Yale University Press, 1987).

[4] Alice Kaplan and Kristin Ross, "Introduction" *Yale French Studies* 73 (1987): 3.

[5] See Robert Gildea and the Team, "Introduction" in *Surviving Hitler and Mussolini: Daily Life in Occupied Europe* edited by Robert Gildea, Olivier Wieviorka and Anette Warring (Oxford and New York: Berg, 2006), 5–6 for reasons for this negligence. Gildea also provides background on the evolution of the history of everyday life as an academic field on pp. 6–9.

and the Fall of the Habsburg Empire.⁶ The following pages use the politics of daily life not only to examine ordinary French residents' support for and rejection of the Vichy regime but also to challenge traditional ideas about xenophobia and antisemitism by exploring the daily construction of "outsider" status during the war.

Some of the best work on France and the Second World War is found in regional studies. The experience of war and occupation varied depending upon one's place of residence, making generalizations about life in France difficult and unwise. The daily experiences of people living in the unoccupied Limousin differed dramatically from those of housewives in occupied Paris, of coalminers in the German-administered northern department of the Pas-de-Calais, or of Michelin employees in Clermont-Ferrand living in Vichy's shadow.⁷ People's lives in the strategically important and German-occupied Loire Valley bore little resemblance to life in Nîmes, where wine and religion had dominated daily lives for centuries.⁸ Discussions of wartime scarcity in these works often appear in early chapters as the background for the discussion of topics such as resistance or public opinion. Only by focusing on a local level does the importance of pragmatic concerns become clear in other areas, such as social relations and the implementation of the "Final Solution" in France.

I owe thanks to many institutions and individuals for their support throughout the long course of this project. At the University of Iowa, a Stanley Fellowship for Graduate Research Abroad funded my first trip to the French archives and allowed me to find the materials that shaped my argument. A T. Anne Cleary Fellowship from the University of Iowa Graduate College and a Lafore Fellowship from the Department of History supported a year of research in Paris, Limoges, and Guéret. A Seashore

---

⁶ Andrew Stuart Bergerson, *Ordinary Germans in Extraordinary Times: The Nazi Revolution in Hildesheim* (Bloomington and Indianapolis: Indiana University Press, 2004); Sheila Fitzpatrick, *Everyday Stalinism: Ordinary Life in Extraordinary Times, Soviet Russia in the 1930s* (New York and Oxford: Oxford University Press, 2000); Maureen Healy, *Vienna and the Fall of the Habsburg Empire: Total War and Everyday Life in World War I* (Cambridge: Cambridge University Press, 2004).

⁷ On Paris, see Dominique Veillon, *Vivre et survivre en France 1939–1947* (Paris: Editions Payot & Rivages, 1995). For the Pas-de-Calais, see Lynne Taylor, *Between Resistance and Collaboration: Popular Protest in Northern France, 1940–1945* (New York: St Martin's Press, 2000). For Clermont-Ferrand, see John F. Sweets, *Choices in Vichy France: The French under Nazi Occupation* (New York and Oxford: Oxford University Press, 1994).

⁸ Robert Gildea, *Marianne in Chains: In Search of the German Occupation 1940–1945* (London, Basingstoke and Oxford: Macmillan, 2002); Robert Zaretsky, *Nîmes at War: Religion, Politics, and Public Opinion in the Gard, 1938–1944* (University Park: The Pennsylvania State University Press, 1995).

Dissertation-Year Fellowship allowed me to dedicate my time to writing without the added pressures of teaching. The careful reading and constructive criticisms of my work in its various stages by Sarah Farmer, Sarah Hanley, and Lisa Heineman have been invaluable. I thank them for their unselfishness, their consistent encouragement, and their continued enthusiasm.

In France, archivists, librarians, and organizations all facilitated my research, and permission to see classified documents further enriched this work. My thanks to the directors, archivists, and librarians of the Archives Départementales de la Creuse and de la Haute-Vienne, the Archives Nationales, the Bibliothèque Nationale de France, and the Centre de Documentation Juive Contemporaine. At the Oeuvre de Secours aux Enfants (OSE), I have to thank Jean-François Guthmann and Michèle Allali for permission to see the organization's records. Jean-Claude Kuperminc at the Bibliothèque de l'Alliance israélite universelle allowed me to view the OSE documents in the Alliance's library. At the Service Historique de la Gendarmerie Nationale, I owe thanks to Laurent Veyssière and his staff.

Without a Charles H. Revson Foundation Fellowship for Archival Research from the Center for Advanced Holocaust Studies (CAHS) at the United States Holocaust Memorial Museum (USHMM), this book would not exist in its present form. As a visiting scholar, I found a rich archival collection, a group of scholars with whom I could share my work, and an environment that made researching and working on such a difficult topic easier. Subsequent research workshops hosted by the CAHS allowed me to work intensively with prominent scholars such as Renée Poznanski, John F. Sweets, and Nechama Tec – a wonderful opportunity for any graduate student. These workshops helped me to refine my ideas and think about my work from different perspectives. At the Museum, I owe special thanks to: Vadim Altskan, Suzanne Brown-Fleming, Martin Dean, Robert M. Ehrenreich, Michael Gelb, Severin Hochberg, Radu Ioanid, Aaron Kornblum, Wendy Lower, Ann Mann Millin, Joan Ringelheim, Claire Rosenson, Paul A. Shapiro, and Madeline Vadkerty. Peggy Frankston in Paris pointed me to invaluable archival collections. (However, the views expressed in this book, and the context in which images from the Photo Archives are used, do not necessarily reflect the views or policy of, nor imply approval or endorsement by, the USHMM.)

I can never fully express my gratitude to the men and women who spent part of their youths in the Limousin and who so openly shared their experiences, memories, and documents with me. I only hope that I have done justice to their stories.

A Research Board Grant from the University of Missouri System and support from the College of Arts and Sciences at the University of Missouri-Rolla (now Missouri S&T) made it possible for me to have a semester out of the classroom to finish the book's revisions. Thank you also to my colleagues in the Department of History and Political Science.

I would also like to thank the editors of *French Historical Studies* and *Holocaust and Genocide Studies* for allowing the republication of material in this book. Earlier versions of Chapter 3 and Chapter 4 have appeared in these journals respectively as " 'They Are Undesirables': Local and National Responses to Gypsies during World War II" and "Refugees and Indifference: The Effects of Shortages on Attitudes towards Jews in France's Limousin Region during World War II."

Many friends have provided intellectual and emotional support throughout the years of researching, writing, and revising: Michelle Bellomy, Jennifer Blackmon, Stacy Denison, Kate Drowne, Karen Egonis, Michele Ford, Allison Gillett, Nat Godley, Kim Henthorn, Mike Innis-Jimenez, Simon Kitson, Joelle Neulander, Kathy Northcut, Becky Pulju, Dana Quartana, Michelle Rhoades, Jesse Spohnholz, Nick Villanueva, and Rebecca Wittmann. The Lancaster-Muckenfuss family graciously welcomed me into their lives and helped make the research possible.

Most importantly, I have to thank my family. My parents taught me to love books and learning when I was young and have been a constant source of strength, love, and support. Heather and Chris bring lots of laughter and perspective to my life. Stéphane's love, energy, patience, understanding, and belief in me have sustained me throughout this project. Tess, through her arrival, and Mom, through her departure, have reminded me of what is most important in life. Thank you all for being the best part of my daily life.

MAP 1. France (1940–44).

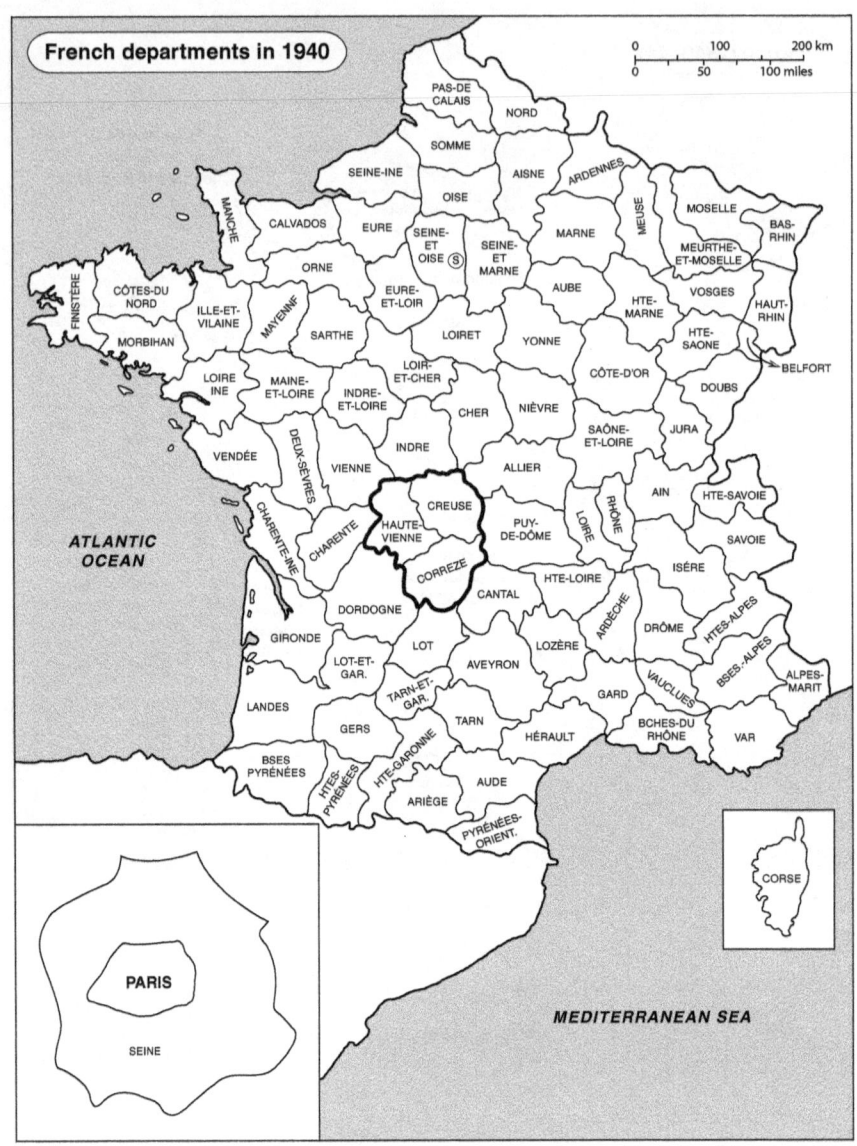

MAP 2. French departments in 1940.

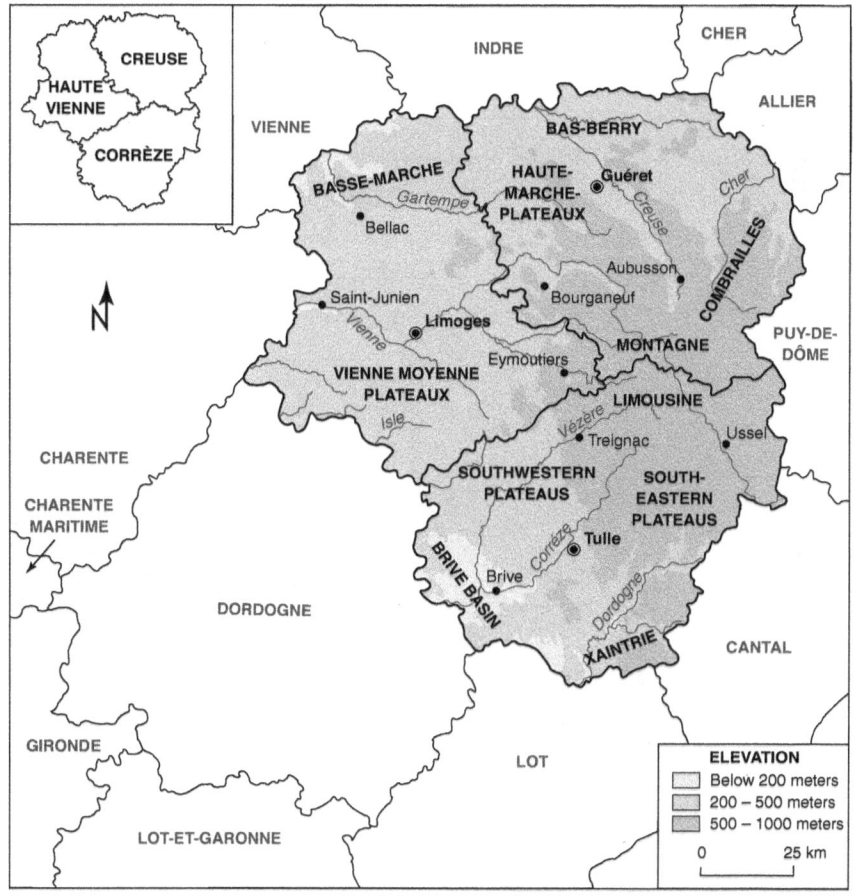

MAP 3. Limousin region.

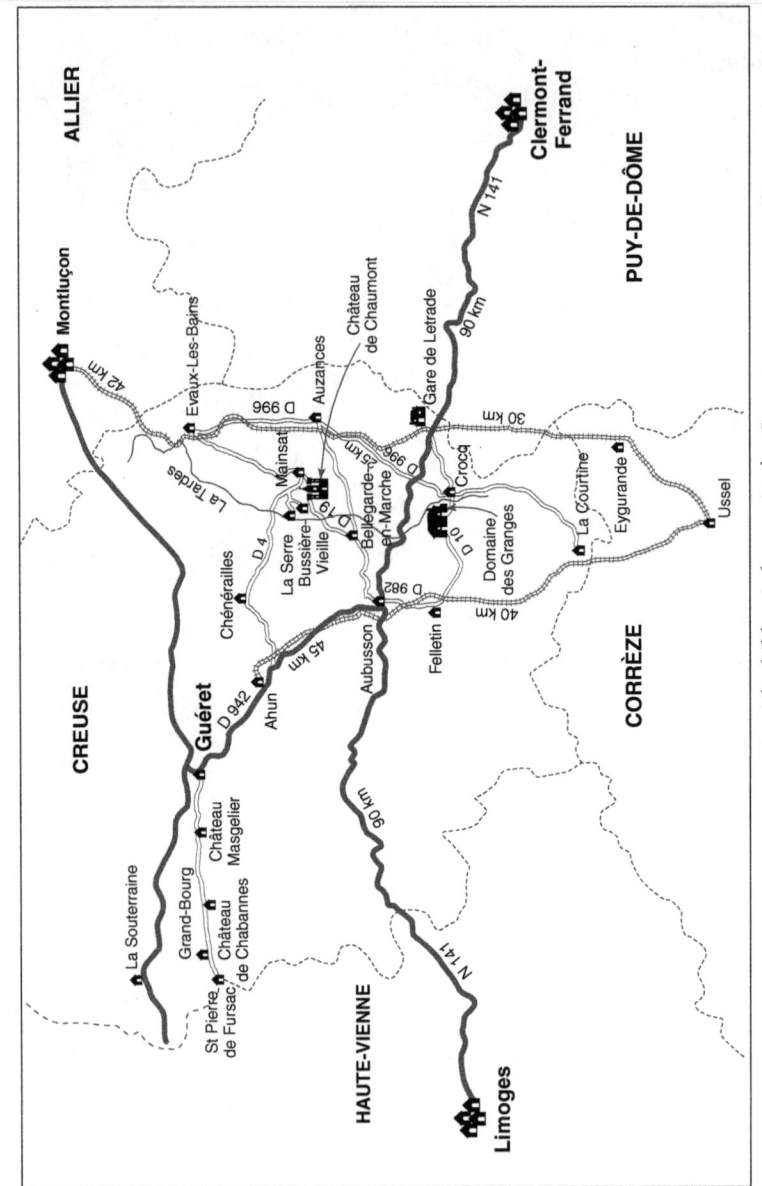

MAP 4. Jewish children's homes in the Creuse.

Introduction

"First place in the population's concerns": The Politics of Everyday Life and the Second World War in France

Charged with monitoring public opinion during the Second World War, prefects in the rural Limousin region of central France regularly reported "supply difficulties still hold first place in the population's concerns."[1] The Vichy regime also employed the *Direction des Contrôles Techniques* in a further attempt to gauge the public's mood. Inspectors opened and read the letters French residents sent each other and then relayed the compiled information to government officials. Complaints about the inadequacy of daily rations and supplies in general appeared in around 5 percent of the letters authorities read in 1941, and just days before the Allied invasion of Normandy in 1944, 24 percent of the recorded opinions mentioned shortages. Even though these numbers may appear modest, provisioning occupied letter writers more than any other issue facing the public throughout the course of the war.[2] The

---

[1] Archives Nationales (hereafter AN) F 1c III – 1197. Rapport mensuel d'information du 1er avril au 30 avril 1942 (May 4, 1942). See also reports dated March 4, 1942, April 5, 1942, June 5, 1942, August 5, 1942, etc. For the Corrèze, see similar comments in AN F 1c III – 1147. See reports from May 2, 1941, May 31, 1941, and December 1943. For the Creuse, see AN F 1c III – 1150, reports dated March 1, 1941, and October 2, 1941. The prefect for the Limoges region also noted the general preoccupation with food in his reports. See AN F 1c III – 1200, reports dated June 15, 1942, July 11, 1942, and September 6, 1942, for examples. John F. Sweets notes that in the fall of 1941, the minister of the interior wrote that life "is dominated essentially – certain Prefects go so far as to write in their reports 'uniquely' – by material preoccupations always concerning the same objects: food, heating, clothing, shoes." Quoted and translated in John F. Sweets, *Choices in Vichy France: The French under Nazi Occupation* (New York and Oxford: Oxford University Press, 1994), 165.

[2] Prisoners of war, the most-mentioned topic after food, usually figured in less than 2 percent of all intercepted letters. For 1941, see AN F7 14926 – Direction des Contrôles Techniques. Secrétariat d'Etat à la Guerre – Cabinet du Ministre – Service Civil des Contrôles Techniques. For 1944, see Inspection générale/régionale de Limoges. Commission de St. Amand Montrond. Rapport Statistique Hebdomadaire. Période du 25 au 31 Mai 1944 (June 3, 1944).

hardships of extreme scarcity also deeply mark the memoirs, testimonies, and memories of ordinary people living in France during the war. Claire Hsu Accomando's account of her childhood in German-occupied Normandy begins with a description of her mother's battle to get the children to eat rutabagas, a staple of their diet, yet again. In an interview conducted fifty-five years after the war's end, Liane Reif-Lehrer vividly remembered the humiliation of being forced to beg for bread when her family's ration coupons ran out. The duty fell to the 5-year-old because bakers in Limoges found it hard to resist the cute little girl with curly brown hair.[3]

Most studies, however, have ignored the day-to-day political effects of shortages in France between 1939 and 1944. The harsh realities of daily life often serve as the context for political and ideological studies rather than as an object of examination.[4] I reverse this perspective to demonstrate the ways in which food became a personal *and* a political issue during the Second World War. Shortages framed daily interactions, influenced governmental and personal decisions, and shaped public attitudes. After the state assumed responsibility for the distribution of goods through rationing and price controls, every attempt to circumvent the restrictions could be – and usually was – considered a political act. The intersection of abstract ideologies with physical realities led to creative and often-contradictory individual responses that directly affected the French political and social structure in ways that made shortages more than a background concern.

The pursuit of ever-decreasing, precious goods forced a variety of strangers to interact on a daily basis, creating tensions and alliances between individuals as a result of material concerns. An examination of these local-level dealings reveals the ways in which shortages shaped, created, and defined interactions between different social, religious, and cultural

---

[3] Claire Hsu Accomando, *Love and Rutabaga: A Remembrance of the War Years* (New York: St. Martin's Press, 1993), ix–x. See also Bonnie G. Smith's *Confessions of a Concierge: Madame Lucie's History of Twentieth-Century France* (New Haven, Connecticut and London: Yale University Press, 1985); *Journal de Louis Aron, directeur de La Maison Israélite de Refuge pour l'enfance Neuilly-sur-Seine 1939, Crocq (Creuse) 1939–1942, Chaumont (Creuse) 1942–1944* edited by Serge Klarsfeld with Annette Zaidman (Paris: Association "Les Fils et Filles des Déportés Juifs de France" and "The Beate Klarsfeld Foundation," 1998); and Isaac Levendel, *Not the Germans Alone: A Son's Search for the Truth of Vichy* (Evanston, Illinois: Northwestern University Press, 1999) for additional examples of the strong presence of shortages in personal accounts. Liane Reif-Lehrer, interview with the author (August 7, 2000). See also Liane Reif-Lehrer, videotaped testimony, Archives of the United States Holocaust Memorial Museum (hereafter USHMM) RG-50-030*186.

[4] See for example Chapter 1 "War, Occupation, and Society" in Sweets, *Choices in Vichy France*.

groups during the war. The wealthy continued to fare better than workers or civil servants living on a fixed income as prices for basic necessities soared and the black market flourished. The wartime shortages also dramatically changed traditional social structures and inverted concepts of privilege as peasants, with their direct access to meat, vegetables, milk, and eggs, claimed a greater standing in society. But even more than socioeconomic status, one's position as a foreigner, "undesirable,"[5] or stranger in a community could affect access to food despite the equality implied by rationing and the state's elaborate system of tickets, cards, and registration. An individual's ability to negotiate the parallel economic world increasingly depended upon personal relationships with those who had access to material goods rather than usual provisioning practices. People on the margins of society such as evacuees, refugees, Jews, and Gypsies had fewer connections and thus fewer opportunities for extra-legal access to food and other supplies.

The experiences of these outsiders are central to understanding Vichy politics and policies and thus form the backbone of this book. Examining the daily interactions between natives and outsiders in the Limousin as shaped by material concerns reveal both strains and alliances in society. A full understanding of the implications of shortages for politics, communities, and families in France during the war requires a comparative, local approach. Therefore, each chapter focuses on a specific group considered to be foreigners, undesirables, or strangers in the Limousin in the attempt both to understand daily life in a specific place and to explore more broadly the ways men and women opposed and/or supported the Vichy regime, developed coping strategies, and related to others in their daily struggle for survival. Studying outsiders in rural communities more generally – Alsatian evacuees, city dwellers in search of food, non-Jewish foreign refugees, Jewish children – allows us to determine the extent to which the treatment of officially persecuted groups was unique or part of a larger phenomenon of materially influenced exclusion.

The general history of France during World War II is now well-known.[6] What is less familiar is the history of daily life during the war and the effects

---

[5] During the war years, the Vichy government designated certain groups as 'undesirable.' Throughout the text, I use the word without quotation marks, but it should be understood that the use of the term refers to Vichy's interpretation and view of these groups.
[6] Two recent syntheses of the Vichy period are Julian Jackson, *France: The Dark Years, 1940–1944* (Oxford: Oxford University Press, 2001) and Richard Vinen, *The Unfree French: Life under the Occupation* (New Haven, Connecticut and London: Yale University Press, 2006).

of scarcity on the social fabric. The political history of the war – the French army's swift defeat, the German occupation, the division of France into zones, the establishment of the collaborationist Vichy regime, and the implementation of its exclusionary National Revolution – cannot be separated from the period's material history. Examining the politics of everyday life, which combines the ideological and the material, thus helps explain the relationship between the public and the French state during the war, clarifies changes in public opinion, and demonstrates how the exclusion of foreigners, Gypsies, and Jews from the national community occurred on a daily basis.

WAR AND SHORTAGES

Shortages of food, clothing, primary resources, and heating materials began with the declaration of war against Germany on September 3, 1939, and eventually touched everyone in France. One could avoid becoming involved in politics, but one could not avoid shortages. In the war's early months, the government of the Third Republic diverted supplies from the home front to the mobilized soldiers protecting France's borders.[7] After the French army's swift defeat and the signing of an armistice in June 1940, Nazi officials demanded that the defeated nation provide agricultural and industrial products to Germany as part of the rational exploitation of the country's economic resources. Furthermore, the northern and coastal portions of France directly occupied by German troops produced the majority of the country's coal, steel, textiles, cereals, milk, sugar, and meat.[8] The terms of the armistice also required Marshal Philippe Pétain's government to pay occupation costs at the rate of twenty million Reichsmarks per day. To fulfill these obligations, additional goods were diverted to Germany. By the end of the war, 2.4 million metric tons of wheat, 891,000 metric tons of meat, and 1.4 million hectoliters of milk had been transferred from France to Germany.[9]

---

[7] The first official restrictions were introduced in November 1939 in order to provide more meat for the mobilized troops. See Dominique Veillon, *Vivre et survivre en France 1939–1947* (Paris: Editions Payot & Rivages, 1995), 36–7, and Hanna Diamond, *Women and the Second World War in France 1939–1948: Choices and Constraints* (London: Longman, 1999), 50.

[8] Polymeris Voglis, "Surviving Hunger: Life in the Cities and the Countryside during the Occupation" in *Surviving Hitler and Mussolini: Daily Life in Occupied Europe* edited by Robert Gildea, Olivier Wieviorka, and Anette Warring (Oxford and New York: Berg, 2006), 17, 20.

[9] Statistics cited in Sarah Fishman, *The Battle for Children: World War II, Youth Crime, and Juvenile Justice in Twentieth-Century France* (Cambridge, Massachusetts and London: Harvard University Press, 2002), 54.

Introduction

As a consequence of the resulting shortages, only 25 percent of the population had sufficient amounts of food, and 55 percent of the French people found provisioning difficult or nearly impossible.[10]

The Vichy government introduced rationing in September 1940 in order to help fulfill German requisitions and to redistribute basic necessities among all French residents. Ration cards provided 1,800 calories a day per person when they first appeared, although the League of Nations estimated that the average adult needed 2,400 to 2,800 daily calories. The number of calories provided by ration cards fell to 1,700 by 1942 and went as low as 900 calories per day for adults as shortages worsened over the course of the war.[11] In principle, age and occupation determined the only differences in amounts of certain goods allocated to individuals. Adults between the ages of 21 and 70 (Category A) received a standard ration, although the amount of goods considered standard varied over the course of the war.[12] Workers who performed heavy labor and fell within the adult age range (Category T) received tickets for supplemental amounts of bread, meat, fats, and wine. Agricultural laborers (Category C) and rural residents were expected to provide for themselves from their land and therefore received a reduced ration. The elderly older than age 70 (Category V) also received less bread than adults, but had a right to slightly more sugar and milk. Children younger than 21 were divided into four different categories

---

[10] Michel Cépède, *Agriculture et Alimentation en France durant la IIe Guerre Mondiale* (Paris: Editions M-Th. Génin, 1961), 372. Cépède estimates that 25 percent of the population, primarily rural farmers, had sufficient food; 20 percent, usually rural, nonagricultural inhabitants, were less well-off but still had relatively easy access to necessary products; 25 percent found provisioning difficult, especially those living in smaller urban areas or people without the means to supplement their rations; and 30 percent residing in large urban areas were extremely disadvantaged.

[11] Cépède, *Agriculture et Alimentation*, p. 151. Category V (the elderly) received even less at the lowest point. Sarah Fishman estimates that "people lacked one-quarter to one-half the necessary daily calories." See Fishman, *We Will Wait: Wives of French Prisoners of War, 1940–1945* (New Haven, Connecticut and London: Yale University Press, 1991), 60 and footnote 16.

[12] As an example, the ration cards distributed in September 1940 came with coupons allowing the following amounts of food: Coupon 1: 350 grams of bread per day; Coupon 2: 500 grams of sugar per month; Coupon 3: 300 grams of coffee blend per month (except children); Coupon 4: 250 grams of pasta per week; Coupon 5: 100 grams of rice per month (children only); Coupon 6: 50 grams of cheese per week; Coupon 7: 100 grams of fatty materials per week; Coupon 8: 360 grams per week of beef, pork, charcuterie, and meat conserves; Coupon 9: 125 grams of soap per month; and Coupon 10: milk. See "Les nouvelles measures de rationnement," *Le Courrier de la Creuse* 65 (September 22, 1940): 1. Variations were published in local newspapers as well as in the *Journal Officiel de l'Etat Français*.

based on age (Categories E, J1, J2, and J3), each of which received some supplemental goods such as sugar, chocolate, jam, and milk.

A ration card did not guarantee that an individual would receive the amount of goods to which he or she was entitled, however. Increasing shortages meant that items disappeared from shelves before everyone's needs were fulfilled. The imprisonment of millions of French soldiers and the physical disruption resulting from the war effort decreased domestic agricultural production significantly. At the same time, British blockades deprived the country of coal supplies and other imports such as coffee, sugar, wool, and cotton. The Allied invasion of North Africa in November 1942 further limited French access to fresh fruits and vegetables. The Germans' subsequent occupation of the "free" zone led to even greater housing shortages and increased competition for scarce items. Allied bombings destroyed even more residences, farmland, and industry. Prohibitive prices also prevented some families from obtaining the items they needed or wanted despite their ration tickets. The search for adequate food supplies occupied every French family's time, drained its income, and became a daily obsession.

Under such conditions, the creation of a parallel economy was inevitable. Individuals turned to the gray market, the black market, and the "Système D" when the government consistently failed to deliver promised goods. On the gray market, items were sold at a price moderately above the legal price, usually to friends or family members. The government tolerated such exchanges as a means to supplement meager rations. The black market had rare goods at a significant mark-up and was available to those with the economic resources and connections to black marketeers. Vichy defined the black market as any "transaction, action, or economic exchange that constitutes an infraction against a state regulation." The proliferation of regulations related to provisioning under Vichy meant that black market activities included, but were not limited to selling or buying items above the legal price; hoarding, selling, or buying items without the proper exchange of ration tickets; and using counterfeit ration documents.[13] The term "Système D" was short for the *système débrouillard*, or making do. Resourcefulness and the ability to make the most of relationships or the goods one had were valued. Such activities could include gardening, raising rabbits and chickens, purchasing goods on the black market, bartering, or making trips to the countryside. These survival tactics often included technically illegal exchanges and challenged the government's authority on a daily basis.

---

[13] Paul Sanders, *Histoire du marché noir 1940–1946* (Paris: Perrin, 2001), 14.

Scholars have explored shortages' political implications in different time periods and other countries in greater depth than examinations of France during the Second World War. Studies of scarcity and the Great War of 1914–1918 often emphasize the political nature of everyday events in total wars in order to challenge "still-dominant assumptions regarding the nature of politics itself as representing a narrow terrain of activity, largely separated from the rest of everyday life, practiced only at particular moments and often by limited segments of society."[14] Scholars utilizing this broader definition of politics have convincingly demonstrated the political importance of material concerns. In World War I Germany, changes in the relationship between state and society based on the intersection of food, identity, and politics played an important part in the German revolution of November 1918. Scarcity also directly contributed to the Habsburg Empire's collapse and the Russian tsar's downfall.[15] During the Great War, the belligerent nations' governments asked citizens to sacrifice in order to sustain the war effort, but some governments' failure to respond to citizens' material needs ultimately undermined their authority, leading to military defeat and governmental collapse. In France, restrictions, prohibitive prices, and the rationing of basic foodstuffs did not begin until 1917, leading at least one historian to conclude that "inconveniences were rarely insupportable [and] the economic problems there were did not provoke major reversals of public opinion or changes in behaviour."[16] The French local and national governments' ability to ease economic and provisioning problems prevented any loss of legitimacy.

If the French Third Republic managed to survive the Great War's material difficulties relatively unscathed, the same cannot be said for the Vichy regime during World War II. The differences between the conflicts, both

---

[14] Belinda J. Davis, *Home Fires Burning: Food, Politics, and Everyday Life in World War I Berlin* (Chapel Hill and London: The University of North Carolina Press, 2000), 3.
[15] Davis, *Home Fires Burning*. Davis also addresses this theme of political legitimacy in "Food Scarcity and the Empowerment of the Female Consumer in World War I Berlin" in *The Sex of Things: Gender and Consumption in Historical Perspective* edited by Victoria de Grazia with Ellen Furlough (Berkeley: University of California Press, 1996) and in her chapter with Thierry Bonzon, "Feeding the Cities" in *Capital Cities at War: Paris, London, Berlin 1914–1919* edited by Jay Winter and Jean-Louis Robert (Cambridge: Cambridge University Press, 1997). For a study of the impact of shortages on the collapse of the Austro-Hungarian Empire, see Maureen Healy, *Vienna and the Fall of the Habsburg Empire: Total War and Everyday Life in World War I* (Cambridge: Cambridge University Press, 2004). On Russia, see Barbara Alpern Engel, "Not by Bread Alone: Subsistence Riots in Russia during World War I" *Journal of Modern History* 69 (December 1997): 696–721.
[16] Jean-Jacques Becker, *The Great War and the French People* translated by Arnold Pomerans and introduced by Jay Winter (Leamington Spa, Heidelberg, Dover, New Hampshire: Berg, 1985), 149.

physical and ideological, help explain how the Third Republic managed to maintain public support while Marshal Pétain's government increasingly lost it. During the First World War, women and the men left behind managed to maintain agricultural production, and the nation continued to have reasonable access to imported goods. Even though prices for basic necessities climbed steadily throughout the war, bread, the nation's food staple, was not officially rationed until January 29, 1918.[17] France during the Second World War experienced rationing and restrictions of many products within months of the war's start. The material difficulties worsened throughout the war, and the problems lacked an acceptable justification. Civilians during the Great War compared their hardships to those of the men in the trenches and found life on the home front relatively manageable. People thus felt a moral responsibility to endure the material shortages at home as long as the men at the front had to face the horrors of war.

Vichy also attempted to equate material shortages with a moral imperative, but, as the following pages will show, without the same success. The actual fighting of the Second World War lasted only six weeks, and civilians found it difficult to accept sacrifices for the abstract "good of the nation" or in order to sustain the German war effort. With the end of fighting, focus shifted to the everyday ideological battles of the new regime's National Revolution. The home front and internal politics thus took on greater significance making a study of shortages and their political implications imperative. Instead of supporting the government and its rationing policies, French residents manipulated the regime's ideology to fulfill material needs, thereby challenging the government's authority within months of its inception. Despite these problems, the Vichy regime managed to survive the war years, which leads to the question of how. Answering this question requires an examination of daily life on the local level.

Hunger was a constant feature of daily life, but the extent of shortages and reactions to the restrictions varied considerably across the country and across time. German occupation led to an immediate drop in agricultural production across Europe due to requisitions, labor shortages, and war damage to countries' infrastructure. French production of grain, potatoes, and meat fell dramatically between 1939 and 1940. By 1943, the amount of land planted with grain was 1.4 million hectares less than it had been in the years before the war. French ration cards consistently provided fewer

---

[17] See Bonzon and Davis, "Feeding the Cities," p. 318. The authors note that there are no historical works on how the Great War affected food supplies and consumption patterns in French cities.

calories than did cards in Germany, Belgium, The Netherlands, Norway, and the Baltic countries despite the fact that France was the largest prewar producer of agricultural goods in Western Europe. The amount of meat and fats provided weekly in France was also lower than that in other countries, and the difference in rations was especially noticeable in the amounts allotted to workers.[18] The French, however, never faced famine and starvation like the residents of countries such as the Netherlands and Greece.[19]

The division of France into different zones (occupied, unoccupied, forbidden, and annexed territories), fuel shortages, and inefficient food distribution contributed to provisioning difficulties. (See Map 1.) Food sitting in port cities like Le Havre often rotted before it could be delivered to hungry urban dwellers.[20] Residents of the large sea port cities of Nantes and Saint-Nazaire in the occupied zone suffered because they were cut off from overseas goods and found it difficult to import food from the surrounding countryside.[21] City dwellers from Paris and other northern cities often ventured to agricultural regions such as Normandy or the Loire Valley in search of food. Those without rural connections or financial means spent hours each day waiting in line to purchase rationed goods.[22]

Shortages were worse in large cities, where the populace relied on products brought in from the countryside, and in the south of France, which produced three-quarters of the country's wine, but little wheat, butter, beef, or sugar. The region around Nîmes near the Mediterranean coast suffered from shortages as early as the summer of 1940. Dependent upon viticulture, the area received most of its produce from other departments, and a commercial blockage of goods coming from other regions in July 1940 meant residents were unable to find essential supplies.[23] Around Clermont-Ferrand, an important agricultural region in the unoccupied zone, food production fell by at least 30 percent, evidence of malnutrition increased, and cases of tuberculosis were twice their prewar levels.[24] Many other cities felt the

---

[18] Voglis, "Surviving Hunger," pp. 20–6.
[19] Famine in these countries resulted from the course of the war and the Nazis' racial ideology and economic exploitation methods. See Voglis, "Surviving Hunger."
[20] Cited in Vinen, *The Unfree French*, p. 221.
[21] Robert Gildea, *Marianne in Chains: In Search of the German Occupation 1940–1945* (London, Basingstoke, and Oxford: Macmillan, 2002), 113.
[22] On queues, see Veillon, *Vivre et survivre*, pp. 127–32; Diamond, *Women and the Second World War*, pp. 53–55; and Paula Schwartz, "The Politics of Food and Gender in Occupied Paris," *Modern & Contemporary France* 7 (February 1999): 36–9.
[23] Robert Zaretsky, *Nîmes at War: Religion, Politics, and Public Opinion in the Gard, 1938–1944* (University Park: The Pennsylvania State University Press, 1995), 76–7.
[24] Sweets, *Choices in Vichy France*, p. 15.

adverse health effects created by penury: Paris saw its mortality rate rise during the war by 24 percent, Lyon by 29 percent, and Marseilles by 57 percent.[25] As residents became desperate for food, polycultural regions in the unoccupied zone, like the Limousin, became increasingly important as sources of food. Thus, the Limousin is an ideal location for the study of the politics of daily life during the Second World War.

THE LIMOUSIN AT WAR

The Limousin region rarely takes center stage in French history. Made up of the departments of the Creuse, Corrèze, and Haute-Vienne, the region is rural and sparsely populated with most of its inhabitants living on farms or in small hamlets and bourgs scattered throughout the rolling countryside. (See Maps 2 and 3.) Limoges, the area's major city, is known internationally for its fine porcelain, but the region's main focus is agriculture.[26] During the Second World War, the Limousin attracted more attention due in part to the geography that usually keeps the region isolated. The mountains of the Massif Central, which cover portions of the Corrèze, the southeastern Haute-Vienne, and the southern Creuse, helped foster the growth of rural guerrilla groups known as the maquis. As a result of the presence of the Resistance in the region, the Limousin was also the site of some of the worst Nazi atrocities in France during the Second World War. German troops moving through the region in response to increased Resistance activity hanged 99 men in the city of Tulle (Corrèze) and deported another 149 on June 9, 1944, in reprisal for attacks. The next day, the troops entered the village of Oradour-sur-Glane in the Haute-Vienne, rounded up the village's residents, divided the men from the women and children, and began a massacre: 642 men, women, and children died that day, either falling under the Germans' bullets or burning to death when the entire village was set ablaze.[27]

---

[25] Vinen, *The Unfree French*, p. 227.
[26] Limoges served as the Limousin's regional capital before and during the war; however, the armistice signed between France and Germany on June 22, 1940, changed the structural administration of the region. In addition to the three usual departments of the Creuse, the Corrèze, and the Haute-Vienne, the Indre and portions of the Dordogne, the Vienne, the Charente, the Indre-et-Loire, the Loir-et-Cher, and the Cher, departments now divided by the demarcation line between occupied and unoccupied France, comprised the Limoges region.
[27] On Oradour-sur-Glane, see Sarah Farmer, *Martyred Village: Commemorating the 1944 Massacre at Oradour-sur-Glane* (Berkeley, Los Angeles, and London: University of California Press, 1999).

Introduction

These dramatic events tend to overshadow the effects of shortages on the social fabric and the importance of daily life in the Limousin during the war years. In 1939, the region was not strategically important, it was not politically influential, and it was of little industrial interest. But it was precisely because of its rural and isolated nature that many refugees found their way to the Limousin during the war. The region thus provides an especially rich context for studying the interactions of diverse populations during a time of extreme shortage. In September 1939, the government of the Third Republic evacuated some 380,000 people from the border regions of Alsace and Lorraine to the French interior, including the Limousin, in preparation for a possible German invasion. When the invasion began in May 1940, millions of residents of northern France fled to southern, rural regions such as the Limousin for safety. After the armistice, the region fell just south of the line of demarcation that divided France into a northern, occupied zone and a southern, unoccupied zone, making it a desirable destination throughout the war for French and foreign Jews fleeing Nazi persecution.

In addition to the political advantages of being in the so-called free zone, the predominantly agricultural Limousin remained relatively privileged in terms of food supply. Unlike many departments in southern France, the region supported mixed agriculture. Farmers grew a combination of wheat, cabbage, beets, carrots, beans, celery, or peas; others raised cattle and hogs. The Limousin, known for its apples and chestnuts, also provided France with a substantial proportion of the country's potatoes. Monocultural regions, such as those that produced the nation's wine, felt the effects of shortages more acutely than the polycultural Limousin.[28] Antoine Perrier, writing in the newspaper *L'Appel du Centre*, called the wartime situation the "Limousins' revenge."[29] After years of denigration by outsiders for being an impoverished and backward region, the French now turned to the people of the Limousin due to the richness of their food production.

---

[28] For an examination of the situation in various departments, especially those hardest hit by shortages, see the sections, "Les Départements 'Affamés'" and "Les Départements en situation 'Intermédiaire'" in "Le temps des restrictions en France (1939–1949)," special edition of *Les Cahiers de l'Institut d'Histoire du Temps Présent*. On shortages in wine-producing regions, see Zaretsky, *Nîmes at War*, and Don and Petie Kladstrup, *Wine and War: The French, the Nazis, and the Battle for France's Greatest Treasure* (New York: Broadway Books, 2001).

[29] Antoine Perrier, "La revanche des Limousins," *L'Appel du Centre* (n.d.) in Archives départementales de la Haute-Vienne (hereafter ADHV) 993 W – 117 – Coupures du presse locale. On Limoges' inferiority complex in the nineteenth- and early twentieth-centuries, see John M. Merriman, *The Red City: Limoges and the French Nineteenth Century* (New York and Oxford: Oxford University Press, 1985).

Agriculture gained an importance it had lacked in the past; however, this newfound respect came at a price. It meant that the government requisitioned and redistributed thousands of tons of agricultural items produced in the Limousin to areas where fresh goods were rare, such as the cities of Paris, Lyon, Nice, and Marseilles.[30] The area's rich food production encouraged some refugees to remain in the region rather than returning to urban cities occupied by German troops where shortages were more severe. Residents of other departments in the unoccupied zone also traveled to the Limousin to purchase vegetables and additional farm products, and relatives living in cities wrote to family members still living on the farm and asked them to send food.

The Limousin's status as a region of varied agricultural production created a situation in which strangers met in the search for food and where the establishment and maintenance of personal relationships took on particular importance. New refugees made their way into the region throughout the war as the situation in the occupied zone worsened and as the Allies made advances in North Africa. Other refugees chose (or were forced) to return to their homes in the occupied zone rather than remain in unfamiliar surroundings once the hostilities officially ended with the armistice in 1940. Cities, towns, and villages in the region saw hundreds or thousands of new inhabitants, but the region also experienced the loss of thousands of prisoners of war and the arrest of Jewish refugees.[31] Native residents who had rarely ventured outside the Limousin now met industrialists from Alsace, Jewish tailors from Paris, refugee families from Belgium, and Jews from Germany seeking a haven from Nazi persecution. Even the area's permanent residents moved about freely. Shortages forced urban residents into rural areas in search of food, residents of neighboring departments in the unoccupied zone visited the Limousin hoping to exchange manufactured goods for foodstuffs, and individuals followed business interests across departmental borders.

---

[30] In his yearly report for 1942, the regional prefect for Limoges detailed the amount of agricultural items sent to departments lacking food: more than 63,000 tons of meat, 200,000 tons of potatoes, close to 20,000 tons of fresh vegetables (since July), 10,000 tons of fresh fruit, 20,461,391 eggs (fresh and conserved), and 997,663 kilograms of poultry. See ADHV 185 W 1–44 – Rapports mensuels du préfet régional au chef du gouvernement. Région de Limoges – Rapport d'Ensemble pour l'année 1942.

[31] The population of the region increased by at least 42,586 people or approximately 5 percent. Statistics from Archives Départementales de la Creuse (hereafter ADC) 297 W1. Secrétariat Général au Ravitaillement. Relève Statistique à la date du 1er Octobre 1943 des Différents Catégories de Consommateurs. The statistics represent only those consumers who had legally registered and thus Jews and résistants living in the area clandestinely are excluded.

The result was a population with different cultural, religious, and social backgrounds in constant flux, all vying for scarce goods.

The departments of the Creuse and Haute-Vienne form the basis of my investigation of shortages and personal relationships. These areas, considered to be the agricultural "twins" of the Limousin, not only shared geographical and economic attributes but also welcomed large refugee populations during the war.[32] Third Republic officials designated the Haute-Vienne as one of the first departments to receive evacuated Alsatians, and the Creuse welcomed refugee Jewish children during the early months of the Phony War. The presence of substantial outsider populations in both the Creuse and the Haute-Vienne, as well as the similarities in food production and supply, provide a common starting point in this case study. The differences in the two departments allow an examination of the variation caused by factors such as population distribution or extent of officials' commitment to the Vichy regime and enforcing its ideals.

THE VICHY REGIME, POLITICS, AND OUTSIDERS

The Vichy regime's conservative National Revolution was predicated on the idea of creating an organic community based on the traditional values of religion, authority, and order.[33] These traditional values also required a return to the earth, a return to conventional gender roles, and the removal of Jewish, communist, and foreign influences from politics and economics. Foreigners and so-called undesirables thus became the object of restrictive legislation, discrimination, and persecution. The simple terms "foreigner" and "undesirable" proved difficult to define, however, and further atomized rather than homogenized French society. "Foreigners" (*étrangers*) included both immigrants and refugees, and the term was even applied to some French nationals, such as evacuees from Alsace and Lorraine. "Undesirables" included a range of individuals including illegal aliens, black marketeers, French and foreign communists, some refugees, strident republicans, Jews, Gypsies, and, according to rural residents, some city dwellers in search

---

[32] The prefect of the Creuse used this label to describe the departments in AN F 1c III – 1150. Rapport Mensuel d'Information du 1er Février au 31 Mars 1943 (March 31, 1943). The Corrèze, on the other hand, compared its agricultural production with other departments in the Massif Central such as its neighbors in the Lot and the Dordogne. See AN F 1c III – 1147, Le Préfet à Monsieur le Sécretaire d'Etat au Ravitaillement (May 31, 1941).

[33] Robert O. Paxton addresses the complexity of defining Vichy's social reform agenda as well as the various components of the National Revolution in *Vichy France: Old Guard and New Order 1940–1944* (New York: Columbia University Press, 1972). See also Julian Jackson's synthesis in *France: The Dark Years*.

of food. At the very least, Limousin natives became more aware of the strangers (*inconnus*) in their midst and Vichy's crusade against foreigners and undesirables provided a means to exclude outsiders from daily life.

Vichy's rhetoric concerning the National Revolution and its commitment to ridding France of detrimental influences often found concrete expression in the issues surrounding provisioning. The French State (*L'Etat français*) used access to food as one means to tighten its control over society and separate "true" French from the undesirables. Ration cards and identity cards stamped "JUIF" or "JUIVE" ("JEW" or "JEWESS") immediately identified the bearer as an undesirable in the French State. Local registers of ration cards could also provide addresses for police and gendarmes involved in the round up of Jews for deportation. By keeping ration cards, authorities increased the probability that Gypsies (another undesirable group) assigned residence in camps would return after a day of work outside, beyond the barbed wire. The threat of arrest for stealing – the best way to get food without a card – proved enough to deter most escapes.[34] In addition to the difficulties of navigating shortages due to their status as outsiders in established communities, marginalized groups also had to contend with Vichy's institutionalized exclusionary tactics related to material concerns.

Historians note the difficulties facing Jews and other marginal groups in their studies of daily life, but the everyday experiences of marginal groups – including the difficulties of provisioning – have not been systematically studied.[35] Michael R. Marrus and Robert O. Paxton demonstrate that officials blamed Jews who immigrated, or were forced into the unoccupied zone, for hoarding, shortages, and increasing tensions within rural society, but local populations did not always express the same sentiments.[36] Renée Poznanski acknowledges the centrality of shortages in shaping relationships between Jews and non-Jews during the war and asserts that the daily material concerns of "Aryans" contributed to their indifference to the Jews' plight.[37] Both Poznanski and Marion Kaplan underline the importance of understanding Jewish experience in terms of daily life as it was in their

---

[34] See Guy Hantarrède, "Les Tsiganes au camp des Alliers (novembre 1940–mars 1946)," *Etudes Tsiganes* 13:1 (1999): 122.

[35] See for example Veillon, *Vivre et survivre*, pp. 231–42 and Robert Gildea's chapter 10: "Sinners" in *Marianne in Chains*.

[36] See Michael R. Marrus and Robert O. Paxton, *Vichy France and the Jews* (New York: Basic Books, 1981).

[37] Renée Poznanski, *Jews in France during World War II* translated by Nathan Bracher (Hanover and London: University Press of New England, Brandeis University Press in association with the United States Holocaust Memorial Museum, 2001), 76.

everyday activities that Jews felt both support and persecution.[38] Yet despite the clear connections between food, persecution, and survival, most examinations of the war period focus on official government attitudes and policies rather than ordinary citizens' responses. The following pages will argue that Limousin natives were not indifferent to their outsider neighbors; rather the experience of daily shortages directly influenced the treatment of new arrivals, often in direct opposition to Vichy's political agenda.

Chapters focus on three major themes based on research into shortages, daily life, and social interactions. First, any study of the period must address the issue of change over time, including changes in public opinion. An assessment of public attitudes at the grassroot level differs significantly from official evaluations demonstrating the distance between the government's ideology and the people's reality. Scholars of France during the Second World War often have been concerned with tracing the evolution of public opinion and its effects on sustaining or destabilizing the Vichy regime. In his ground-breaking study of the period, Robert Paxton argues that public opinion "offered a broad basis of acquiescence within which active participation in the Vichy regime was made legitimate" until the spring of 1943.[39] Roderick Kedward also sees 1943 as the major turning point in citizen-state relations after the institution of the Compulsory Labor Service (Service de Travail Obligatoire, STO) in February and the government's subsequent ruthless pursuit of work draft evaders.[40] John F. Sweets, however, documents a noticeable decline in public support for Pétain's regime in the Clermont-Ferrand region as early as the first half of 1941, and Robert Gildea sees June 1941 as a turning point in Franco-German relations in the occupied Loire Valley.[41] Julian Jackson's synthesis of public opinion under Vichy describes the French as "immediately hostile to Germany, and progressively disillusioned with Vichy, [but] much slower to lose confidence in Marshal Pétain."[42] Other

---

[38] See Poznanski, *Jews in France*, Marion A. Kaplan, "When the Ordinary Became Extraordinary: German Jews Reacting to Nazi Persecution, 1933–1939" in *Social Outsiders in Nazi Germany* edited by Robert Gellately and Nathan Stoltzfus (Princeton, New Jersey and Oxford: Princeton University Press, 2001) and Kaplan, *Between Dignity and Despair: Jewish Life in Nazi Germany* (New York and Oxford: Oxford University Press, 1998).

[39] Paxton, *Vichy France*, pp. 240–1.

[40] Roderick Kedward, "The Maquis and the Culture of the Outlaw (with Particular Reference to the Cévennes)" in *Vichy France and the Resistance: Culture & Ideology* edited by Roderick Kedward and Roger Austin (London and Sydney: Croom Helm, 1985), 242.

[41] Sweets, *Choices in Vichy France*, p. 155. Gildea, *Marianne in Chains*, pp. 17–8.

[42] Jackson, *France: The Dark Years*, p. 278.

scholars locate the population's definitive break with Vichy in the summer of 1942 after the arrest and deportation of Jews in both occupied and unoccupied France.[43] These debates raise several important points: First, public opinion assessments vary depending upon both the geographical region and the population under investigation; second, the chosen subject matter – the Vichy regime, Marshal Philippe Pétain, the German occupiers, antisemitism – influences the interpretation; and third, implicit in discussions of public attitudes are questions about how to understand French attitudes during the war and their relationship to the larger issues of resistance and collaboration.

The second, related theme is discussions about the extent of public complicity with Vichy's agenda. By focusing on the intersection of shortages and ideology, I argue that rejection and acceptance of Vichy's policies often existed side by side, complicating our ideas about resistance and collaboration. Local, daily concerns held greater weight for individuals than abstract national ideals and responses to local problems could either undermine Vichy's moral agenda or support it. The political issues of collaboration and resistance have been the subject of numerous historical studies focusing on the Vichy period. Scholars continue to debate the very definition of resistance as well as its extent in France during the war years. One area of contention is how to classify the 96 percent of the population that neither actively collaborated nor actively resisted. Examining people's daily choices related to provisioning further enhances our understanding of resistance and collaboration under oppressive regimes by detailing how men and women negotiated the quotidian within political constraints. Decisions to accept or reject certain ideals of the government's National Revolution had their roots in individual, daily experiences.

Even though French residents increasingly engaged in illicit activity related to their material concerns, we cannot consider their activities resistance in the traditional sense. Most scholars agree that the term "resistance" only applies to active, intentional attempts to overthrow an

---

[43] See Sweets, "Jews and Non-Jews in France During the Second World War" in *Nazi Europe and the Final Solution* edited by David Bankier and Israel Gutman (Jerusalem: Yad Vashem, 2003), 371; Pierre Laborie, *Les Français des années troubles: De la guerre d'Espagne à la Libération* (Paris: Desclée de Brouwer, 2001), 158; Renée Poznanski, "French Public Opinion and the Jews during World War II: Assumptions of the Clandestine Press" in *Facing the Nazi Genocide: Non-Jews and Jews in Europe* edited by Beate Kosmala and Feliks Tych (Berlin: Metropol, 2004), 124.

oppressive regime.⁴⁴ But concepts such as *Eigen-Sinn* and duplicity and complicity reject the resistance/collaboration dichotomy and provide a theoretical basis for explaining how rampant illegal provisioning undermined Vichy's authority while providing the government with the acceptance fundamental for its survival. *Eigen-Sinn,* or "movements of evasion," allows ordinary people to challenge power relations, yet it differs from open opposition to authoritarian regimes by allowing individuals to demonstrate their personal freedom while continuing to sustain oppressive institutions.⁴⁵ In Vichy France, illegal food transactions often represented individual, willful acts, but they did not evolve into a widespread repudiation of the Vichy government or its policy of collaboration. The concepts of complicity and duplicity also help explain the ways in which ordinary people both uphold and undermine repressive governments through their daily activities. Duplicity, "willful, conscious behavior in which social actors are aware of their intentions," occurs at the same time as complicity, where "Social actors may, out of fear, indifference, or alienation, actively or passively 'aid and abet' that in which they do not believe or with which they do not concur."⁴⁶ Limousin residents often acted in a duplicitous manner in order to escape the government's laws and sanctions. However, by deliberately concealing their actions or opinions, they became complicit in perpetuating the Vichy regime and its ideology. Unlawful material activities reveal not a deep seeded rejection of Vichy politics but rather the banalization and normalization of illegality during the war that ultimately served to undermine the government's moral regeneration program.

---

⁴⁴ See for example Detlev J. K. Peukert, *Inside Nazi Germany: Conformity, Opposition, and Racism in Everyday Life*, translated by Richard Deveson (New Haven, Connecticut and London: Yale University Press, 1987), 119–20. On the difficulty of defining Resistance in the French context, see François Bédarida, "Sur le concept de Résistance" in *Mémoire et Histoire: la Résistance* edited by Jean-Marie Guillon and Pierre Laborie (Toulouse: Editions Privat, 1995); François Marcot, "Réflexions sur les valeurs de la Résistance" in *Mémoire et Histoire: la Résistance* edited by Jean-Marie Guillon and Pierre Laborie (Toulouse: Editions Privat, 1995); and Pierre Laborie, "L'idée de Résistance, entre définition et sens; retour sur un questionnement," *Les Cahiers de l'Institut d'histoire du temps présent* 37 (December 1997).

⁴⁵ Alf Lüdtke, "What Happened to the 'Fiery Red Glow'? Workers' Experiences and German Fascism" in *The History of Everyday Life: Reconstructing Historical Experiences and Ways of Life*, edited by Alf Lüdtke, translated by William Templer (Princeton, New Jersey: Princeton University Press, 1995), 226. See also Andrew Stuart Bergerson, *Ordinary Germans in Extraordinary Times: The Nazi Revolution in Hildesheim* (Bloomington and Indianapolis: Indiana University Press, 2004).

⁴⁶ Gail Kligman, *The Politics of Duplicity: Controlling Reproduction in Ceausescu's Romania* (Berkeley, Los Angeles, and London: University of California Press, 1998), 14.

The third and final theme explored in the following pages is the importance of community and family in navigating the war years. A regional study reveals the contrasts between national and local ideas about community and belonging and demonstrates how membership in a community affected survival. Marshal Pétain considered the family the "essential unit" of the community in his new social order, but often families developed strategies that contradicted traditional ideals in the daily attempt to fulfill material needs.[47] Communities responded to the influx of refugees not only as strangers but also as potential benefits or threats to their economic and material well-being. These reactions often undermined the Vichy regime's attempts to exclude so-called undesirable groups from the national community demonstrating that all responses to outsiders cannot be explained by political ideology, xenophobia, or antisemitism. In addition to material concerns, cultural differences, race, and age also clearly shaped social experiences, and the following pages demonstrate the vital importance of exploring these categories in order to fully understand war experiences in the twentieth century.

Politics – and especially the politics of the Left – matter in the French Limousin. But during the Second World War, everyday concerns took precedence over political ideology as material shortages increasingly dominated daily life. The policies of the Vichy regime thus became the background against which the quotidian played out. Pragmatic concerns about survival often trumped political loyalty, antisemitism, and social differences. For French residents on the margins of society including refugees, evacuees, Gypsies, and Jews, the politics of daily life mattered. Even though the government legally circumscribed lives between 1939 and 1944, shortages helped define the relationship between citizens and the state, created the very definition of who was an "insider" and an "outsider" in local communities, and shaped the manner in which native and refugee populations interacted. Studying the daily anxieties created by penury clearly reveals why shortages held "first place in the population's concerns" and how they undoubtedly became a political matter.

---

[47] Philippe Pétain, *Discours aux Français 17 juin 1940-20 août 1944* edited by Jean-Claude Barbas (Paris: Albin Michel, 1989), 71.

I

"Life has never been so good": Shortages, Public Opinion, and Urban-Rural Interactions

In August 1942, someone stole potatoes from one of Jean Lalande's fields. The farmer contacted the Gendarmerie Nationale's local battalion to file a report, and in the course of their investigation the gendarmes questioned both Lalande and his neighbor, Jean Barthélemy. When asked if they had any suspicions as to who could have committed the crime, both men said "no." Undoubtedly none of their neighbors from the rural village of Buxerolles in the Haute-Vienne would have done such a thing, but they believed the thief could be "one of the numerous persons from the surroundings of Limoges who come to the villages daily in order to provision themselves [*se ravitailler*]."[1] Located in the commune of Couzeix, approximately six kilometers from the center of Limoges, Buxerolles was just one rural village that city dwellers visited in their daily search for food. Instead of bringing their goods to town and city markets, rural inhabitants remained at home and customers came to them, reversing traditional provisioning patterns and increasing the possibility of thefts. Both these tactics became vital strategies for survival during the Second World War.

Viewed from the provinces, the history of shortages during the war years takes on a different appearance than histories of Paris and other major cities under the Occupation where the memory of endless food lines predominates. These differences have led one regional historian to conclude that "the image of food queues should be replaced by the image

---

[1] Service Historique de la Gendarmerie Nationale (hereafter SHGN) Box 12706 – BT Limoges – Procès-verbal number 1796 (August 20, 1942). Similar cases and declarations can be found in SHGN Box 12708 – BT Limoges – Procès-verbaux numbers 906 (May 20, 1943), 917 (May 21, 1943), and 1675 (August 28, 1943).

of bicycles and trailers scouring the countryside."[2] Yet the more common experience for French men and women living in small cities, towns, and villages during World War II consisted of waiting in line for rationed goods *and* venturing into the surrounding countryside in search of food on a regular basis. As Jean Lalande's police report indicates, theft also became a regular aspect of provisioning during the war years. Daily interactions changed as strangers met and sometimes came into conflict when Limousin natives, newly arrived refugees, residents of neighboring departments, and foreigners combed farms for items to supplement their meager rations.

As markets and provisioning patterns changed during the war, the relationship between French urban dwellers and their rural counterparts also underwent a transformation. Exploring the manner in which French natives with similar regional and cultural identities dealt with each other within this confusing world of supplying and increasing shortages sets the stage for the examination of how undesirable outsiders fared in the continual battle over scarce resources. The establishment and maintenance of personal relationships between native French urban and rural dwellers also led to illegal provisioning tactics. Studying these tactics reveals the simultaneous alliances *and* divisions within French society created by the various methods of acquiring necessary goods, by the fear of sanctions, and by the moral agenda espoused by the Vichy regime.

Government officials further complicated relationships between peasants and townspeople throughout France by tying material shortages to Vichy's ideological agenda. Peasants held the responsibility of feeding the nation and exemplifying all that was good in French society. Propaganda glorified peasants as the repository of "true" French values while urban dwellers accused them of being selfish and exploiting others' misery for profit. To people in cities, facing shortages and recriminations for decadence, it appeared that

---

[2] Robert Gildea, *Marianne in Chains: In Search of the German Occupation 1940–1945* (London: Macmillan, 2002), 419. The articles in a special edition of *Les Cahiers de l'Institut du Temps Présent* devoted to shortages during the war provides a department-by-department examination of the period and also describes both queues and trips to the countryside. See "Le temps des restrictions en France (1939–1949)," special edition of *Les Cahiers de l'Institut d'Histoire du Temps Présent* Vols. 32–3 edited by Dominique Veillon and Jean-Marie Flonneau (Paris: Institut d'Histoire du Temps Présent, 1996). On queues, see Dominique Veillon, *Vivre et survivre en France 1939–1947* (Paris: Editions Payot & Rivages, 1995), 127–32; Hanna Diamond, *Women and the Second World War in France, 1939–1948: Choices and Constraints* (London: Longman, 1999), 53–5; and Paula Schwartz, "The Politics of Food and Gender in Occupied Paris." *Modern & Contemporary France* 7 (February 1999): 36–9.

"life [had] never been so good" for peasants.³ While many peasants did profit from the new situation, they also felt pressure from Vichy's demands for increased production (despite the shortages of farming supplies and labor) and from the requests of potentially hostile strangers for food. The National Revolution called for sacrifices in the name of the common good, but self-interested attempts to gain more food or the highest price for products often overrode such calls. This tension between personal interests and national interests led to the creation of survival strategies that manipulated Vichy's ideologies to serve individual needs.

The evolution of shortages in the Limousin during the war can be divided into four general stages. Although there is some overlap in the characteristics of each phase, they also exhibit distinctive traits that distinguish one from the other. Phase one began in September 1939 with the Third Republic's declaration of war on Germany and the evacuation of Alsatians and Lorrainers to the French interior and lasted until September 1940. During this period, shortages were directly related to preparations for war and the arrival of the first evacuees and refugees in the Limousin. Material conditions worsened with the Nazi invasion and subsequent civilian exodus in May 1940 and were only ameliorated by the repatriation efforts of the new Vichy regime in July and August 1940. Phase two, characterized by increased government regulation of supplies and the resultant social divisions and alliances, began with official rationing on September 23, 1940. Lasting until the spring of 1942, this stage demonstrates the creative and contradictory strategies Limousin residents employed in their daily provisioning struggles. Extreme penury first affected the region during this time period, and locals' refusal to submit to harsh rationing laws forced the Vichy government to tolerate extra-legal activity. During phase three, between the spring and fall of 1942, supplying strategies increasingly shifted from questionable activities to outright illegality. As the Vichy government imposed harsher punishment for food infractions, the local population demonstrated greater social solidarity against the regime. Yet the rejection of certain aspects of the National Revolution in the name of provisioning often existed simultaneously with acceptance of other ideals and did not result in the complete collapse of the regime's legitimacy. Phase four is strongly characterized by fear, violence, and thefts. Beginning in the fall of 1942 and lasting

---

³ On the idea of a True France, see Herman Lebovics, *True France: The Wars over Cultural Identity, 1940–1945* (Ithaca, New York and London: Cornell University Press, 1992). For the quote, see Archives Départementales de la Haute-Vienne (hereafter ADHV) 185 W 1–206. Synthèses hebdomadaires du coordinateur du service civil des contrôles techniques (August 8, 1942).

until the war's end, Vichy increasingly lost control of supply issues and faced direct attacks on provisions from the organized Resistance. Despite the discontent, there were no food riots in the region or governmental collapse. Examining each phase reveals the connection between increasing shortages, public opinion, and decreasing legitimacy.

WAR, REFUGEES, AND SHORTAGES: SEPTEMBER 1939–SEPTEMBER 1940

The arrival of refugees and evacuees defined the first period of shortages experienced in the Limousin. Within days of the evacuation order forcing residents of Alsace and Lorraine from their homes along the German border, local Limousin authorities reported difficulties provisioning the refugees in items such as meat, sugar, and coffee.[4] Rather than resorting to a rationing system, the Third Republic restricted the days on which certain items could be sold. Alfred Sauvy argues that the Great War of 1914–1918 psychologically influenced the French government's response in 1939: "[There was] a strong anxiety of men concerning deprivations and a general desire to escape them."[5] Unlike the leadership in other belligerent nations, Third Republic officials did not immediately institute rationing with the declaration of war, reflecting the government's hope of escaping deprivations and its hesitance to create changes in daily life. Instead, the government chose to restrict the sale of certain food items at a time when the goods were already scarce due to the refugee situation. Beginning in December 1939, a decree prohibited the sale or consumption of meat and charcuterie in public establishments on Fridays. This came in addition to earlier decrees that had restricted the sale of different cuts of meat on Mondays and Tuesdays. Justified by French soldiers' increased need for meat on the front lines, such restrictions immediately redistributed goods from women, children, and the elderly to healthy, adult men. Touted as "easily supportable" and as a substitution for ration cards, officials expected the population to accept the necessary restrictions with grace.[6] A new wave of restrictions appeared later in the Phony War (the period after war had been declared in September 1939, but before fighting broke out) in March 1940: pastry, confectionary, and chocolate shops were

---

[4] ADHV 187 W – 18. Le Sous-Préfet de Wissembourg à Monsieur le Préfet de la Haute-Vienne (September 10, 1939).

[5] Alfred Sauvy, *La vie économique des français de 1939 à 1945* (Paris: Flammarion, 1978), 12.

[6] "Les vendredis sans viande," *Le Courrier de la Creuse* number 92 (December 14, 1939), 1.

to be closed on Tuesdays, Wednesdays, and Fridays. The public sale and consumption of alcoholic beverages was forbidden on Tuesdays, Thursdays, and Saturdays. Restrictions also affected the amount of bread and food served in restaurants as well as the types of bread, pastry, and chocolate produced. Eventually closings extended to bakeries, which were only permitted to sell day-old bread starting in July 1940 in the attempt to encourage the French to eat less of this staple item. People violating the new decree-laws were threatened with fines and forced shop closings.

By April 1940, even before the outbreak of hostilities and the civilian exodus, the Third Republic prepared the population for future hardships. All French residents had to register for ration cards by April 1. The cards, to be delivered at a later date, would be issued to each individual and used for all goods subject to restriction. Local papers informed consumers that ration quantities would be determined by age and occupation, but it quickly became apparent that restrictions would extend beyond food products to encompass nearly every aspect of daily life. The same month, *Le Courrier du Centre*, the Limousin's most important newspaper, announced the government's ban on central heating during the months of April through October as well as the law limiting hot water use to only three days a week. Severe shortages of gas, wood, and coal would make heating and cooking extremely difficult in towns, especially during the war's unusually harsh winters. In attempts to ameliorate the worsening material situation, residents turned to direct purchases between buyers and sellers at the farm or outside official markets early in the war.

Millions of civilian refugees fleeing the German invasion in May and June 1940 only worsened gas, food, and housing shortages as they flooded towns and cities in southern France. The subsequent urban shortages sent more individuals searching for food at the source. The situation was so critical in July 1940 that authorities forbade anyone without a residence in the Creuse or without proper authorization documents to enter the department. Individuals coming from other departments for the express purpose of provisioning were formally prohibited, and roadblocks at the department's borders turned searchers away.[7] On June 22, 1940, France signed an armistice with Germany to end the fighting, and on July 10, the National Assembly voted itself out of existence by granting full powers to Marshal Philippe Pétain. These political changes did not drastically change the material situation for Limousin residents. The documents that still exist from this tumultuous period demonstrate that shortages of gas, meat, and wheat

---

[7] SHGN Box 12536 – Creuse, Grpt Guéret. R/2. Note de Service. (July 5, 1940).

became severe and prices for basic items skyrocketed with the refugees' continued arrival. An official telegram sent on July 23, 1940, estimated the population of the Haute-Vienne at 300,000 and stated that centers in Limoges served more than 40,000 meals daily. Officials worried about potential incidents resulting from food shortages and the continued influx of refugees.[8]

Only refugee repatriations ameliorated the food situation at the end of July and beginning of August 1940. By the end of August, the prefect reported that two-thirds of the refugees had left the Haute-Vienne, leading to a noticeable improvement in provisioning.[9] Official rationing followed close on the heels of repatriation. Individual departments throughout France had already chosen to institute ration cards for some goods; however, mandatory ration cards for the entire country did not go into effect until September 23, 1940, under pressure from German authorities.[10] Bread, sugar, coffee, pasta, rice, cheese, dietary fats, meat, soap, and milk all required coupons to purchase the allowed amounts. Intended to show national solidarity and help build a strong future, Vichy touted restrictions and the establishment of ration cards as evidence of the government's commitment to a new France where "the necessary sacrifices would be equally borne by all."[11] Rationing, restrictions, and price controls also fit neatly within the National Revolution's ideological commitment to centralize the economy and subordinate individual concerns to the larger national well-being.

The start of official rationing marked a turning point in material concerns during the war. For the first time, the political decisions of the Vichy regime touched every resident directly and concretely. Previously shortages were largely a consequence of the refugee situation and the need to provision French troops. After the French defeat and the resultant armistice, refugees began to return to their homes in the newly designated occupied zone, and the army no longer needed supplies. Clearly, the material changes were related to political events – defeat, occupation, the Vichy regime – but they were not concurrent. Restrictions gave way to rationing and as the upheaval of the first months of the war settled into an everyday routine, individuals began to employ strategies intended to supplement their insufficient rations.

---

[8] ADHV 185 W 1–45 – Rapports du préfet de la Haute-Vienne au ministère de l'Intérieur. Telegramme Officiel. Préfet Limoges à Intérieur Cabinet Vichy (July 23, 1940).
[9] Ibid., Telegramme Officiel. Préfet Limoges à Intérieur Cabinet Vichy (August 31, 1940).
[10] Veillon, *Vivre et survivre*, p. 112.
[11] See "Les Sacrifices," *Le Courrier de la Creuse* number 67 (October 6, 1940): 1.

PROVISIONING ON FOOT AND BY MAIL: SEPTEMBER 1940–MARCH 1942

During the second phase of material concerns, the Vichy regime attempted to impose its National Revolution while French residents struggled to survive and adapt to the new political reality. Between September 1940 and spring 1942, the Vichy government increasingly regulated material goods, and ordinary citizens responded by manipulating the system more and more, often against the moral ideals of Pétain's regime. Officials noted the earliest incidents of urban-rural animosity during this time period while public opinion reports recorded the first instances of extreme shortages. Individual actions also contributed to the national government's institution of a law related to the black market on March 15, 1942, effectively ending this stage.

Despite the relative agricultural wealth of the Creuse and the Haute-Vienne, people in the region's towns and villages often found it difficult to obtain the goods required for daily life. The Vichy government provided supplemental ration tickets for people without direct access to rural products, but residents of Limoges and smaller towns throughout the Haute-Vienne and the Creuse such as Bellac, Rochechouart, Guéret, and La Souterraine frequently faced empty shelves at groceries, butcher shops, and bakeries, forcing them to develop alternative means of acquiring goods. When the official efforts at equitable distribution of material goods through rationing quickly failed to fulfill the needs and expectations of these urban populations, people turned to two legal means of procuring goods: trips to the countryside and family packages (*colis familiaux*). Individuals soon manipulated both of these activities, transforming them into extra-legal and illegal enterprises in order to meet their material needs as shortages worsened. In so doing, survival strategies contradicted certain ideals of the National Revolution, prompting officials to institute further provisioning policies in hopes of ensuring the equal division of necessities. Local and national initiatives, often contradictory and inconsistently enforced, attempted to control the two new forms of acquiring food with varying degrees of success. While providing city dwellers with essential items and peasants with additional income, these trips to rural areas and family packages also had the unintended consequences of limiting the number of items sold at legitimate markets, creating tensions and alliances between rural producers and urban consumers, and fostering black market activities.

Initially, officials did not discourage individuals from seeking additional food on farms since ration cards alone could not meet daily nutritional needs. In theory, the purchase of reasonable quantities of nonrationed items such as chickens, rabbits, and vegetables directly from farmers did not pose a problem for authorities. It did, however, pose a problem for the individuals who spent their time searching for something to eat. The hunt for food could become a full-time occupation. Searchers often had no destination in mind upon setting out from their homes. All they knew was that the chance of finding something to eat was better when one went directly to the source as rationing and restrictions tightened. The process was by no means easy. Due to shortages of gas, most expeditions took place on foot or by bicycle. Unpaved roads, out-of-the-way farmhouses, and patrols of law enforcement officers checking for purchases of rationed or excessive amounts of goods made the task even more difficult. Furthermore, there was no guarantee of returning home with any more than one left with.

As local stores and markets proved unable to provide adequate goods after rationing began, many urban residents spent their days roaming the countryside in search of food. The shortages caused by the refugee situation during the Phony War had already prompted Limousin residents to call on peasants directly for purchases, a tactic that intensified under Vichy. One's possibility for success in returning with precious food items often depended upon connections and luck; thus, people with family, friends, or acquaintances living on farms often fared better. The Orieux family, living in the rural commune of Le Moustier about thirty kilometers southwest of Limoges, provides an example of daily provisioning difficulties and the importance of personal relationships. Though he lived in a rural area, Jean Orieux worked in Limoges and did not farm or have direct access to coveted countryside products. To supplement the family's food supply, his sisters cultivated relationships with local peasants in exchange for food. An older couple in Saint-Laurent-sur-Gorre enjoyed the young women's company and asked them questions about the latest news and about the novels they had read over a bowl of soup or an omelet. From time to time, the women would help the couple in the fields and always left these occasions with food packages (which they paid for, of course). The family's relationship with a widow who made goat cheese also proved valuable. Jean Orieux knew the importance of maintaining a friendship with the woman, "not for her cheese, but for the brilliant relationships she had with the farmers in the area. Thanks to her we could have access to an inexhaustible reserve of potatoes, lard, eggs, rabbits, and chickens. She was also the friend of a miller!"[12] Even though they enjoyed the woman's company and her colorful

---

[12] Jean Orieux, *Souvenirs de campagnes* (Paris: Flammarion, 1978), 336–9. Quote from p. 339.

stories, the Orieux family self-consciously fostered the relationship for material ends. People in search of food exploited any available resource, and the levels of acquaintance and intimacy ranged from repeat customers, former employees, military buddies, and business relations to family members.[13]

Local officials initially allowed nonrural inhabitants to go to farms, but the phenomenon's generalization by the spring of 1941 led peasants to believe that it was no longer necessary to bring their goods to market. As a result, the lack of vegetables, poultry, and other farm items in town markets forced residents to look elsewhere. One letter writer felt that this "vicious circle" created by buyers going to the country and sellers remaining at home was bound to continue because one cannot "reason with people who are hungry."[14] Peasants chose to stay on their farms not only because it eliminated the time and expense of transporting their products to local markets but also because they could avoid state regulations imposed at the marketplace. Hungry urban dwellers then ventured to farms despite laws and decrees prohibiting such actions.

In *Souvenirs de campagnes*, Jean Orieux described a typical market day in a Limousin village in the years preceding the Second World War. For Orieux, the animation of these days contrasted sharply with the quiet, reserved atmosphere that usually reigned in the rural village where he lived. On market days,

The people of the town came out of their shell and scampered in the streets; those from the countryside, with their ramshackle carts, their cows and their calves, invaded squares and markets. All of them milling around, standing about, talking, mooing. Impossible to advance in this crowd. They formed small groups in the middle of the street that devoted themselves, without worry, to the excitement of conversation. The cars stopped and honked. No one moved. [...] The odor of stables entered the houses of the city, the streets became a farm yard. It is a form of solidarity. All these people gorged themselves with the delights of noise and bustle.[15]

---

[13] For examples of repeat customers, see SHGN Box 12725 – Haute-Vienne, BT Nexon, procès-verbal number 189 (May 24, 1942); SHGN Box 12754 – Haute-Vienne, BT Saint-Léonard-de-Noblat, procès-verbaux numbers 349 and 352 (August 24, 1942); and SHGN Box 12756 – Haute-Vienne, BT Saint-Léonard-de-Noblat, procès-verbal number 137 (March 30, 1943). For employees and military relationships, see SHGN Box 12707 – Haute-Vienne, BT Limoges, procès-verbaux numbers 2587 (December 9, 1942) and 278 (February 28, 1943). For business relationships, see SHGN Box 12709 – Haute-Vienne, BT Limoges, procès-verbal number 2007 (October 14, 1943). For family, see SHGN Box 12710 – Haute-Vienne, BT Limoges, procès-verbal number 90 (January 6, 1944).

[14] ADHV 185 W 1–205. Commission de Contrôle Postal. Rapport Mensuel No. 60 (March 1942), 12.

[15] Orieux, *Souvenirs de campagnes*, p. 102.

The market was a prewar form of sociability and economic exchange that brought the city and the countryside into contact on a regular basis. Men brought and sold livestock while peasant women furnished the market with eggs, poultry, ducks, and vegetables. Bargaining and gossiping often took place in the regional patois during the day, culminating in an evening shared in the local eating and drinking establishments.

The Second World War transformed both the nature of local markets and forms of urban-rural sociability. Shortages, the structures put into place to collect farm products for repartition, and the potential for increased profit by staying at home discouraged peasants from bringing their goods to market. Markets did not disappear, but under Vichy market days were no longer joyous occasions. Familiar haggling over prices disappeared after legislation in October 1940 required the posting of items' government-determined, fixed prices. The number of cows, chickens, eggs, and vegetables brought by the peasants diminished sharply, and the goods that would be available at each market varied unpredictably. Gone was the bustle of the street, replaced instead by long queues for scarce items. Trains, trams, buses, and stations replaced markets and fairs as the focal points of sociability. Jean Orieux remembered the Limoges train station as a farmyard where one heard and smelt the animals (just like the streets of the prewar market days), but where one did not see the rabbits and chickens hidden in passengers' baskets and bags. On the trains themselves, people with little in common save their hunger, exchanged news about the war, the latest gossip and recipes, and information on where to find food.[16]

The market also became one of the public spaces in which the authoritarian French State attempted to regulate citizens and control prices. Gendarmes in uniform patrolled markets in hopes of discovering infractions and discouraging any illicit acts, a duty that was sometimes hampered by their inability to understand the region's patois.[17] Furthermore, when civilians spotted the authorities, all transactions often ceased, lending to the somber air. This led more than one officer to suggest that men in plain clothes be used to stop clandestine activity.[18] Authorities also monitored queues in

---

[16] Ibid., pp. 330–3.
[17] Officials noted such problems in Limoges. See SHGN Box 12647 – Grpt Haute-Vienne, Limoges. R/4. Rapport sur l'état d'esprit des populations (May 28, 1941).
[18] SHGN Box 12640 – Grpt Haute-Vienne, Limoges, R/2, Rapport du Capitaine Lotte sur la Police économique pendant la période du 1er au 20 décembre 1940 (January 6, 1941); SHGN Box 12741 – Battalion St. Germain-les-Belles, R/4, Rapport sur l'état d'esprit des populations (May 30, 1941); and SHGN Box 12647 – Grpt Haute-Vienne, R/4, Rapport sur l'état d'esprit des populations (May 28, 1941).

places like Limoges' central market to gauge public opinion. As early as March 1941, police reported shortages' negative effects on morale and authorities' inability to control the situation: "In buyers' lines, the exercised surveillance has not been able to detect the presence of suspect individuals who can provoke discontent and criticism of Marshal Pétain's work concerning questions having to do with supplying and rationing measures."[19] Thus, urban residents, rural sellers, and government representatives all met within the context of fulfilling material needs. The shift of business from official markets to the privacy of individual farms made these forms of surveillance even more difficult. In the spring of 1941, the prefect of the Haute-Vienne attempted to make surveillance and provisioning easier by outlawing the purchase of items at the farm and instead allowing families to buy two dozen eggs, rabbits, and chickens a half an hour before the official markets opened.[20]

At the heart of attempts to eliminate direct sales on the farm in April 1941 were concerns about the continuing diminution of goods in local markets, increasing prices for necessary items, and the proliferation of the black market. Although officials had reported an amelioration in shortages' extent during the fall of 1940 due to repatriation efforts, the winter months of 1940–1 proved difficult for Limousin residents. Milk, oil, butter, fruit, vegetables, meat, and potatoes became scarce or completely nonexistent in shops and markets. Residents also complained about coal and gasoline shortages. In February 1941, the prefect of the Haute-Vienne reported to Vichy's interior minister that the department's residents truly suffered from restrictions for the first time.[21] Rather than improving the situation, the spring only added new burdens: Bread rations were reduced by 20 percent in March, and by April rabbits, poultry, and eggs had disappeared from markets. The loss of these staple items only further encouraged urban residents to seek food at its source: the rural barnyard. It was in this atmosphere that the Haute-Vienne prefect issued his decree attempting to regulate the sale of eggs and other rural products by outlawing direct sales on the farm.

---

[19] ADHV 185 W 1–45 – Rapports du préfet de la Haute-Vienne au ministère de l'Intérieur. Le Commissaire Central à Monsieur le Préfet de la Haute-Vienne (March 26, 1941), 5.
[20] Prefectoral decree of April 16, 1941. See SHGN Box 12741 – Grpt Haute-Vienne, St-Germain-les-Belles, R/4, Rapport sur l'état d'esprit des populations (May 30, 1941) and SHGN Box 12647 – Grpt Haute-Vienne, Limoges, R/4, Rapport sur l'état d'esprit des populations (April 28, 1941).
[21] ADHV 185 W 1–45 – Rapports du préfet de la Haute-Vienne au ministère de l'Intérieur. Rapport Mensuel (February 3, 1941), 1.

Increasing regulations in the attempt to improve the food supply often had the opposite effect, however. By early 1941, the complex laws related to food supply clearly played a role in discouraging peasants from bringing their goods to town thereby forcing city dwellers out into rural areas. The prefect of the Creuse complained that the corpus of regulations in force appeared extremely complex to farmers, preventing them from bringing their agricultural products to market out of fear of violating the law.[22] Within two weeks of the Haute-Vienne prefect's decree outlawing direct farm purchases, gendarmes in Limoges reported that "the ban on going to buy at the farm produced an effect completely opposite to that expected by inciting people to do it and to buy at any price."[23] The new law did not take into consideration or make provisions for the fact that many communes held markets only once a month, and consumers had no other choice than to travel to neighboring farms for basic food items when they disappeared from store shelves. Even two years after the law prohibiting trips to the countryside went into effect, individuals continued to venture into the countryside because markets remained empty. "By not providing what is promised," observed the Limoges gendarmerie report in February 1943, "we provide people with an excuse to get it for themselves in an illicit manner."[24] Acknowledging the failure of the rationing system and the laws intended to ensure fair distribution, authorities were left with little choice but to permit familial provisioning at the source in order to avoid harsh criticism and food riots. Individual actions forced political accommodations.

Even though authorities allowed direct provisioning to continue, they did try to keep prices down and catch black marketeers by policing transactions on the farm. Yet the gendarmes responsible for monitoring sales found it nearly impossible to catch the authors of illegal price increases and other supply law infractions. Having become dependent upon peasants for survival, the residents of towns and villages hesitated to denounce their suppliers no matter what price the farmers charged. The legal ramifications facing the buyer as well as the seller also discouraged people from reporting price increases to officials. By purchasing items on the farm, city dwellers violated the law and were thus unwilling to expose themselves to possible sanctions. Though the gendarmerie heard rumors and received

---

[22] AN F 1c III – 1150. Rapport du Préfet (March 1, 1941).
[23] SHGN Box 12647 – BT Limoges, R/4, Rapport sur l'état d'esprit des populations (April 28, 1941).
[24] Ibid., Rapport sur l'état d'esprit des populations (February 23, 1943).

indirect information about peasants charging more than the official price for items, they were unable to take action "because we cannot collect any official statements."[25] The departmental director of general supplies for the Haute-Vienne admitted in October 1941 that although his services cited people for more infractions, "the real black market is not touched."[26]

Thus, by the spring of 1941, less than a year after the Vichy regime had come to power, the government faced serious material challenges with social and political consequences. On one hand, the shortages had created a form of social solidarity in which hungry urban dwellers worked in concert with rural peasants to ensure their food supplies in direct opposition to government authorities. On the other hand, authorities began to notice the first serious divisions between the urban and rural population in this second stage of shortages. In November 1940, the prefect of the Haute-Vienne reported, "There is a [...] scission between urban populations and those from the countryside. For the former whose earnings are, in general, reduced (reduction of work, limited profits), the fear of privations is, in effect, much larger than for the latter who see products from the soil within their reach."[27] Rather than equally sharing the burden of wartime shortages, the French noticed the inequalities created by rationing and restrictions. By December 1941, authorities feared a "gulf" between suffering city dwellers and prospering peasants that would work "to the detriment of the task of national renovation."[28] The government continued its attempts to ease shortages and ameliorate social divisions by largely ignoring illegal provisioning trips, but this did little to remedy the shortage of goods in the traditional marketplace.

The new year saw an increasing atomization of society as jealousy, selfishness, and suspicion prompted Limousin residents to denounce their neighbors for provisioning infractions. Concerns about denunciations first become

---

[25] SHGN Box 12721 – BT Nexon, R/4, Rapport sur l'état d'esprit des populations (May 21, 1942). Gendarmes in the Creuse also complained, "Infractions are difficult to record, [due to] buyers and sellers acting in full agreement." SHGN Box 12557 – Grpt Creuse, Cie Guéret, R/4, Rapport du Capitaine Chaumet sur la physionomie de la Section au cours du mois de Juin (June 24, 1942).

[26] ADHV 185 W 1–74 – Rapports Mensuels du directeur départemental du Ravitaillement Général. Rapport du Directeur Départemental du Ravitaillement Général de la Haute-Vienne à Monsieur le Préfet Régional (October 1941).

[27] ADHV 185 W 1–45 – Rapports du préfet de la Haute-Vienne au ministère de l'Intérieur. Etat d'esprit, Rapport mensuel (November 3, 1940).

[28] SHGN Box 12557, BT Guéret, Rapport du Capitaine Chaumet sur la physionomie de la Section de Guéret au cours du mois de Décembre 1941 (December 26, 1941).

apparent in public opinion reports in 1940, but the rash of denunciations in 1941 led to official attempts to limit their use that year. By year's end, denunciations had so thoroughly permeated French society that Pétain included the subject in his New Year's radio message.[29] Motivated by material gain, ideological commitment, self-preservation, or petty differences, residents picked up their pens and regularly informed the government of their neighbors' and acquaintances' immorality and misdeeds. Individual willingness to resort to denunciations created an atmosphere in which officials noted that "Few people dare to talk. One has a tendency to see in his neighbor a possible denunciator."[30] Even though denunciations could provide information on food infractions that were admittedly difficult to police, they also created an atmosphere of fear and suspicion that opposed the ideals of the National Revolution. Rather than building a stronger community through the purge of harmful elements such as black marketeers and hoarders, denunciations encouraged lying, dissimulation, and self-interested actions.

Authorities had to deal with these growing divisions in society, but they also continued to face provisioning problems. One factor that discouraged peasants from selling their farm products in traditional markets was urban dwellers' trips to the countryside. The official decree in 1941 allowing peasants to send family packages to urban relations also had the unexpected consequence of further reducing the number of items available at local markets. After sending goods to cities, peasants had fewer items to take to market, further reinforcing the need for town residents to visit the countryside. Residents of rural towns and cities also ventured into the countryside in search of items to send in packages to relatives living in cities harder hit by shortages such as Paris or Marseilles. The lack of goods in urban markets hit people without rural connections hardest, and family packages did little to lessen their difficulties.

The creation of so-called *colis familiaux* in 1941 reflected the demographic realities of France in the middle of the twentieth century as well as the new government's ideology. Forced to abandon farms by the depression in the 1930s and the organization of the agrarian market, enough city dwellers still had connections to rural relatives to make family packages a

---

[29] During the Vichy era, French residents sent between three and five million signed and anonymous denunciation letters. See André Halimi, *La délation sous l'Occupation* (Paris: Editions Alain Moreau, 1983), 7.

[30] SHGN Box 12557 – Grpt Creuse, Cie Guéret, R/4, Rapport sur la physionomie de la Section au cours du mois de Juin (June 24, 1942).

viable option for increasing rations during the Second World War.[31] Besides ameliorating shortages for some, family packages also reinforced Vichy's cultural agenda outlined in the National Revolution. Marshal Pétain called family agriculture "the principal economic and social base of France"[32] and encouraged a "return to the soil" to combat moral decadence and to promote the nation's regeneration. The French State glorified the peasant and farm life, introduced credits and subsidies for farmers, and created rural work camps (*Chantiers de la Jeunesse*), all with the belief that a strong and valued peasantry would build a strong nation. *Colis familiaux* underlined the important role peasants played in supporting French families as well as the advantages of living in a rural area. However, family parcels ultimately failed in both their material and their ideological purposes.

Rural residents soon manipulated the system, transforming it from a legal to an illegal provisioning tool. In March 1941, gendarmes in the Creuse stopped a man carrying a suspiciously large pack. Upon investigation, the gendarmes discovered a quantity of poultry, eggs, butter, and a rabbit, all intended to be sent to Paris, breaking the order concerning the "circulation of contingent foodstuffs and the constitution of family packages."[33] Ernest-Pierre Jouanneton admitted he was sending nonauthorized items and had even gone so far as to hide the butter inside a chicken and in the rabbit's stomach to avoid detection. He insisted, however, that his goal was not financial gain but rather service to his relatives and friends. A year later, gendarmes posted at a rural train station also stopped a man trying to conceal the contents of parcels. This time the accused, Maurice René, failed to print the contents of the package on the attached ticket (required by

---

[31] Between 1900 and 1936, the rural population in France decreased from 22,715,000 to 19,935,358 due largely to a rural exodus, although the fact that 673,700 male farmers were killed in the First World War certainly contributed to the decrease. Statistics from Cépède, *Agriculture et Alimentation*, p. 14. This continued a trend initiated in the late nineteenth century by patterns of migration and improved national infrastructure. See Eugen Weber, *Peasants into Frenchmen: The Modernization of Rural France, 1870–1914* (Stanford, California: Stanford University Press, 1976), especially Chapter 16, "Migration: An Industry of the Poor." On the troubles facing peasants in the interwar years, see Robert O. Paxton's chapter, "The Triple Crisis of the French Peasantry, 1929–1939," in *French Peasant Fascism: Henry Dorgères's Greenshirts and the Crises of French Agriculture, 1929–1939* (New York and Oxford: Oxford University Press, 1997).

[32] Quoted in Paxton, *Vichy France*, p. 206. See *Vichy France* for a discussion of peasants and the National Revolution as well as Lebovics, *True France* on Vichy's traditionalism and glorification of all things rural.

[33] ADC 976 W – 387. Procès-verbal dated March 16, 1941.

order) and falsified the return addresses so the sender's last name matched the recipient's. In this manner, and in keeping with the rules concerning family packages, it appeared that members of the same family were involved. He denied knowingly sending items illegally and also justified the packages as merely helping friends with no desire for recompense.[34] In both cases, the food in question was confiscated and turned over to the official supply repartition and distribution office for the department.

Though both men clearly knew they were acting illegally, proven by their efforts at dissimulation, their defense of acting in favor of their family is telling. For Vichy, the French family was a central pillar of the National Revolution and the essential building block of society. Both men tried to capitalize on this ideology while denying the financial potential of their activity, thus simultaneously acknowledging and attempting to minimize concerns about the black market. They used Vichy's own rhetoric of the family to defend illegal activities related to *colis familiaux*. Maurice René, the man caught in a rural Creuse train station, went even further than his declaration to the gendarmes in justifying the family nature of his activities. Just a month earlier, gendarmes had stopped René at the train station closest to his home and charged him with sending a package that included pork and butter, both unauthorized as parcel contents. In the attempt to avoid legal ramifications, René wrote to both the prefect of the Creuse and the department's head of supplies explaining, "I made the shipments with the sole goal of supplying my eighty-year-old mother, my sister, my son, and two old friends."[35] Furthermore, he was making a sacrifice in his own food supply in order to help his family members (two of whom, he pointed out, were career military men). Admitting to receiving a little money from his friends in order to cover his expenses, Monsieur René did not think he was actually at fault since he had declared the pork to the village mayor. Apparently the threat of prosecution did not deter René from continuing his activities; he merely took his packages to another train station.

These two Creusois men were not the only French residents sending illegally constituted family packages, thus demonstrating a clear decline in Vichy's authority. Peasants mailed millions of packages containing tons of food, but authorities soon discovered it was impossible to regulate the parcels – estimates place the number of packages sent to urban residents at

---

[34] Ibid. Procès-verbal dated March 24, 1942.
[35] ADC 976 W – 387. Letter dated March 4, 1942, making reference to a procès-verbal dated February 2, 1942.

13,500,000 in 1942 alone.³⁶ It is not possible to determine how many people with access to farm products sent parcels or how many urban residents received the precious items. Mailing and receiving parcels required connections; one had to know someone living in the country. Money often facilitated such acquaintances and "families" grew, as did tensions between producers and consumers and between individuals and the state. Though called family packages, they were often in fact sent to acquaintances or even to complete strangers willing to pay for the service. An intercepted letter from a woman in the department of the Jura implored a Creuse inhabitant to resume sending food in light of increasing difficulties in provisioning in July 1941. She had not had the "pleasure of receiving a package" from him in quite a while.³⁷ The polite tone of the letter as well as the employment of formal language including the use of "*vous*" and "*monsieur*" suggests that the sender and recipient were not close friends or family members, but merely acquaintances. The fact that postal controllers transcribed the entire letter demonstrates their concern that individuals were abusing the program in order to supply people outside their immediate family. In fact, officials opened packages, looking for rationed items or excessive amounts of food, and monitored telegrams and letters requesting farm products. They soon discovered, however, that attempts at regulating packages' contents and the number of parcels expedited did little to end abuse of the system. Profit appeared to play a larger role in many peasants' decision to send goods than did a genuine desire to help French families.

The prefect of the Creuse, Jacques-Henry, took an especially proactive approach to ending fraudulent shipments. In the desire to end black market exchanges while allowing legitimate family packages to continue, Jacques-Henry issued order number 201 on February 9, 1942. The first article required senders to write their return address on all packages and postal workers and railroad services to verify the return information by matching it to the name and address on the senders' ration cards. Article two stated packages could only be sent from the post office or train station closest to the expediter's residence. Any infractions were subject to sanctions, and various authorities in the department were authorized and expected to enforce the order. In April, the minister of the interior wrote to the secretary of state for communications in favor of Prefect Jacques-Henry's actions. Finding the order to be effective in the prevention of black market activities without

---

³⁶ Antoine Lefébure, *Les Conversations secrètes des Français sous l'Occupation* (Paris: Plon, 1993), 85.
³⁷ ADC 44 W 16. Letter dated July 18, 1941.

creating serious inconveniences for honest citizens, the minister recommended extending the practice to the rest of France.[38]

The timing of Prefect Jacques-Henry's attempts to halt black market sales reflected a shift in the national government's stance toward illicit purchases. Although the government had issued decree after decree throughout 1941, nothing seemed to stem the illegal flow of food or to prevent unlawful activity.[39] On January 1, 1942, Marshal Philippe Pétain clearly stated his position on the black market when he took to the airwaves for his annual New Year's address. Focusing on the need for national solidarity in the face of the "second winter of the armistice and of misery," Pétain claimed it was his duty to consider black market traffickers as "adversaries" to French unity.[40] Yet by the time of his speech, pinpointing black market activity and catching its animators was becoming increasingly difficult due, ironically, to French residents' unity against the government.

The dual strategies of trips to the countryside and *colis familiaux* often fell into Vichy's broad definition of black market activities. Peasants selling or mailing unregulated quantities of rationed bread, milk, eggs, pork, and beef at prices significantly above the state-imposed tax or trading agricultural products for manufactured items such as shoes and clothing constituted illegal transactions. The wide repertoire of activity that officials considered unlawful represented a continuous threat for the ordinary French citizen in search of food and other supplies. Citations for food infractions or black market activity could result in fines, confiscation of the contraband items, or imprisonment.

By the spring of 1942, the extent of the parallel economy and the complicity of sellers and buyers in abusing the state's decrees forced the government to accept minor infractions committed in the name of family food

---

[38] The text of the order can be found in AN F 1c III – 1150. Rapport Mensuel d'Information du 1er au 28 février 1942 (March 2, 1942). See also the letter from le Ministre, Secrétaire d'Etat à l'Intérieur to Monsieur le Secrétaire d'Etat aux Communications (April 18, 1942). It is unclear whether the order was revoked or extended. A gendarmerie report from the Creuse in 1943 makes reference to a "decree from October 22, 1942 which provides that all parcel senders are obliged to prove their identity." SHGN Box 12539 – BT Guéret, R/2, Le Chef d'Escadron Rivals aux commandants de section (September 1, 1943).

[39] For examples, see AN F 9–5578. Loi du 28 Juin 1941 conférant au Gouvernement des pouvoirs spéciaux en matière de prix et de ravitaillement. *Le Journal Officiel de l'Etat Français* (August 1, 1941), 3210 and Décret du 10 Novembre 1941 instituant une commission interministérielle chargée de proposer l'internement des individus dont les manoeuvres sont de nature à compromettre le ravitaillement du pays. *Le Journal Officiel* (November 30, 1941), 5166.

[40] Philippe Pétain, *Discours aux Français 17 juin 1940–20 août 1944*. (Paris: Albin Michel, 1989), 212.

supply. The law of March 15, 1942, relative to the black market thus marked a turning point in provisioning and citizen-state relations. Though internally divided along class, geographical, and racial lines, the French public was united in its quest for additional supplies in opposition to the Vichy regime, forcing the government to respond to local needs. The new black market law distinguished between broad-scale selling for profit and the small-scale activities of individuals concerned with family welfare. The severe penalties described for black market infractions, including 2, to 10 years in prison and fines ranging from 2,000 to 10,000 francs, applied only to those in search of profit and not to those who "aim only to satisfy their familial supplying needs."[41] In order for France to flourish in the new European order, French families also had to thrive.[42] Hence, the efforts of women and men to find additional food for their families ensured the survival of both the family unit and France. By allowing illegal trips to the countryside and family packages to continue in the best interest of certain French families, however, Vichy implicitly recognized its own failure to provide sufficient amounts of food for its citizens, leading to a third phase in provisioning.

INCREASING ANIMOSITY AND CULTIVATING ILLEGALITY: MARCH 1942–FALL 1942

Despite official concern with the black market, the proliferation of supply laws, and the increasing complicity and simultaneous divisions in society, the French population continued to engage in illegal activities. Following the law concerning the black market in March 1942, the food situation in France only worsened. Public opinion reports from the summer and fall of 1942 record the growing animosity between urban and rural residents as well as the fact that even country residents felt shortages' effects. Yet the Vichy government did not bear the brunt of the criticism concerning supplying, and strained relationships never reached the breaking point. French residents worked together against the Vichy regime's restrictive provisioning laws, but

---

[41] Loi numéro 405 du 15 mars 1942 tendant à réprimer le marché noir. *Le Journal Officiel de l'Etat Français* volume 67 (March 19, 1942), 1076.

[42] On the role of families in general (and women in particular) in the National Revolution, see Paxton, *Vichy France*, pp. 165–8; John F. Sweets, *Choices in Vichy France: The French under Nazi Occupation* (New York and Oxford: Oxford University Press, 1994), 42+; Miranda Pollard, *Reign of Virtue: Mobilizing Gender in Vichy France* (Chicago and London: The University of Chicago Press, 1998); and Francine Muel-Dreyfus, *Vichy et l'éternel féminin* (Paris: Seuil, 1996).

they still worked within the system. Even government officials accepted extra-legal activities as a daily fact of life during the war. This simultaneous adaptation on the part of individuals and the government allowed the government to continue to function but created a culture of illegality that directly countered the National Revolution and helped facilitate active resistance.

Notwithstanding the continually growing corpus of supply regulations, officials – including those charged with combating food infractions – often turned a blind eye to minor transgressions when the result was the survival of certain French families. Gendarmes in Nexon (just twenty kilometers southwest of Limoges and the site for the department's camp for undesirables) reported in May 1942, "Some people from the cities supply themselves a little in the countryside, either in vegetables or sometimes in eggs or poultry. When it has to do with the normal supplies of a family, it is good to close your eyes a little, because certain people are really in critical situations."[43] In Saint-Germain-les-Belles, thirty-six kilometers from Limoges and near the border of the department of the Corrèze, the situation was much the same:

Sunday nights and often during the week, it is not unusual to see at the train stations, either in the direction of Brive or Limoges, a large quantity of people, and one easily guesses that each traveler carries in his suitcase a dozen eggs and a chicken. It is from a little black market that one does not dare reprimand, but often repeated, it is an obstacle to the good division of these products.[44]

Gendarmes suspected these individuals of violating the law on various levels: Eggs were rationed, the prefect of the Haute-Vienne had outlawed purchases at the farm, and, in all likelihood, purchasers paid far more than the official price for the items. Authorities clearly followed the black market law that distinguished between profit and survival, but demonstrated their inability to provide foodstuffs or to stop extra-legal activity.

In this third period, officials recorded the growing abuse of trips to the countryside and family packages as material conditions continued to worsen. In March 1942, gendarmes reported that supplying was "more and more difficult" for those who did not grow their own food, and collection brokers bought most farm products thereby depriving markets of goods and forcing consumers out into the countryside.[45] One letter writer remarked in

---

[43] SHGN Box 12721 – Grpt Haute-Vienne, BT Nexon, R/4, Rapport sur l'état d'esprit des populations (May 21, 1942).

[44] SHGN Box 12741 – Haute-Vienne, BT Saint Germain-les-Belles, R/4, Rapport sur l'état d'esprit de la population et la police économique (March 20, 1943).

[45] SHGN Box 12647 – Grpt Haute-Vienne, BT Limoges, R/4, Rapport du Chef d'Escadron Rebour sur l'état d'esprit des populations (March 20, 1942).

May that "one must move, comb the countryside starting at four in the morning and beg from door to door," just in order to survive.[46] In April, the postal control reported, "Numerous are the city dwellers who call on their country friends and acquaintances to supplement the supply insufficiency. Each day numerous communications have as an object the sending of provision packages (principally butter and eggs)."[47] Farmers responded to the requests for food: The director of food supply for the Haute-Vienne reported that in one month that summer, 27,000 eggs were declared in packages sent from the train station in Eymoutiers. He believed, however, that this was only half of the number of eggs that were actually mailed from the station.[48] The interception of letters and packages demonstrated the commercial rather than private nature of many interactions, further confirming the government's fears about black market activities and profiteering.[49] Individuals with access to rural areas bought items at farms (often at elevated prices) and sent them to city dwellers who would reimburse the expenses – including fines incurred for breaking laws concerning food supply. The sheer numbers of packages prevented the verification of all contents and although parcels were to include only nonrationed items, precious goods like butter and meat often slipped through. Still reports repeatedly remarked on officials' tolerance of trips to the countryside and indulgence of the black market. With the overwhelming generalization of these supply tactics, there was little the government could do to stop clandestine activity.

When trips to the countryside and family packages fell short of meeting needs, some city dwellers could turn to bartering. Roland du Chalard exchanged his tobacco ration tickets for cheese by mailing his tickets to a family acquaintance in the Aveyron. Du Chalard did not smoke while the farmer did, thus the exchange of tickets for cheese from the Cantal benefited both parties.[50] Marie Gatard's family also exchanged their tobacco tickets

---

[46] Portion of letter quoted in ADHV 185 W 1–205. Commission de Contrôle Postal. Rapport Mensuel No. 62 (May 1942), 7.
[47] Ibid., Commission de Contrôle Téléphonique de Limoges. Rapport Mensuel No. 16 (April 1942), 5.
[48] ADHV 185 W 1–74 – Rapports Mensuels du directeur départemental du Ravitaillement Général (July 23, 1942).
[49] ADC 976 W – 387. Letter from le Ministre, Secrétaire d'Etat à l'Intérieur à Monsieur le Secrétaire d'Etat aux Communications (April 18, 1942). See also AN F 1c III – 1150. Rapport Mensuel d'Information du 1er au 28 février 1942 (March 2, 1942) and ADHV 185 W 1–63 – Rapports mensuels du directeur régional du ravitaillement général. Report from June and July, 1942 (July 25, 1942).
[50] Claude Lacan, Georges-Marie Proux, and Roland du Chalard, *Le Limousin de la Défaite et de l'Occupation. Chronique des années 1940–1944* (Limoges: Editions René Dessagne, 1978), 231.

for food. In addition to supplementing the family's rations by buying food in the countryside while performing his duties as an inspector for the Central Office of the Distribution of Industrial Products, her father traded his tobacco ration for a liter of milk per day from a grocer in Limoges.[51] However, as one anonymous Limousin author observed, happy "are those who have something to exchange, but in order to do that one must have relatives and friends in the countryside."[52] Judging by postal control service reports, many French residents did have the rural contacts necessary for bartering and were taking full advantage of them by the spring of 1942. Censors regularly intercepted letters proposing exchanges, and residents of other departments brought cheese, wine, tires, and other regional products into the Limousin in exchange for potatoes and other goods.[53]

Despite the government's obvious failure to provide food and the resultant need for French residents to act illegally in order to ensure their food supply, the Vichy government did not bear the brunt of public criticisms related to shortages. Citizens expected Vichy to rectify inequalities, but urban French regularly blamed "selfish" peasants for the shortages, and the whole nation believed that Nazi requisitions contributed to the country's suffering. The Vichy regime, committed to collaboration with the Germans and to notions of the peasantry's gallantry, often held Jews responsible for the country's supplying woes. A special report on the public's attitude in Limoges toward restrictions, prices, and provisioning conducted in March 1942 concluded that even though citizens expressed criticisms, "They are perfectly aware that the severe measures that are applied are the inevitable consequence of our defeat and the Government's prestige is not affected."[54] In contrast, the Postal Control Commission in Limoges noted blatant anger and violent threats directed at the peasants who failed to bring their goods to market. Various authorities recognized the antagonism that existed between the rural and

---

[51] Marie Gatard, *La guerre, mon père* (Poitiers: Mercure de France, 1978), 35–6.

[52] ADHV 185 W 1–205. Commission de Contrôle Postal. Rapport Mensuel No. 62 (May 1942), 7.

[53] On the rapid development of bartering in 1942, see ADHV 185 W 1–206. Synthèses hebdomadaires du coordinateur du service civil des contrôles techniques (January 31, 1942–November 4, 1943). Report dated May 30, 1942. See also ADHV 185 W 1–205 especially Contrôles Techniques – Synthèse Hebdomadaire du 17 Novembre 1941; Commission de Contrôle Postal de Limoges, Synthèse des Renseignements No. 5 du Mois de Mai 1943; and Commission de Contrôle Postal de Limoges, Synthèse des Renseignements No. 9 du Mois de Septembre 1943.

[54] ADHV 185 W 3–15. Services départementaux des renseignements généraux – Haute-Vienne. Le Commissaire Spécial à Monsieur le Commissaire Principal, Chef de Service (March 24, 1942).

urban populations and recorded virulent condemnations of the peasantry: "The peasants do nothing for the supplying of the cities, they prefer to sell to the highest bidder, the dirty bastards! If we hang a few of them, that would change but no one says anything to them" or "The peasants starve the people of the cities and they are short of nothing, they earn incredible amounts, [and] that should not be permitted."[55] The letters' authors wanted to see the government take action against the "dirty bastards"; however, most of the anger was directed at the rich peasant who, it appeared, was not suffering from the wartime restrictions. Despite the complaints articulated in presumably private letters, public expressions of hostility were rare as urban residents depended upon farmers for food. The "have-nots" acknowledged peasants to be the new "kings of the situation"[56] with the power to withhold valuable items, and buyers could not afford to alienate their suppliers. The shortages thus simultaneously divided and allied the French population.

The criticism of the peasantry reflects both historical animosities between urban and rural populations in times of crisis and moral objections to privilege in periods of scarcity. During the Great War, teachers on fixed incomes regularly expressed bitterness toward the farmers who "were 'stuffed with gold,' [and] were making 'fabulous' profits," yet other segments of society felt peasants deserved more money for the hard work that kept the country relatively well supplied.[57] Despite farmers' best efforts during the Second World War, supplies could not keep up with demands, and no one defended the profits made through selling items at higher prices. The French people viewed the sacrifices of the First World War as necessary and rightfully shared between the fighting front and the home front. Farmers under Vichy did not have the same motivation; their hard work supported seemingly ungrateful city dwellers and the foreign occupier. As hard as

---

[55] ADHV 185 W 1–205. Commission de Contrôle Postal de Limoges. Rapport Statistique Mensuel du Mois de Décembre 1943, p. 10. See also prefect's reports, gendarmerie reports, and general information reports for examples of urban-rural antagonism.

[56] Ibid. Quote from a letter cited in Commission de Contrôle Postal de Limoges. Rapport Mensuel No. 55 (October 1941), 10.

[57] Jean-Jacques Becker, *The Great War and the French People* translated by Arnold Pomerans with an introduction by Jay Winter (Leamington Spa, Heidelberg, and Dover, New Hampshire: Berg, 1985), 121. Such antagonism between urban and rural dwellers in times of shortages extends back centuries in French history. See for example Cynthia A. Bouton's examination of food riots in 1775 in *The Flour War: Gender, Class, and Community in Late Ancien Régime French Society* (University Park: The Pennsylvania State University Press, 1993). Georges Lefebvre explores urban-rural attitudes during the French Revolution in *The Great Fear of 1789: Rural Panic in Revolutionary France* translated by Joan White (London: NLB, 1973).

they tried, officials failed to adequately justify the sacrifices or to evenly distribute their effects, further adding to the tensions between city and countryside.

Economic, material, and ideological concerns as well as long-standing attitudes all affected the complex relationships between urban and rural dwellers. Increasingly reliant on their connections with rural acquaintances for survival as official rations decreased, city residents came to resent peasants' advantages. But concerned with their own problems, inhabitants of towns and villages failed to take the difficulties facing peasants fully into account before launching their criticisms. In order to meet German demands, the Vichy regime imposed ever-growing production quotas on peasants despite severe labor shortages. In 1940, approximately 1.6 million men were being held as prisoners of war in Germany. At least 500,000 of these men were farmers between the ages of 20 and 40. In other words, 13 percent of the active male agricultural population was now absent.[58] Women, the young, the elderly, and refugee laborers tried to maintain farms in the absence of the missing men and in a situation worsened by shortages, the disruption of the war, and the Occupation. The short supply of seeds and fertilizer for the fields, gas and oil for farm machinery, and fodder for the animals rendered farms' daily operations even more difficult.

Official reports from the Limousin first consistently noted agricultural labor shortages in the war's third spring and summer. A survey conducted by the Agricultural Services in the Creuse in March 1942 revealed a shortage of over 3,000 male and female farm workers in the department.[59] From April through August, the prefects of the Creuse and the Haute-Vienne both reported on locals' complaints about labor shortages to the national government in Vichy. Marshal Pétain's government attempted to ameliorate the

---

[58] Prisoner-of-war numbers cited in Sarah Fishman, "Waiting for the Captive Sons of France: Prisoner of War Wives, 1940–1945" in *Behind the Lines: Gender and the Two World Wars* edited by Margaret Randolph Higonnet, Jane Jenson, Sonya Michel, and Margaret Collins Weitz (New Haven, Connecticut, and London: Yale University Press, 1987), 182. Farmer statistics in Cépède, *Agriculture et Alimentation,* p. 210. For a local example, see SHGN Box 12631 – BT La Souterraine R/2, Etat de renseignements concernant les hommes de 18 à 27 ans. In the communities surrounding the town of La Souterraine in the Creuse, 104 of the 650 men aged 18–27 (16 percent) were prisoners of war at the beginning of 1941. The prefect also estimated that four-fifths of the 9,000 prisoners of war from the department were farmers. See AN F 1c III – 1150, Rapport Mensuel d'Information du 1 au 30 Novembre 1941 (December 2, 1941). In the Haute-Vienne, there were 6,600 agricultural prisoners of war. See AN F 1c III – 1197, Rapport Mensuel d'Information du 1er mai au 31 mai 1942 (June 5, 1942).

[59] ADC 25 W – 44. Requisition de main d'oeuvre agricole. Commission d'Utilisation de la Main-d'Oeuvre agricole (March 28, 1942), 1–2.

FIGURE 1. Loading hay, Creuse. Ingeborg Haas, a Jewish refugee living at the Château de Chabannes, helps load a hay wagon at a farm where she worked for local residents (1941–3). Photo credit: USHMM, courtesy of Angela Schneider.

situation by encouraging a reverse migration from cities to the countryside. Propaganda associated the "return to the earth" with France's moral regeneration, but the campaign also had utilitarian functions. Rural employment initiatives required male city dwellers to discover themselves in the countryside. Urban workers, drafted as farmhands during labor-intensive periods of the agricultural cycle such as planting and harvesting, could also provide much-needed help and would ensure larger yields. Officials further encouraged young men and the unemployed to seek positions on farms. An announcement from the Peasant Restoration Mission printed in the regional newspaper in April 1942 promised urban dwellers a better life without worries for the future, without food concerns, and with all the joys of family if they went to work on farms.[60] Even René Bousquet, Vichy's General Secretary of the Police, ordered young, unemployed Jews in the unoccupied zone – excluded from most jobs by Vichy's antisemitic legislation – to be put at the disposal of rural work collectives on July 21, 1942.[61] (See Figure 1.) But such actions often resulted in greater tension between the populations as the workers with no agricultural knowledge proved useless to farmers, and

---

[60] See *Le Courrier du Centre* number 79 (April 1, 1942): 2.
[61] ADC 25 W – 44. Requisition de main d'oeuvre agricole. Le Secretaire Général à la Police à Messieurs les Préfets zone sud (July 21, 1942).

the farmers began to reject aid offers.[62] The results of Vichy's financial incentives designed to encourage the cultivation of new farmland were not much more successful. The program attracted only 1,561 families throughout France, a quarter of whom failed to remain on the land.[63]

Thus, the rhetoric and celebration of a "return to the earth" articulated in the National Revolution failed to attract new farmers, and, in fact, immigration to urban areas continued during the war despite the shortages. Financial realities once again proved stronger than idealism and ideology. The porcelain, textile, and shoe making industries in Limoges had drawn peasants from the rural Haute-Vienne and Creuse to the city throughout the nineteenth and twentieth centuries. Due to shortages of primary materials, including coal for the porcelain kilns and leather for shoes, the traditional industries suffered during the war, but Limoges and other towns continued to attract rural inhabitants. Authorities complained that the need for additional members of the police force and the generous pay provided for such services enticed agricultural laborers to leave farms for the cities at a time when rural labor was already stretched thin.[64] The prefect of the Haute-Vienne reported that in Magnac-Laval, the installation of a garrison of infantrymen created a demand for workers in the town. Offering wages well above those in agriculture, the military installation created a "massive departure" from the surrounding countryside to the town by the spring of 1942.[65] In this manner, Vichy's own institutions for surveillance and the maintenance of order contradicted its domestic program for a social and cultural rebirth exemplified by the peasant way of life.

City dwellers also resented the pride of place Vichy awarded to peasants and the rural lifestyle, though peasants found the distance between rhetoric and reality hard to reconcile. Pétain's government offered peasants the respect and support the Third Republic had denied them. After the disintegration of rural life hastened by the Great Depression in the 1930s, the

[62] ADHV 185 W 3–15. Services départementaux des renseignements généraux. Report dated July 24, 1942, p. 4. See also *Le Courrier du Centre* number 116 (May 13, 1942): 1.
[63] Paxton, *Vichy France,* p. 208.
[64] The delegate prefect of the Haute-Vienne estimated that 2,500 agricultural workers left the countryside for cities during 1941. See AN F 1c III – 1197, Rapport Mensuel d'Information du 1er mai au 31 mai 1942 (June 5, 1942). On people leaving the countryside for police forces, see ADHV 185 W 3–15. Services départementaux des renseignments généraux. Report dated July 24, 1942, p. 4; AN F 1c III – 1197. Prefect's report (August 5, 1942); and SHGN Box 12691 – BT Limoges, R/4, Rapport sur l'état d'esprit (May 21, 1942). Certain members of the state's policing forces were also entitled to "T" ration cards. See *Le Journal Officiel de l'Etat Français* (February 22, 1942).
[65] AN F 1c III – 1197. Rapport Mensuel d'Information du 1er février au 28 février 1942 (March 4, 1942).

"*Life has never been so good*" 45

French State's promises to develop family farms, to ensure the comfort, hygiene, and prosperity of peasants, and to return the peasantry to their rightful place in society appealed to many farmers.[66] Associating the peasant soul with the soul of France, prominent members of the government gave rural inhabitants hope for a bright future while angering some city dwellers. A number of urban residents, especially civil servants with fixed salaries, took offense at the solicitude authorities displayed toward the newly rich peasants.[67] Many farmers experienced monetary gains, but without Vichy's aid. The material conditions – shortages of foodstuffs, labor, and farming supplies; requisitions; and low official prices – soon disabused peasants of the notion of a better life under the new regime. Officials intercepted a letter in April 1942 complaining that "the return to the soil is all well and good, but with 350 grams of bread and no wine for plowing or mowing all day, they can tighten their belts."[68] Only by breaking rationing laws (and thereby the principles of the National Revolution's moral regeneration) could the peasant achieve the promised prosperity.

Despite obvious social tensions, the rift between urban and rural residents and between citizens and the government never became unbridgeable. The social fabric held because the split was largely superficial and because the multiple fractions in society (urban, rural, refugees, French Jews, foreign Jews, Gypsies, resisters, collaborators) diffused criticism. While voicing complaints about each other, urban dwellers relied on rural residents for food, and farmers often preferred selling their goods to individuals rather than turning their products over to the state. Such activities created links between the populations that prevented true ruptures. Although authorities emphasized the divisions between city dwellers and producers in the countryside, food shortages could actually bring the urban and rural populations together in common cause against the Vichy regime and the Germans. Furthermore, the German occupiers provided the average French citizen with a

---

[66] Pierre Caziot, Vichy's minister of agriculture, outlined the government's program for the "return to the soil." See the article, "Le Problème Agricole d'après-guerre." *Le Courrier de la Creuse* number 53 (July 28, 1940): 1. See also Caziot's postwar statement on agriculture under Vichy in *France during the German Occupation 1940–1944: A Collection of 292 Statements on the Government of Maréchal Pétain and Pierre Laval, Volume 1* translated by Philip W. Whitcomb (Stanford, California: Stanford University Press for The Hoover Institution on War, Revolution, and Peace, 1957), 250–70.
[67] AN F 1c III – 1150. Rapport Mensuel d'Information du 1er février au 31 mars 1944.
[68] ADHV 185 W 1–207. Services des contrôles techniques de Guéret. Le Préfet du Département de la Creuse. Synthèse des interceptions (1ère quinzaine de Avril, 17 Avril 1942), 3. On peasants' disaffection with Vichy in other regions, see Sweets, *Choices in Vichy France*, pp. 77–9 and Gildea, *Marianne in Chains*, pp. 125–30.

convenient and convincing scapegoat. German officials estimated in March 1942 that merchandise worth more than 100 million francs passed from the unoccupied to the occupied zone clandestinely each day. Over the course of the war, the Germans spent approximately 127 billion francs on black market purchases, far outweighing any individual family purchase.[69] One did not need direct interactions with the Germans to place the blame for shortages on the occupier. The weekly summary from the coordinator of the *Service civil des contrôles techniques* at the end of May 1942 noted, "Supplying difficult because ninety-three million Germans eat from our plates. The restrictions are becoming intolerable (*intenables*)."[70] Of course Vichy could never publicly acknowledge German culpability due to the regime's commitment to collaboration and its own inability to maintain political and material sovereignty.

Placing blame on individuals and the German occupiers helps explain how the Vichy government was able to maintain its authority and why the regime allowed illegal supplying to continue. Even though a government may be able to prevent uprisings on the short term, failure to respond adequately to material demands ultimately undermines its authority and legitimacy. The Vichy government's failure to provide and/or to maintain adequate levels of goods fostered an atmosphere in which deceit and dissimulation became invaluable despite their incongruity with the National Revolution's ideals. Public opinion developed in ways that were often related to the extent of shortages, and local ideas about community based on material interactions served to further weaken the Vichy government's moral agenda and legitimacy. Daily tensions changed the nature of urban–rural interactions and altered social hierarchies, shifting power to the peasantry. Finally, the French State's attempts to control illegal material transactions facilitated and justified its intrusion into daily lives but ultimately demonstrated the supremacy of personal concerns over national ideals.

THIEVES AND TERRORISTS: FALL 1942–SUMMER 1944

Beginning in the fall and winter of 1942, the greatest material threats facing many locals were thieves and the organized Resistance. The increasing extent of shortages also raised a question for the Vichy regime: Was the rejection of rationing and restrictions by both men and women a form of political

---

[69] Numbers cited in Simon Kitson, *Vichy et la chasse aux espions nazis 1940–1942: complexités de la politique de collaboration* (Paris: Editions Autrement, 2005), 29.

[70] ADHV 185 W 1–206. Synthèses hebdomadaires du coordinateur du service civil des contrôles techniques (May 30, 1942), 2.

expression, or did it constitute Resistance against an oppressive regime?[71] Men and women had become habituated to negotiating the quotidian within political constraints and decisions to accept or reject certain ideals of the government's National Revolution had their roots in individual, daily experiences.

The government was fully aware of shortages' political implications by the fall of 1942 and the ways in which material concerns could aid the organized Resistance. The prefect's report from the Haute-Vienne in October explicitly outlined the concerns: "Almost indifferent to the national repercussions of exterior events, the population judges these only from a utilitarian angle and complains bitterly about the war's prolongation which makes the privations more and more noticeable." Delegate Prefect Popineau feared "grave events" due to the shortages of cheese and fatty goods in the fall, his fear further supported by "particularly intense" Resistance propaganda in September that focused on the theme of famine and called for a civil war. He re-emphasized the threat noting,

> This propaganda must be followed attentively and its authors tracked and punished without pity, if not the country will face extremely grave events. But this repression [...] must not make the administration forget its first duty: to help those who suffer, to simplify as much as possible the formalities concerning supplying, to avoid carefully everything that could be considered by the public as vexation or negligence.[72]

Throughout France, there was a "stirring of civil disobedience in the countryside in the second half of 1942" including "the widespread retention of foods which were subject to requisitioning."[73]

By 1942, the Limousin and its hills of the Massif Central had become a center of organized Resistance activity by rural guerrilla groups known as the maquis. Clandestine life required these illegal fighters to depend upon the local population for food, clothing, shelter, and supplies especially after new ration cards went into effect on January 1, 1942. Usually organized by the region's Communist Party, the maquis shifted from political resistance such as propaganda and demonstrations to more active forms of resistance like thefts and bombings in the fall of 1942.[74] Spectacular and brazen acts, intended to

---

[71] The political issues of collaboration and resistance have been the subject of numerous historical studies focusing on the Vichy period. For a historiographical overview of these issues, see John F. Sweets, "Hold that Pendulum! Redefining Fascism, Collaborationism and Resistance in France," *French Historical Studies* 15:4 (Fall 1988): 731–58, and Jackson, *France: The Dark Years*.

[72] AN F 1 c III – 1197. Rapport mensuel d'information (October 6, 1942).

[73] H. R. Kedward, *In Search of the Maquis: Rural Resistance in Southern France, 1942–1944* (Oxford: Clarendon Press, 1993), 13.

[74] For an overview of the party's activities in the Limousin, see Sarah Farmer, "The Communist Resistance in the Haute-Vienne" *French Historical Studies* 14:1 (Spring 1985): 89–116.

thwart Vichy and the Nazis, also sought to win the public's support in the struggle against these authoritarian governments. As a result, communists throughout France focused on the population's daily concerns about provisioning. By the time the maquis decided to undertake active resistance, the population had become increasingly comfortable with illegal activity, and locals' silence was imperative for the Resistance to survive. But life outside the law often put an increased material strain on local populations as the maquis "requisitioned" food from Limousin farmers and demanded supplies.

The communists were among the first in France to oppose the Nazis, the war, and, later, the Vichy regime. Outlawed on August 26, 1939, after the Nazi-Soviet Pact, the Communist Party went underground, producing the first edition of its clandestine newspaper, *L'Humanité*, on October 26, 1939. From the beginning, communists drew on the concerns of daily life in their attempt to mobilize the French population against the war, a continuation of the party's interwar focus on "bread and butter" issues. By the fall of 1942, criticism of the government's handling of material allocations and supplying was a familiar and predictable refrain in *L'Humanité*. The articles placed blame for shortages (on the Third Republic, the Vichy regime, Adolf Hitler, or the Germans depending on the month), called for increased rations, and linked daily life to political goals. One article reminded readers, "the battle for bread, it is not only the present battle for family life, it is also the battle for the future, the battle for liberty and for peace."[75] Most of the articles on supplies – an issue essential to maintaining the family – were addressed specifically to French women. Lise Ricol, a member of the communist Resistance during the war, recalled organizing "Feminine Committees" in the southern suburbs of Paris. She explained, "Like a certain number of women, I asked myself: why 'feminine' committees? In fact it was the only way to mobilize women against Vichy and the occupying forces, starting with the real problems of everyday life."[76] The Communist Party hoped that female opposition to individual provisioning policies could be extended to include a condemnation of the government as a whole. The communists (and the Vichy government) assumed that women held the primary responsibility for providing their families with food and thus focused on women. But much of the active Resistance, especially in rural areas, remained a male preserve.

---

[75] *L'Humanité* no. 112 (May 8, 1941) in *L'Humanité clandestine, 1939–1944* edited by Victor Joannes and Jean Burles (Paris: Editions sociales, 1975).

[76] Ania Francos, *Il était des femmes dans la Résistance* ... (Paris: Stock, 1978), 121. On the role of women in the Resistance and the Communist Party see especially, Paula Schwartz, "*Partisanes* and Gender Politics in Vichy France" *French Historical Studies* 16:1 (Spring 1989) and Schwartz, "Redefining Resistance: Women's Activism in Wartime France" in *Behind the Lines*.

"Life has never been so good"   49

By 1942, rural communism and Resistance had well-established roots in the Limousin. Since the French Communist Party's (Parti Communiste Français, PCF) establishment in 1920, the Limousin proved to be a region that consistently supported the PCF. The increasing urbanization of French society in the 1920s and 1930s marginalized the rural population socially, economically, and politically, and many peasants turned to communism.[77] Despite Vichy's rhetoric extolling the virtues of the peasant way of life and its promises to revalorize rural labor, the Communist Party in the Limousin remained a force to be reckoned with during the war years because "From the beginning, Communists recognized that the Pétain regime was dominated by their principal enemies from the prewar period."[78] As early as November 1940, local officials observed that communists in the Haute-Vienne were distributing copies of *L'Humanité*. Throughout 1940 and 1941, officials arrested communists in the Creuse and Haute-Vienne, and communist propaganda calling Vichy authorities *affameurs* (starvers) appeared in the region. After the Nazis launched their offensive against the Soviet Union on June 22, 1941, the Hitler–Stalin Pact no longer prevented PCF members from opposing the Nazis. Some scholars see this event as a major turning point in Franco-German relations,[79] but there was neither a noticeable increase in communist agitation nor Resistance activity in the Limousin judging from the political opinion reports. The shift from political to active Resistance came in 1942, with the first spectacular antigovernment actions taking place that fall.

Georges Guingouin would emerge as a leader of wartime communist activity in the Limousin early in the war. Dismissed from his position as a schoolteacher in the southeastern Haute-Vienne town of Saint-Gilles-les-Fôrets in September 1940 due to his political affiliation, Guingouin printed the region's edition of *L'Humanité* and began organizing rural Resistance networks in the Limousin at the end of 1941. By October 1942, Guingouin headed a group of partisans ready to engage in active Resistance to the Vichy regime. One of their first targets was the baling machines sent into the region by the Ravitaillement Générale (General Supply Services) to requisition and remove hay from the area. Guingouin explained the rationale for such attacks in his memoirs: "[T]he German war machine will be weakened and the peasants will keep their hay. It is a new threshold in the action."

---

[77] For a detailed account of the Communist Party's strength and development in the Limousin, see Laird Boswell, *Rural Communism in France, 1920–1939* (Ithaca, New York, and London: Cornell University Press, 1998). On interwar attitudes, see p. 9.
[78] Farmer, "The Communist Resistance," p. 94.
[79] Gildea, *Marianne in Chains*, pp. 17–18.

Citing the low prices offered by the government and the arbitrary requisitioning system, Guingouin justified the sabotage as protecting local peasants' economic interests. The initial attacks were followed by additional bombings of baling machines in the spring, leading the charismatic Guingouin to proclaim: "They will not bale any more hay for the Germans in this region!"[80]

The political situation in the Limousin underwent major changes during the fall of 1942 and spring of 1943, coinciding (although not directly correlated) with the increase in communist Resistance activity. On November 11, 1942, German troops crossed the demarcation line into Free France as a result of Allied landings in North Africa. The occupation of the entire country effectively ended many of the political advantages previously associated with living in the unoccupied territories and further limited the Vichy regime's autonomy and authority. Resistance activities, however, now could be aimed directly at the foreign occupier rather than just at its French agents or indirectly at the German war machine. With total occupation came greater demands: Germany raised occupation costs to 25 million Reichsmarks and required larger numbers of French workers to be sent to the Reich to support the war effort. As a result, the Vichy government instituted the STO (Service du travail obligatoire, or Compulsory Labor Service) on February 16, 1943, which conscripted workers to fulfill German labor needs. Rather than facing "deportation" to German factories, many young men took to the hills, where some joined the maquis.

These political changes had material consequences as the French prepared to face their fourth winter at war. In general, the food situation was worsening throughout the country after years of requisitions and shortages of fertilizer, feed, farmhands, and other necessary raw materials. The Allied invasion of North Africa also meant that the metropole was now cut off from its colonies and their foodstuffs. As local residents tried to stock up for the long winter months, officials reported that large businesses from the neighboring Midi region had grouped employees' ration cards in order to buy potatoes in bulk, above the government-set price.[81] By November, the Postal Control asserted, "Opinion is unanimous: supplying is becoming more and more difficult, restrictions are making themselves felt more than last year, and villagers complain almost as much as city dwellers."[82] Shortages of butter, milk, fruits,

---

[80] Georges Guingouin, *Quatre ans de lutte sur le sol limousin* (Paris: Hachette, 1974), 64, 69.
[81] ADHV 185 W 1–206 – Synthèses hebdomadaires du coordinateur du service civil des contrôles techniques. Report written by Pujol (October 3, 1942), 3.
[82] ADHV 185 W 1–205. Contrôle postal. Commission de Contrôle Postal de Limoges. Rapport Mensuel No. 68 (November 1942), 6.

and vegetables persisted, but food was not the only item in short supply. The regional prefect for Limoges noted in his report for August 1942 that the housing situation in the region remained critical.[83] The German troops' arrival in Limoges on November 11, 1942, exacerbated food and housing shortages. A report intended to provide information about German actions to resisters living outside France described the situation in the city. On the day of the invasion, the Germans occupied the majority of hotel rooms, they established a presence at the train station, installed a special police service, and demanded space at the local slaughterhouse to butcher thirty animals daily.[84] Within a month, local officials commented regularly on housing shortages created by German requisitions and on residents' fears about the adverse effects of an additional drain on the food supply. The supply situation in cities was so critical that officials described it as creating a "revolt psychosis."[85] By the spring of 1943, even rural portions of the population previously sheltered from the war's harshest effects began to feel shortages' strains due in part to the Occupation and the STO.

The deteriorating food situation led many residents to resort to thievery. Farmers like Jean Lalande, mentioned at the beginning of this chapter, filed report after report with the gendarmerie: chickens, rabbits, ducks, geese, fruits, and vegetables disappeared with alarming regularity. For the most part, gendarmes listed the crime as committed by an "unknown author." In other cases, thefts occurred after peasants turned away urban residents in search of food empty handed. A rural woman caught two men stealing a pair of ducks after their effort to "procure a little food" in a small hamlet outside Limoges produced no results. Many French citizens often had no intention of stealing, yet they could not resist snatching a chicken or duck wandering along the side of the road due to the desperate provisioning situation. One pair of unemployed men even stole a sheep they inadvertently stumbled upon while looking for a job.[86] By the fall of 1942, thefts had become just another tool residents used in their struggle to get by. Survival required creativity and stretching the law's limits – lessons already learned from

---

[83] ADHV 185 W 1-44. Rapports mensuels du préfet régional au chef du gouvernement. Rapport régional – août. Lemoine (August 1942), 5.

[84] AN F 1a 4000 – Région de Limoges. Bulletin Hebdomadaire de Renseignements. PHX 5 2739/12 (November 11, 1942).

[85] ADHV 185 W 1-206 – Synthèses hebdomadaires du coordinateur du service civil des contrôles techniques (31 janvier 1942–4 novembre 1943). Limoges, Période du 17 au 24 Avril 1943 (April 24, 1943), 1.

[86] On the duck theft, see SHGN Box 12710 – BT Limoges. Procès-verbal number 90 (January 6, 1944). On the sheep theft, see SHGN Box 12708 – BT Limoges. Procès-verbal number 1406 (July 25, 1943).

the government's mixed messages on family packages and trips to the countryside. As early as December 31, 1940, Marshal Philippe Pétain had called on "Frenchmen's ingenuity so that they themselves improvise the means to supplement [*completer*] their diet."[87] Such imperatives contradicted justifications for rationing and encouraged egoism rather than French unity.

Illegal activity such as thefts also helped contribute to the "culture of the outlaw" that was necessary for the Resistance's survival. This outlaw culture "embodies the conviction that the established law has exceeded its rights and has itself become illegal, so that real authority, real justice and legitimacy, now lie with those who have technically become outlaws."[88] In this case, the outlaws were the maquis living in woods and planning attacks on strategic targets in opposition to Vichy's legal authority. The creation of a positive outlaw culture required cohesion between the maquis and local communities, both urban and rural. In his study of the Cévennes region in southern France, Roderick Kedward sees these connections occurring when urban workers drafted for the STO fled to rural areas to avoid going to Germany.[89] In the Limousin, one way in which Georges Guingouin hoped to strengthen this cohesion and increase his maquis' authority and legitimacy was to focus on the material situation. The peasantry's access to food proved vital to sustaining and propagating active Resistance movements; therefore, Guingouin actively cultivated relationships between his band of Resistance fighters and local farmers.

The relationship between the maquis and the peasantry required delicacy, however. Choosing to live life outside the law meant abandoning your family, your friends, your employment, and your ration cards. It meant adjusting to life among men, in the open, and on the run. Those in hiding relied on the local population for both food and silence. Some rural residents, such as Madame Ribiéras, the grocer in Sussac (forty-four kilometers southeast of Limoges) had access to valuable goods such as sugar, but also aided the Resistance for more personal reasons. Guingouin explained, "Her husband is a prisoner in one of Hitler's stalags. For her, the cars' rumblings evoke known faces. She knows that the more numerous these men are, the more blows they will strike at the German war machine, and the sooner the papa of her small boy will return."[90] But in addition to organized Resistance groups, the hills of the Haute-Vienne sheltered *réfractaires* – young men

---

[87] Pétain, *Discours aux Français* (December 31, 1940), 108.
[88] Roderick Kedward, "The Maquis and the Culture of the Outlaw (With Particular Reference to the Cévennes)" in *Vichy France and the Resistance: Culture & Ideology* edited by Roderick Kedward and Roger Austin (London and Sydney: Croom Helm, 1985), 244.
[89] Ibid., pp. 246–9.
[90] Guingouin, *Quatre ans de lutte*, p. 97.

fleeing the STO but not organized into partisan bands – that engaged in pillaging and thievery. The maquis relied on friendly peasants, but often poor and facing shortages themselves, they could not provide the supplies necessary to feed the growing bands. So Guingouin's maquis would "requisition" goods from peasants known to be Vichy sympathizers or steal money from the government to pay for their purchases.[91] Officials reported increasing thefts by "terrorist" bands in the early months of 1943 including an incident in which fifteen armed men attacked a truck carrying requisitioned calves and stole three of them.[92] Such activities were justified in the maquis' eyes because feeding the Resistance, the homeland's protectors, had greater legitimacy than turning French farm products over to the Germans.

By the summer and fall of 1943, the Limousin maquis became more active in its search for food and in establishing itself as a genuine alternative to the Vichy regime. With nearly one hundred and fifty maquis to feed clandestinely, Guingouin found provisioning the group more difficult. New tactics included using vehicles to transport food, stealing ration cards from town halls, and harassing merchants, activities that all undermined Vichy's authority. Guingouin also used familiar tactics: with the harvest season came the destruction of threshing machines reminiscent of the sabotage aimed at baling machines the previous year. The activity that garnered the most attention from officials, however, was raiding town halls to steal ration cards and tickets. With official documents, the maquis could "legally" purchase food, clothing, and other supplies. The gendarmerie chief in the Creuse reported in September 1943 that since January there had been six attacks on town halls or their employees with the object of stealing ration cards. As a result, 25 of the Creuse's 265 communes stored the cards at the local gendarmerie post each night in the attempt to prevent thefts of the precious commodity. Officials urged local communities without gendarmerie posts to store the cards in different locations each evening, in a safe if possible, or to distribute the cards immediately upon their arrival. By October and November, armed gendarmes in the Creuse and Haute-Vienne protected the transport and distribution of ration cards.[93]

---

[91] Ibid., pp. 85–6, 111–12.

[92] ADHV 185 W 1–44 – Rapports mensuels du préfet régional au chef du gouvernement. Rapport Régional Avril 1943 (May 6, 1943), 6–7.

[93] SHGN Box 12540 – Grpt Creuse – Guéret, R/2, Compte-rendu du Chef d'Escadron Rivals, sur la conservation des titres d'alimentation (September 23, 1943); Note Préfet Régional No. ABR.00.53/M/V. Copie conforme transmise par le Chef d'Escadron Rivals au Commandant de Section à Guéret. Pour notification et exécution en ce qui le concerne (October 26, 1943). ADHV 185 W 1–63 – Rapports mensuels du directeur régional du ravitaillement général. Le Général de Brigade Bois Commandant la 2ème Brigade de la Garde à Monsieur le Préfet Régional de Limoges (November 13, 1943).

Despite the guards, the thefts continued through the winter and into the spring of 1944, demonstrating the complicity of local residents and the gendarmerie as Vichy's legitimacy waned.[94] While undermining the regime's authority through thievery, Guingouin attempted to increase his own influence by naming himself the "Préfet du Maquis." Under his guidance, the maquis fixed its own prices for agricultural products, well above the low prices offered by the government, and posted the new prices at the entrance to town halls throughout the Limousin. These fixed prices were intended to give peasants a fair price for their products while allowing urban workers to purchase goods without resorting to the black market. Sellers caught breaking the maquis-imposed price limits paid a fine and were required to leave a poster outlining their crime affixed to their door for eight days. The Vichy regime had attempted to stop the black market for years and eventually turned a blind eye to small-scale illegal transactions, publicly demonstrating its inability to stop the black market or adequately provision the country. The Resistance exploited the government's political and material failure to boost its own standing and prove that "outlaw culture" had a greater legitimacy than the legally constituted government in power. But not until after the D-Day invasion began on June 6, 1944, would the region finally come under the complete control of the Resistance.

PUBLIC OPINION AND URBAN-RURAL RELATIONS

Placing political events within the context of the material situation rather than vice versa highlights the ways in which the public's habituation to illegality in daily life eroded the Vichy government's authority and legitimacy over an extended period of time. Within months of the regime's inception, individuals challenged its provisioning policies based on local needs and concerns. Material shortages were necessary in creating an atmosphere for the Resistance to exist, but they were not sufficient in and of themselves to lead most French civilians to reject the Vichy regime. This does not mean that shortages should be relegated to secondary status as the background against which political events played out. They directly shaped public opinion and affected relationships between urban and rural residents. They also forced government officials to respond to citizens and affected political decisions.

From the first days of the Phony War and throughout the war years, inadequate food supplies, ineffective distribution of rations, and the

---

[94] Kedward provides examples of gendarme complicity in the escape of *réfractaires* in "The Maquis and the Culture of the Outlaw," p. 243.

government's moral agenda all played a role in shaping the complex interactions between the Limousin's urban and rural inhabitants. Urban dwellers resented rural privilege in material and ideological terms, but they also became increasingly dependent upon peasants for survival. Though tension between the communities mounted throughout the war, it did not erupt into violence, and theft represented the limit of attacks aimed specifically at the peasantry. Relationships became intertwined as urban and rural worked together to feed and clothe themselves and to avoid Vichy's sanctions. Some city inhabitants relied heavily upon their rural relatives for food, whereas others cultivated new relationships through visits to the countryside or correspondence. The organized Resistance in the Limousin also fostered links and tensions between the city and the countryside as raids provided additional resources for men evading compulsory labor service in Germany. Residents throughout the region turned Vichy's own traditionalist rhetoric against the regime in order to justify their illicit purchases, further undermining the government's legitimacy and authority.

As provisioning became more and more difficult, individuals searched for ways to make ends meet creating both alliances and divisions. People with goods, money, or connections, and those willing to resort to dishonest and unlawful means were able to provide for their families. Manifestations of tensions within urban and rural communities themselves further fragmented society and worked against Vichy's desire for a national rebirth. The sous-préfect of Rochechouart, at the western-most border of the Haute-Vienne, summarized the situation in 1943 and the deep sense of demoralization resulting from worsening conditions: "The majority of people no longer concern themselves with the reforms necessary to prepare the future of the country, but live from day to day, only worried about escaping as much as possible the increasingly severe privations imposed by restrictions."[95] Material issues clearly trumped politics in the daily lives and concerns of individuals forcing the government to make accommodations to demands from ordinary citizens.

[95] ADHV 185 W 1–58. Sous-Préfecture de Rochechouart – Rapport Mensuel (December 24, 1943).

2

"Where we are from, that is for pigs": Alsatian Refugees in the Interior

As September 1939 came to its close, Annie and Gritou Vallotton received a letter from their uncle, a doctor and the man responsible for the sanitary conditions of refugees recently evacuated from Alsace and Lorraine to the French interior. In the letter, he described the new committee that would provide much-needed material goods and health services and would also serve as the liaison between the evacuees and the native population. Two weeks before Christmas, Annie and Gritou left the southern coastal town of Sanary after completing Red Cross training and arrived in the Limousin to help their uncle in these tasks. Making rounds on behalf of the committee, both women witnessed firsthand the difficulties facing Alsatians in the Limousin, including the tension that existed between the two populations. After a day of visiting evacuees in the countryside around Limoges, Annie noted her impressions in her journal:

> A lot of incomprehension between those who take in and those who are taken in! The Limousins offer their Jerusalem artichokes and their chestnuts, and the Alsatians reply: 'Where we are from, that is for pigs.' The Limousins, in the Alsatians' eyes, are dirty, use very little water, rarely speak of washing, but say to them: 'These Alsatians are dirty! Imagine that they have their toilets in the house! That is disgusting!'[1]

Annie Vallotton pinpointed a crucial source of cultural misunderstanding between these French men and women: material issues. The complaints about food and accommodation described – in material terms – the cultural

---

[1] Gritou and Annie Vallotton, *C'était au jour le jour: Carnets (1939–1944)* (Paris: Editions Payot & Rivages, 1995), 41 (December 20, 1939). Though technically "evacuated" from their home region, officials, reporters, and individuals used the terms "evacuee" and "refugee" interchangeably in reference to the men and women from Alsace and Lorraine.

differences between the evacuees and the people of the Limousin that marked and shaped their relationship throughout the course of the Second World War.

When Nazi Germany invaded Poland on September 1, 1939, the French government announced the immediate evacuation of civilians from towns and cities along the French–German border. Military strategists believed the German army would attack France at the Maginot Line and the population would be safer in the French interior, far from the front. The evacuation proceeded haphazardly and without adequate physical or mental preparation on the part of the evacuees or the host populations. Limited to only thirty kilograms of baggage and often with only a few hours notice, entire families hurried onto trains bound for unknown destinations in central France, including the Haute-Vienne.[2] The confusion continued as the evacuees arrived in the interior departments where local officials also proved ill equipped to deal with the recent events. Preparing for the possibility of war, the prefect of the Haute-Vienne had initiated a building inventory in his department on August 10, 1939, in order to locate structures that could be used to house French refugees, especially residents from the dangerous border region. The responsibility of gathering this information fell to the Gendarmerie Nationale, and brigades received an order to conduct a discreet investigation (so as to avoid worrying the population) on August 21, 1939. The prefect requested final reports on available housing in each commune by September 18.[3] Needless to say, an organized system for matching evacuees with available accommodation did not exist when the first trains from Alsace arrived in the Limousin during the night of September 2.

Evacuee policy undertaken by the government of the Third Republic and perpetuated under Vichy continued to be marked by improvisation and contradictions. This lack of official preparation and coordination created

---

[2] For a description of the evacuation plan and the evacuation itself, see Henri Amouroux, *La grande histoire des Français sous l'occupation*, Vol. 1 "Le peuple du désastre, 1939–1940" (Paris: Éditions Robert Laffont, 1976), 158+. Approximately 600,000 inhabitants of Alsace and Lorraine from 417 communes within ten to fifteen kilometers of the German border were relocated to the interior departments of the Haute-Vienne, Dordogne, Landes, Charente, Charente-Inférieure, Indre, Lot-et-Garonne, and Gers. See Laird Boswell, "Franco-Alsatian Conflict and the Crisis of National Sentiment during the Phoney War," *Journal of Modern History* 71 (September 1999): 558. On the planning and consequences of the government's evacuation plan, see Nicole Ann Dombrowski, "Beyond the Battlefield: The French Civilian Exodus of May–June 1940." Ph.D. Dissertation, New York University, 1995.

[3] Service Historique de la Gendarmerie Nationale (hereafter SHGN) – Box 12647 – Groupement Haute-Vienne, R/4, Le Chef d'Escadron Médina aux commandants de Section. (August 2, 1939).

material difficulties – shortages of housing and schools, for example – that hampered the integration of the Alsatian–Lorrainers into local communities. Efforts encouraging cultural exchanges between Alsatians and Limousins and misunderstandings about evacuees' rights and duties (such as allocations and employment) further demonstrate the extent to which the daily conflicts over cultural differences and material issues affected relationships. Although government officials attempted to reconcile the two populations and encourage unity, daily experiences proved to be more influential in forming alliances and creating tensions between new neighbors. Rather than completely accepting the evacuees as fellow French citizens in distress, the Limousin residents worried about the economic and cultural consequences of welcoming these strangers into their towns, villages, and homes.

The Alsatian evacuees' arrival in the Limousin in September 1939 marked the beginning of wartime shortages as well as the beginning of interactions between the region's natives and outsiders. Government officials assigned former residents of the Bas-Rhin to approximately 145 different towns and villages scattered throughout the Haute-Vienne. By the end of September, nearly 60,000 evacuees found themselves in the department's rural communities, immediately straining the local population's ability to provide the necessary housing, bedding, and house wares.[4] The massive influx of refugees also placed stress on the food supply, exacerbating shortages already created by the restrictions designed to prepare France for war. As French troops awaited the German attack during the winter of 1939–40, French residents searched for affordable food. Shortages of butter, coffee, and eggs started almost immediately and caused prices to soar.[5] The shortages only worsened over time, and the governments of the Third Republic, and later that of Marshal Philippe Pétain, struggled to meet the alimentary, housing, clothing, and heating needs of the entire French population.

In addition to safeguarding the evacuees' material needs, policy initiatives needed to consider and address the cultural differences between the two communities. The relocation of families from the border regions to the interior brought dissimilar cultures into close contact. The Limousin and Alsace-Lorraine were two culturally distinct areas of France. Known for its

---

[4] For a list of the Bas-Rhin communes evacuated to the Haute-Vienne as well as the names of the newly assigned towns, see Archives Nationales (hereafter AN) F 23 221. "Liste des communes évacuées avec indication des communes de correspondance" (no date). For statistics, see AN F 23 – 225.

[5] Gritou and Annie Vallotton, *C'était au jour le jour*, pp. 39–40 (December 18, 1939), 50 (January 24, 1940), 52 (January 25, 1940). Butter cost 7 francs 90 and eggs were 12 francs a dozen in the countryside as compared to 17 francs in Limoges.

porcelain and enamel, the region around Limoges was primarily rural, secular, and politically left leaning. The region also had a reputation for being poor, isolated, and underprivileged, whereas the industrial and agricultural strength of Alsace-Lorraine created prosperity for its inhabitants.[6] The Limousins' secular and anticlerical attitudes also contrasted with the religious devotion of refugees from Alsace and Lorraine. In addition to practicing Catholics and Protestants, a strong Jewish community with a long history in the two provinces inhabited the area.[7] The border region's history as an area of contention between France and Germany also influenced Alsatian culture. Annexed to Germany between 1871 and 1918, many Alsatian refugees, particularly the older generations, spoke either German or a related regional dialect.

Little did the Limousin people know in September 1939 that the Alsatian evacuees represented the first wave of culturally, socially, and religiously different populations that would seek refuge in the area during the war. Xenophobia, antisemitism, and anticlericalism influenced local attitudes: The Alsatians, though French, often appeared foreign with their German dialect and strong religious beliefs.[8] The Alsatian evacuees' linguistic, cultural, and religious differences clearly influenced how the Limousins perceived them, but these intangible concerns cannot be separated from the period's material shortages. For evacuees who "protested first and foremost about their difficult material situation," the amelioration of their living

---

[6] On the region's prewar leftist politics, see Laird Boswell, *Rural Communism in France, 1920–1939* (Ithaca, New York, and London: Cornell University Press, 1998). For a contemporary newspaper article making allusions to the region's history of poverty and destitution, see the clipping from *L'Appel du Centre*, "La revanche des Limousins" (no date) in the Archives Départementales de la Haute-Vienne (hereafter ADHV) 993 W 117. See also John M. Merriman, *The Red City: Limoges and the French Nineteenth Century* (New York and Oxford: Oxford University Press, 1985) and Jean Bourdelle, *Limoges (1870–1919): la mémoire ouvrière* (Périgueux: Pierre Fanlac, 1984) for a discussion of the region's history and its reputation throughout France.

[7] In 1936, approximately 21.5 percent of the population in Alsace was Protestant, the majority of whom were Lutheran; 2 percent of the population was Jewish; and the remainder was Catholic. See Alfred Wahl and Jean-Claude Richez, *La vie quotidienne en Alsace entre France et Allemagne 1850–1950* (Paris: Hachette, 1993) for an overview, especially Chapter 5, "Le pluralisme confessionnel." For histories of the Jews in Alsace-Lorraine see especially: Paula E. Hyman, *The Emancipation of the Jews of Alsace: Acculturation and Tradition in the Nineteenth Century* (New Haven, Connecticut, and London: Yale University Press, 1991); Vicki Caron, *Between France and Germany: The Jews of Alsace-Lorraine, 1871–1918* (Stanford, California: Stanford University Press, 1988); and Freddy Raphaël and Robert Weyl, *Juifs en Alsace: Culture, société, histoire* (Toulouse: Privat, 1977).

[8] See Boswell, "Franco-Alsatian Conflict and the Crisis of National Sentiment during the Phoney War," pp. 564, 571, 578.

conditions required immediate attention.⁹ Official policy toward the evacuees acknowledged the tensions that resulted between refugees and natives due to different cultural expectations *and* the physical hardships of the period and worked to address both issues simultaneously. Yet the government's attempts to integrate the communities or to provide for their physical needs often reinforced rather than diminished the differences between the groups. The difficulties experienced by these French citizens under the Third Republic set the stage for their treatment under Vichy and prepared Limousins for the arrival of future outsiders. Contradictions in official policy, individual reactions, and local results remained a hallmark of the war years that began with the Alsatian evacuation in 1939.

CULTURAL AND MATERIAL ENCOUNTERS DURING THE PHONY WAR

The declaration of war on September 3, 1939, began the long period of waiting known as the *drôle de guerre* or Phony War that lasted until the Nazi invasion of France on May 10, 1940. During this period, the Alsatian evacuees discovered that their language, religion, and attitude did not correspond to their hosts' expectations for men and women from the most "patriotic" French region.¹⁰ Politically, linguistically, religiously, economically, and culturally Alsace had as much (if not more) in common with Germany as it did with France. Thus, attempts to educate the general public about Alsace-Lorraine's political and cultural history began almost immediately after the evacuees' arrival in the Limousin. This educational process coincided with the imposition of restrictions and the first encounters with shortages in the region.

At a time when anything that vaguely resembled German aroused suspicion, the evacuees' regional dialect caused disquiet and discomfort. Unprepared for the fact that a French region, and especially one so important to the nation-building myth, could speak anything but French, local officials began a campaign to reassure Limousins. A major tool employed in the campaign was the regional press. *Le Courrier du Centre* first addressed the issue of Alsatian language on September 7, 1939, less than a week after the evacuations began.¹¹ The arrival of patois-speaking refugees from the regions of Wissembourg and

---

⁹ Ibid., p. 560.
¹⁰ Ibid., pp. 571, 578.
¹¹ One source estimates the daily run of *Le Courrier du Centre* as 64,000 issues. See AN F1a 4000. France-Politique 8. "La Presse de la Région du Centre" (June 6, 1943). Claude Bellanger reports the same number in *Histoire Générale de la Presse Française Vol. 4 (1940–1958)* (Paris: Presses Universitaires de France, 1975), 74.

Niederbronn prompted military authorities to remind the native population that "these unfortunates are excellent Frenchmen," forced to leave everything behind due to the current circumstances. The article continued, "It will be very unfortunate if our compatriots in misery feel isolated, suspected, or even unjustly worried because they speak a dialect [patois] that resembles German. One can speak German and be 100 percent French. That, do not forget, is the case of our refugees."[12] By continually referring to the refugees in nationalistic terms such as "Frenchmen from Alsace," local officials emphasized the new arrivals' patriotism. Even the Haute-Vienne's prefect assured the region's inhabitants that by conserving their regional language, Alsatians demonstrated resistance to the imposition of German language in the provinces during the annexation of 1871–1918 rather than pro-German sentiment.[13]

But throughout the war years, fear played an important role in daily life, and for many Limousin natives and government officials, the arrival of Alsatian-speaking French men and women raised immediate concerns of a "Fifth Column" invading the region. On September 12, just ten days after the first evacuees arrived in the Haute-Vienne, the general director for national security sent out a memo on behalf of the minister of the interior warning prefects that "among the evacuated French populations, certain individuals of questionable morality slipped in." General Director Bussière thus advocated close surveillance of these unnamed individuals.[14] This call for scrutiny echoed the Wissembourg sous-prefect's suggestion that despite the progress being made integrating the evacuees into Limousin society, "surveillance must never become lax." Many former Wissembourg residents had possessions and relatives in Germany, and despite their "incontestable" loyalty and patriotism, their attitudes could be misinterpreted especially due to the evacuees' clumsiness with the French language and their use of Alsatian.[15]

While the Limousin residents feared German spies, Alsatian refugees rightly feared that a few ill-chosen words might poison natives' attitudes toward the evacuees. In December 1939, the mayor of Lembach, evacuated to Droux in the northern Haute-Vienne, complained that following a Lorraine woman's anti-French remarks, he and his administrators were

---

[12] "À propos des réfugiés," *Le Courrier du Centre* number 245 (September 7, 1939): 4. Articles concerning language in the first weeks after the evacuation also appeared in number 247 (September 9, 1939): 4, and number 251 (September 13, 1939): 4.

[13] Amédée Ducombeau, "Un appel du Préfet à la population du département,"*Le Courrier du Centre* number 247 (September 9, 1939): 4.

[14] AN F 23 229. Le Ministre de l'Intérieur à Messieurs les Préfets (September 12, 1939).

[15] ADHV 187 W 18. Le Sous-Préfet de Wissembourg à Monsieur le Préfet de la Haute-Vienne (September 10, 1939).

regarded "as *boches* [a derogatory term usually applied to Germans] and Hitler's agents."[16] Anti-French remarks naturally raised suspicions, but even patriotic Alsatians faced discrimination. One Alsatian woman speaking to Annie Vallotton bitterly noted in December 1939: " 'My grandfather fought with the French Army for nine years and died on the boat on his way home. Now, his sons are mobilized. And they call *me* "Boche?" ' "[17] When expectations – both Alsatian and Limousin – did not meet reality, the local and national government attempted to ameliorate the situation and build understanding between the two communities.

In an effort to educate the people of the Limousin about their new neighbors, Michel Walter, a national deputy and the president of the General Council of the Bas-Rhin, wrote a series of articles for *Le Courrier du Centre*. Designed to "explain [...], in all truth, loyally and very simply, our character and our manner of living," the articles focused on the Alsatians' language, patriotism, religion, and home life.[18] Trying to allay xenophobic fears, officials denied the "Germanness" of the evacuees and emphasized their "Frenchness" by equating the Alsatian patois with other regional dialects found in France. Despite the concerted effort to educate the general public about Alsatian patois and culture, contradictions in policy and in attitudes remained. While publicly equating the conservation of the regional dialect with resistance to Germanization, officials initially forbade the use of patois in phone conversations because those monitoring the conversations could not understand it. In Oradour-sur-Vayres, the mayor voiced his own frustration with the language differences in January 1940. Describing the situation with the refugees as a "nightmare," the mayor complained about an official letter he received written in Alsatian. Finding the situation "disgraceful," the mayor returned the offending letter and asked, "Can they not speak French?" It seemed to him that the situation

---

[16] Ibid. Monsieur Hetzel, Maire de Lembach à Monsieur le Sous-Préfet de Wissembourg (December 25, 1939).
[17] Gritou and Annie Vallotton, *C'était au jour le jour*, p. 41 (December 20, 1939).
[18] See Michel Walter, "Ce que sont les Français d'Alsace," *Le Courrier du Centre* number 276 (October 8, 1939): 1; "Pour mieux connaître nos Frères d'Alsace: Le dialecte alsacien," *Le Courrier du Centre* number 285 (October 17, 1939): 1 and 3; "Pour mieux connaître nos frères d'Alsace: l'Alsace a le Culte du Foyer et l'Amour des Demeures Confortables," *Le Courrier du Centre* number 304 (November 5, 1939): 1; "Entre Alsaciens, Limousins ou Périgordons, Une Amicale Compréhension Réciproque doit s'instituer," *Le Courrier du Centre* number 319 (November 20, 1939): 2; "Noël 1939," *Le Courrier du Centre* number 353 (December 24, 1939): 1. A response to Walter was written by L. Taponnet, "Notre chère Alsace," *Le Courrier du Centre* number 291 (October 23, 1939): 2. Quote from "Ce que sont les Français d'Alsace," p. 1.

created the perfect opportunity for the Alsatians to "properly" learn French; instead they continued to speak their patois.[19] The government in the Limousin agreed that refugees should learn French and officials expected that the language classes established in the area would have "the best results for the evolution of spirits."[20] Despite official efforts to persuade the public to accept the evacuees' use of dialect, the government expected linguistic assimilation. The use of patois on a daily basis created difficulties and suspicions that undermined the official rhetoric displayed in the regional newspapers and created apprehension on the part of locals already fearing a German invasion.

Even though many residents initially offered to help the refugees, finding housing proved difficult. Residents of Limoges, the major distribution point of the Alsatians to various towns and villages in the interior, eagerly provided food and aid at the city's train station in the evacuation's early weeks. The prefect of the Haute-Vienne and social service organizations also established various forms of aid and food relief, while urgent calls for housing and other supplies, especially bedding and mattresses, went out to individuals. Locals generously provided warm meals, financial contributions, and moral support but proved to be more hesitant about opening their homes to strangers. The mayor of Oermingen, relocated to Bersac-sur-Rivalier in the central portion of the Haute-Vienne with the rest of his village, complained to the sous-prefect of Wissembourg that "a lot of people here close their homes and do not want to let the refugees have rooms." The mayor of Rochechouart in the western Haute-Vienne threatened to requisition furniture and rooms if the town's population did not volunteer these items after his second appeal on September 8. By September 21, some officials believed that the first stage of personal, local assistance in ameliorating conditions was over.[21] Calls for external aid received a fairly positive response, but when it came to welcoming the evacuees into their homes, the Limousins demonstrated more restraint.

As the *drôle de guerre* continued, the government searched for long-term accommodation solutions for the approximately 63,000 Alsatian refugees in the Haute-Vienne. The answers proposed by officials, journalists, and

---

[19] Gritou and Annie Vallotton, *C'était au jour le jour*, p. 54 (January 31, 1940).
[20] AN F 23 225. Letter from Le Contrôleur Général de la Sûreté Nationale à Monsieur le Ministre de l'Intérieur (Direction Générale de la Sûreté Nationale) à Paris (February 15, 1940).
[21] The administrative structures of each evacuated town remained intact in their corresponding town of refuge. See ADHV 187 W 18. Letter from Le Maire d'Oermingen à Monsieur le Sous-Préfet de Wissembourg à Bellac (September 18, 1939). For the mayor's appeal see "Deuxième appel en faveur des réfugiés français," *Le Courrier du Centre* number 246 (September 8, 1939): 4. On the fear that aid was over, see ADHV 187 W 18. Letter from Le Sous-Préfet de Wissembourg à Monsieur le Préfet de la Haute-Vienne (September 21, 1939).

Alsatians reveal a hierarchy of refugees based on nationality, but justified by material concerns. In order to provide additional living quarters for the French evacuees, the Limousin people called for the repatriation of the 2,700 refugees from the Spanish Civil War who had been living in the area since February 1939. Although some had chosen to return to Spain, approximately 1,400 Spanish refugees still remained in camps or "accommodation centers" in the Haute-Vienne when the Alsatian refugees arrived in September.[22] Already rare resources were stretched to their limits. Thus, officials and inhabitants faced questions of who would receive priority – French or foreign refugees? Though foreign, the culture of Spanish refugees seemed closer to Limousin values than the conservative, religious, and Germanic traits of the Alsatians. The left-wing, anticlerical, and Latin nature of most of the Spanish refugees aided their acceptance in the southwestern regions where many of these ideals were shared.[23] Yet despite similarities in political sympathies between the Limousins and the Spaniards, the public and local officials favored the Alsatians over the Spanish refugees.

The finite amount of resources led to competition and conflict between the refugee populations. The Spanish refugees had created material difficulties that were exacerbated after the evacuation of Alsace and Lorraine: The prefect noted "damages" inflicted by the Spanish refugees at vacation colonies in the department where they had been housed and shortages of shoes and bedding materials.[24] These were the same items – housing, bedding, and clothing – that Alsatians needed after their arrival. An official report on the evacuation of the Alsatians–Lorrainers also blamed the Spanish for the hesitancy of Rochechouart's population to house the French refugees: "the area was sacked by the Spanish refugees and today the Alsatians suffer the consequences of this bad memory. The Limousin peasant, in general distrustful [*méfiant*], is not perceptive enough to know the difference."[25]

[22] Statistics reported by the squadron head commanding the Haute-Vienne company of the Gendarmerie Nationale. SHGN Box 12639, R/2, État des renseignements sur les évacués hébergés sur le territoire de la Compagnie (October 11, 1939). He estimated the number of Alsatian refugees (all from the Bas-Rhin) to be 63, 253.

[23] Boswell, "Franco-Alsatian Conflict and the Crisis of National Sentiment," p. 579. Local officials and the prefect noted local communists were encouraging the refugees to stay in the region rather than return to Spain. See reports in ADHV 4M 275.

[24] ADHV 4 M 275. Compte rendu de la réunion du mercredi 10 mai 1939 qui s'est tenue dans le Cabinet de Monsieur le Préfet, à 16 heures, au sujet de l'application des nouvelles instructions de Monsieur le Ministre de l'Intérieur, relatives aux réfugiés espagnols (May 10, 1939) and Situation des réfugiés espagnols dans le département de la Haute-Vienne (May 15, 1939).

[25] AN F23 225. Rapport Fredault sur les évacuations de septembre 1939. (No date, probably late January/early February 1940).

The natives did, however, differentiate between the two populations. A writer for *Le Courrier du Centre* asked, "could we not, in order to facilitate the accommodation of our brothers from Alsace, hasten a little more the repatriation of the Spanish that General Franco is accepting today without restriction?" At the end of September, the town of Le Châtelard "evacuated" the remaining Spanish refugees to other villages in order to offer more housing to the Alsatians.[26] Clearly, "our brothers from Alsace" took precedence over foreign Spanish refugees from both the official and local perspective.

Complaints about Spanish refugees did not come solely from the Limousin's native population. Alsatians themselves also wanted the rapid repatriation of Spanish refugees. Having been in the region longer, the Spaniards had first access to accommodations, and abandoned schools, military establishments, and châteaux had been refurbished to meet their needs. Unprepared for the sudden influx of internally displaced persons, the government in the Limousin had not undertaken repairs or designated housing for the Alsatians. It thus appeared that the government favored foreigners over French evacuees. Camille Chautemps, the vice-president of the council in charge of evacuees, promised that the French government would resolve the issue as quickly as possible.[27] For the government, the status of the people from Alsace and Lorraine as forced *evacuees* outranked the status of foreign *refugee*, even though both populations appeared "foreign" to Limousin residents. The material and the cultural were thus linked in popular conceptions and in the government's policies.

Beyond Spanish repatriation, local and national officials attempted to ameliorate the dire housing situation. Despite the best efforts of aid organizations, the disrepair of available housing often added to the refugees' sense of alienation. Officials noted the general lack of bathrooms and running water in refugees' accommodations, a contrast with the more industrial and modernized departments of Alsace.[28] The unusually cold winter of 1939–40 also contributed to the evacuees' malaise. While most lodgings came equipped with some form of heating, it "was not judged to be sufficient

---

[26] Pierre Davesnes, "Le problème des réfugiés alsaciens," *Le Courrier du Centre* number 254 (September 16, 1939): 4 and "L'évacuation des réfugiés espagnols logés au Châtelard," *Le Courrier du Centre* number 263 (September 25, 1939): 4.

[27] "L'hébergement des évacués d'Alsace," *Le Courrier du Centre* number 285 (October 17, 1939): 2.

[28] See for example the report in AN F 23 225, Le Contrôleur Général de la Sûreté Nationale à Monsieur le Ministre de l'Intérieur (Direction Générale de la Sûreté Nationale) à Paris. (February 15, 1940). Only 18 percent of homes in rural communities throughout France had indoor plumbing for running water (the rest made use of outdoor pumps or wells) and only 2 percent had bathrooms. Statistics cited in Dominique Veillon, *Vivre et survivre en France 1939–1947* (Paris: Editions Payot & Rivages, 1995), 200.

by the Alsatian evacuees used to better heating conditions."[29] Even Michel Walter, in his third article for *Le Courrier du Centre*, acknowledged that this attitude could be misunderstood by the Limousin population: "[W]e look a little like spoiled children in the eyes of the inhabitants of some towns and villages."[30] He further explained that the evacuees, accustomed to modern comforts, complained about their current living situation because of the material differences and not as a criticism directed toward the Limousin's people. But the complaints, based upon real concerns, testified to the evacuees' low morale and increasing tensions between the host and evacuated communities during the war's first winter.

Beyond the psychological effect of abandoning their well-kept homes for smaller, more primitive ones, the refugees contended with serious shortages and dangerous living conditions as well. A report from the Chamber of Deputies issued over a month after the evacuations began called for an urgent amelioration of the refugees' situation, noting that "offices and health organizations are insufficient, bedding is completely lacking, supplying is difficult, teaching is not organized, and the refugees suffer from their inactivity."[31] Living arrangements were, in fact, abominable for many evacuees. By November 1939, Camille Chautemps informed the prefect of the Haute-Vienne that no more refugees would be sent to his department due to the "very bad" living conditions. Informed of the "use of unhealthy premises, the packing together of numerous people, the systematic refusal of locals to put certain available premises to use, and too often, a lack of understanding of the duties that the war imposes on all citizens," Chautemps demanded the redistribution of the evacuee population to areas of the department that had been reserved for future needs.[32] The order does not appear to have ameliorated the situation dramatically. In the course of her activities on the refugees' behalf, Annie Vallotton visited as many as fifty-seven farms and families in a day, and her descriptions paint a dismal picture. In March 1940, thirty-five rooms in the château in Neuvic-Entier (approximately thirty-five kilometers southeast of Limoges) still remained unoccupied in anticipation of their future use as a hospital, while approximately a dozen families lived in the stables on the grounds. Vallotton described the living quarters in her

---

[29] AN F 23 225. Rapport Fredault.
[30] Walter, "L'Alsace a le Culte du Foyer et l'Amour des Demeures Confortables," p. 1.
[31] AN F 23 225. Letter from Le Président de la Délégation [des Présidents de Groupes de la Chambre des Députés] Ref. no. 93 DPGr (October 11, 1939).
[32] ADHV 187 W 9 – Letter from Le Vice-Président du Conseil à Monsieur le Préfet de la Haute-Vienne (November 18, 1939).

diary: "In the stables, each family has two stalls, one for the beds, the other for a kitchen, separated by see-through racks. No windows. One has to open the door, or make do with the light from the stove. In winter, with −15 degrees, just imagine!" Other families found themselves four kilometers from town or seven kilometers from their nearest neighbors in houses that left much to be desired. A Doctor Schneider reported forty-five refugees sharing a single, dark room with only straw as bedding and rats as neighbors.[33] Evacuees were isolated from each other, felt abandoned by their government, and were often treated as suspicious outsiders in their new communities.

Between September 1939 and the outbreak of war in May 1940, the issue of refugee allocations played a central role in shaping public opinion and the evacuees' initial integration into the local population. The Third Republic attempted to ease the financial burden on the evacuees by providing a refugee allocation. These allocations went through a series of stages shaped by the war's course, ideological concerns, and financial considerations. All official evacuees – those required to leave their home rather than those who voluntarily chose to relocate – received allocations between September 1939 and May 1940. Things began to change after the German invasion prompted approximately eight million French and foreign citizens to take to the road ahead of the Nazi advance. All displaced persons were eligible for state aid from May until October 1940 at which point the new Vichy government encouraged the repatriation of internally displaced refugees to their homes in the northern, occupied zone by withdrawing aid from those who were eligible to return. Starting in November 1940, refugees excluded from the northern zone based on political, racial, or ethnic discrimination had to work in order to receive state aid. This arrangement lasted until April 1941 when Vichy abolished refugee allocations altogether on paper, although many evacuees from Alsace-Lorraine continued to receive aid.[34]

As the first French citizens to face displacement, the residents of Alsace-Lorraine remained at an advantage over other refugee populations, but many did not see immediate benefits. Allocations often negatively affected public perception of the refugees as well as their integration into local communities. The amount of allocations remained modest throughout the war. Initially, adult evacuees had the right to 10 francs a day while

[33] Gritou and Annie Vallotton, *C'était au jour le jour*. See entries on p. 71 (April 10, 1940) for activities; p. 68 (March 14, 1940) on Neuvic-Entier; pp. 40 (December 20, 1939) and 42 (December 29, 1939) for scattered conditions; and p. 67 (March 14, 1940) for the doctor's report.
[34] Dombrowski, "Beyond the Battlefield."

children received 6 francs. For a family of four, this meant 32 francs a day.³⁵ With rising food and housing prices – as much as 90 percent increases were reported by February 1940 – the evacuees often found it difficult to make ends meet even with state aid. In August 1940 during the period of universal aid eligibility, two Alsatian men, fathers of large families, were caught stealing potatoes in Magnac-Laval in the northern plains of the Haute-Vienne. The region's newspaper report harshly criticized the men: "These 'repliés' receive allocations, the one, 2,235 francs and the other, 1,800 francs per month. They are housed, clothed; furniture and pots and pans have been given to their family. As one can see, they are not contented with this large hospitality."³⁶ Annie Vallotton recorded in her journal a conversation with the mayor of Oradour-sur-Vayres who also criticized the Alsatian refugees for their greed in January 1940: "'They are also demanding: 10 francs, it appears, is not enough for them. Here on our farms I am convinced that one could live on 5 or 6 francs. The Spanish were given 8 francs and on top of that they paid for wood, electricity, and rent.'"³⁷ While money was intended to help the evacuees deal with the difficult material situation, it could also hinder relationships between the new neighbors. Within months of their evacuation, the Alsatians faced hostile public reactions related to state relief, demonstrating the strained relationships between the communities.

The allocations also added to the perception of difference between Alsatians and Limousins. The region's natives often falsely assumed that Alsatians were lazy and preferred to live on their allocations rather than work. A woman in the mayor's office in Veyrac (sixteen kilometers northwest of Limoges) complained that the Alsatians "do not want to work" and contrasted the work ethic of Limousins ("Here, on the farms, one gets up early

---

35 This is equivalent to approximately 13 euros a day or 390 euros a month in 2004 prices. "Pouvoir d'achat de l'euro et du franc." Institut national de la statistique et des etudes économiques. < http://www.insee.fr/fr/indicateur/achatfranc.htm >. The allocations were as follows in 1941 after several augmentations: 15 francs per day for the head of the family; 10 francs for the wife or other person in the charge of the head of the household; 12 francs for children aged 13–20; and 10 francs for children younger than 13. There was an additional amount of 2 francs per day per person for housing, and if a woman's husband was a prisoner of war, she had a right to an additional 10 francs per day. See "Les droits des expulsés d'Alsace et de Lorraine," *L'Écho des Réfugiés* number 28 (September 7, 1941): 1. Converting the 1941 amounts to euros in 2004, a family of four evacuees would receive approximately 14.37 euros a day or 431 euros a month.
36 "Le cas des Alsaciens," *Le Courrier du Centre* number 222 (August 9, 1940): 2.
37 Gritou and Annie Vallotton, *C'était au jour le jour*, p. 54 (January 31, 1940). The mention of wood, electricity, and rent is a reference to the fact that the Alsatians received additional money above the daily allocation to help offset these costs.

and goes to bed late") with Alsatian girls who lounged in bed until noon.[38] The reality, however, was more complex. One report in February 1940 acknowledged that "numerous are those refugees who, desiring to find work in order to ameliorate their situation and that of their family, hesitate to occupy a fixed position with an average salary fearing a noticeable reduction in their allocation."[39] By March, the government attempted to prevent this situation by compelling refugees to accept any reasonable job. Despite this official declaration, some refugees sought jobs yet could not find anything, while others succumbed to demoralization and inactivity as a result of their situation.[40]

The presence of nonworking refugees proved particularly difficult to accept for some Limousins due to the region's agricultural nature and the military mobilization of farmers. A letter from a government official published in *Le Courrier du Centre* in April 1940 urged evacuees to provide much-needed labor on the farms in the region. Arguing that one could learn the ways of agricultural service as quickly as one could learn the ways of military service, Robert David asserted that the service rendered by the evacuees on the farm would physically help the natives who had so kindly opened "their doors and their arms" and would also help build closer relationships between the groups.[41] Due to the military mobilization of male agricultural laborers, the situation on farms became so desperate that the law of February 23, 1940, prevented evacuated farmers from practicing any profession other than those related to agriculture.[42]

The Alsatians, however, were not the only ones accused of greediness with respect to allocations. In January 1940, *Le Courrier du Centre* printed

---

[38] Ibid., p. 51 (January 24, 1940).
[39] AN F 23 225. Le Contrôleur Général de la Sûreté Nationale à Monsieur le Ministre de l'Intérieur (Direction Générale de la Sûreté Nationale) à Paris (February 15, 1940).
[40] AN F 23 220. Le Sous-Secrétaire d'Etat à Messieurs les Préfets. Circulaire No. 36. Instructions Générales pour le Reclassement au Travail (March 30, 1940). On unsuccessful searches, see SHGN Box 12753 – Haute-Vienne, BT Saint-Léonard-de-Noblat. Procès-verbal number 418 (September 10, 1941). On inactivity and morale, see Gritou and Annie Vallotton, *C'était au jour le jour*, p. 45, and the report of the Comité Français de Service Social, *Journées d'Etudes de Service Social. Paris, 24–25 Février 1940. Le Travail Social auprès des Evacués dans les Départements d'Accueil* (Paris: Edition Sociale Française, n.d.). Available at the Bibliothèque de documentation internationale contemporaine (BDIC).
[41] "La main d'oeuvre agricole et les évacués alsaciens et lorrains," *Le Courrier du Centre* number 96 (April 5, 1940): 3. David was an "Ancien député et sous-secrétaire d'Etat à l'Intérieur."
[42] AN F 23 220. Le Sous-Secrétaire d'Etat à Messieurs les Préfets. Circulaire No. 36. Instructions Générales pour le Reclassement au Travail (March 30, 1940). The government also intended to move refugees with agricultural knowledge to rural departments in need of farmers in order to maintain agricultural production.

an announcement from the prefect about price surveillance in the department. Reports of unusually high prices for basic necessities coincided with the days refugees received their allocations, troubling local authorities. Sure that only a "minute minority of shopkeepers without scruples" could be involved in such deeds, the prefect promised immediate sanctions and increased policing of prices.[43] Local shopkeepers, uninhibited by personal relationships with the Alsatians, tried to profit from the arrival of these outsiders rather than treating them as equals. Although some shopkeepers exploited the evacuees' misfortune by raising prices, popular Alsatian author Benjamin Vallotton described how allocations might be viewed as a source of rapprochement between the two communities. Published in 1941, *Feuilles dans le vent* (*Leaves in the Wind*) is a fictional account of an Alsatian town's evacuation to the Haute-Vienne told from the point of view of a bilingual female nurse (much like his journal-writing daughters, Annie and Gritou). After regular allocation distributions, the unnamed narrator describes the interactions: "Warehouses, lean-tos, outbuildings, abandoned houses, all bring in money. The grocery never empties. The 'general store' is full. The hardware store overflows. There is a line in front of the butcher's. And the smiles blossom. The Alsatians take advantage of it."[44] Thus, depending on one's perspective, allocations either created greedy natives and lazy evacuees or they helped foster relationships based upon economic and material needs.

Official reports and government assessments often reflected this ambiguity making it difficult to summarize the overall mood in the Limousin during the Phony War. Differences also existed between official and local interpretations of events, a situation that would continue for the next five years. As early as September 10, 1939, the sous-prefect of Wissembourg reported a "very close merging" of the evacuee and native populations, and a month later, the prefect of the Haute-Vienne declared that the relationships between the hosts and hosted represented a "unanimous display of French solidarity."[45] Despite assurances that the natives warmly welcomed the displaced evacuees, the actions undertaken by local officials tell another story. Public and private organizations worked to create situations that would bring natives and outsiders together. Yet lack of organization, cultural assumptions, and material shortages continued to work against the assimilation of Alsatian evacuees into the Limousin community.

---

[43] "Surveillance des prix," *Le Courrier du Centre* number 10 (January 10, 1940): 4.
[44] Benjamin Vallotton, *Feuilles dans le vent*, p. 112.
[45] ADHV 187 W 18. Le Sous-Préfet de Wissembourg à Monsieur le Préfet du Bas-Rhin (September 10, 1939) and Le Préfet de la Haute-Vienne à Monsieur le Sous-Préfet de Wissembourg (October 4, 1939).

Government officials viewed children as one means to help bring natives and outsiders together. Born in the years following the Great War in a region that was once again part of the French Republic, most Alsatian children were bilingual. In his address to Haute-Vienne inhabitants at the beginning of September 1939, Prefect Ducombeau outlined the role of children: "In our towns where they will quickly take their place among the young men and women of our towns and villages, they will serve as links and interpenetrations between their parents and the Limousin population."[46] The youngest evacuees would serve as the means to overcome the language barrier that separated the two populations, bringing them together in the service of the French nation. In addition to serving as interpreters and connections between adult Limousins and Alsatians, the government expected children to befriend each other. In theory, one place young people from Alsace and the Limousin would interact was the classroom. Cultural and material concerns as well as policy decisions limited the amount of contact between the youngsters, however. Officials soon discovered that lack of physical space to accommodate the new students served as a major obstacle to education. The French Social Service Committee noted in February 1940 (six months after the evacuation of the border region) that Alsatian students in Saint-Yrieix in the southernmost portion of the Haute-Vienne were left to their own devices during the day because the local school did not have enough classrooms and an Alsatian school had not yet been established.[47] In some towns, Alsatian students used rooms in buildings other than the school, while barracks were eventually constructed for the evacuees' use in other locations.[48] Separate classes for Alsatians and Limousins were counterproductive to the stated intention of bringing the children together.

Even if local governments could overcome the lack of space, they faced another issue: ideological differences concerning pedagogy. In Alsace, religious education remained an accepted and expected part of the curriculum. This concession on the part of the French government after the provinces' recovery from Germany represented an important part of Alsatian and Lorrainer culture

---

[46] Ducombeau, "Un appel du Préfet à la population du département," p. 4. L. Tapponet, in response to Walter's article about the Alsatian dialect, also acknowledged the role of children as interpreters in the article, "Notre chère Alsace," p. 2.
[47] Comité Français de Service Social. *Le Travail Social auprès des Évacués dans les Départements d'Accueil*, p. 26.
[48] The Controller General of National Security reported that the barracks were being built near public schools so that they could be used as recreational facilities after the war. By February 1940, twelve such barracks had been built in the Haute-Vienne. See AN F 23 225. Letter from Le Contrôleur Général de la Sûreté Nationale à Monsieur le Ministre de l'Intérieur (Direction Générale de la Sûreté Nationale) à Paris (February 15, 1940).

unique to that region. It also meant that Protestant (Lutheran and Reform), Catholic, and Jewish children usually attended separate classes. Such divisions were impractical in the Limousin where various religious and geographical communities mixed in the towns of refuge. Beyond practical considerations, the Limousin was one of the least religious and stridently secular regions of France. The juxtaposition of the crucifix (organized religion) and Marianne (the French Republic) in the same space was unacceptable to some. Reports from the Haute-Vienne went so far as to suggest that Alsatian and Limousin children attend different facilities in order to prevent friction.[49] Separate facilities or dividing the school day with Alsatians attending class in the morning and Limousins in the afternoon (or vice versa) helped resolve the problems over religious instruction but limited the contact between the children.

Government officials recognized the Alsatian children's isolation and took steps to bring the groups together in other areas. After all, the children were supposed to be the greatest potential link between the native and refugee communities. Drawing on the Alsatian cultural tradition of celebrating Christmas with a festively decorated pine tree, the national government saw the holiday as an opportunity to bring the populations together. Camille Chautemps issued a circular to the prefects in host departments suggesting a distribution of toys and warm clothes for the holiday in 1939. With no idea how long their exile would last, many Alsatians came to the Limousin unprepared for the winter. Thus, the celebration would fill the dual role of providing material and moral support for the evacuees. Children would get the warm clothes they needed while participating in a familiar tradition. Chautemps made a third role explicit: "This *fête* must, as much as possible, be put to profit for gathering and combining the local population and the refugees."[50] Not only would the children from Alsace mix with their Limousin counterparts, their parents would as well.

The directive came from the national level, but local officials had to determine the logistics and provide the materials. On December 13, 1939, the prefect of the Haute-Vienne sent a response to Chautemps assuring him that he would study the best means to achieve the celebration. On the same day, the prefect also sent a letter to the primary academic inspector outlining the purpose and potentials of a Christmas celebration for Alsatian and Limousin children. For the prefect, the celebrations were to be primarily a

---

[49] AN F 23 225. Letter from Contrôleur Général (February 15, 1940).
[50] AN F 23 220. Le Vice-Président du Conseil à Messieurs les Préfets des Landes, du Gers, du Lot-et-Garonne, de l'Indre, de la Haute-Vienne, de la Dordogne, de la Charente, de la Charente-Inférieur. Circularie numéro 12 (n.d.).

"*Where we are from, that is for pigs*" 73

cultural exchange where the children would share songs and dances from their own regions. In addition to providing a distraction for the "little exiles," the celebration would also be "an occasion for the two populations to better know each other, appreciate each other, and be united in the same fondness for a homeland [*patrie*] so varied, [and] so rich in diverse beauties."[51] The prefect charged the inspector with examining the possibilities for the cultural exchange and reporting back to him with a plan for its realization. Aid societies in the Limousin called for the organization of relief efforts in view of Christmas as early as December 2, 1939, and an "Alsatian Day" held in mid-December raised funds from the sale of Alsatian insignias to donate to the refugees.[52] The war's first holiday would be used to demonstrate French camaraderie and create it, if necessary.

In Limoges, La Fusion Amicale des Réfugiés d'Alsace et Lorraine sponsored the celebration as well as the Christmas tree, drawing about two thousand participants. The stated purpose of La Fusion as an organization was to introduce the Limousin people to the beauties of Alsace and vice versa in order to foster understanding and mutual appreciation. Many Limousin residents had never seen a Christmas tree, as the tradition had an Alsatian origin (drawing from the Germanic tradition).[53] The tree was just one form of cultural exchange; dressed in regional costumes, the Alsatian and Limousin children also performed songs and dances from their respective provinces. In addition to the cultural sharing, 837 Alsatian and Limousin children received toys. The committee's president concluded his holiday speech by reminding the people of the link children created in the two communities: "Your children are our children, just as our children are your children, because they are all children of France, and it is for this reason that La Fusion Committee is happy to give Christmas presents to all these precious little ones!"[54] The war's first Christmas was thus spent in the

---

[51] ADHV 187 W 9. Letter to Le Vice-President du Conseil (Direction Générale des Services d'Alsace et de Lorraine) (December 13, 1939) and quote in letter from Le Préfet de la Haute-Vienne à Monsieur l'Inspecteur d'Académie et Madame Baeremback, Inspectrice Primaire (December 13, 1939).

[52] "Noël alsacien," *Le Courrier du Centre* number 331 (December 2, 1939): 4.

[53] For a discussion of the origins of the Christmas tree in Alsace, see Wahl and Richez, *La vie quotidienne en Alsace*, pp. 131–2. Claude Lacan, Georges-Marie Proux, and Roland du Chalard briefly mention the peasant introduction to Christmas trees in their study, *Le Limousin de la Défaite et de l'Occupation* (Limoges: Editions René Dessagne, 1978), 9.

[54] "Arbre de Noël de la fusion amicale des réfugiés d'Alsace et Lorraine," *Le Courrier du Centre* number 1 (January 1, 1940): 4. Articles about Alsatian-Limousin Christmas celebrations also appeared in the newspaper on December 27, 1939, January 3, 1940, January 4, 1940, and January 7, 1940. Benjamin Vallotton also includes a fictional description of Christmas celebrations in *Feuilles dans le vent*, pp. 121–4.

Limousin in the continuing quest to build relationships between the evacuee and native populations by recognizing and celebrating cultural differences and providing some material support.

Sustained efforts to make the Alsatians feel more comfortable in the Limousin followed the initial efforts to bring the diverse communities together. The first Christmas also emphasized the growing realization that the evacuees could be away from their homes for an extended period of time. The longer the *drôle de guerre* continued, the more the efforts of cultural and material accommodation were needed. Increased organization and an effort to maintain the Alsatian–Lorrainer sense of community and identity replaced the chaos and confusion of the evacuation period. Despite the heterogeneity of the Alsatian community and the geographic dispersal of evacuees, the experience of evacuation and their refugee status remained a common bond.

A meeting of social service workers held in Paris in February 1940 addressed both the material and moral concerns of evacuees from Alsace and Lorraine. A session dedicated to evacuees' social life acknowledged that material concerns made life difficult for the evacuees, but intangible worries also contributed to their low morale:

> There is a malaise of the evacuees that can coexist with their physical suffering and their material needs, but that is distinguished from it. Not a malaise that comes from cold, destitution of clothing, bedding, and utensils, or from housing inconveniences; but one that is necessarily born from a change of milieu and habits, from the distance from the places and people one loves, and the forced contact with people one does not understand any better than one can make oneself understood by them.[55]

Aid organizations proposed to ameliorate these problems by establishing institutions to meet the community's psychological needs. Social service workers and women's newspapers suggested warm, light-filled buildings with various forms of distractions in which Alsatians could visit with others of similar cultural and linguistic backgrounds.

Foyers, or clubs, were one of the earliest arenas in which men, women, and children from Alsace could interact with other evacuees in the Limousin. In addition to providing for the emotional needs of the community, the *foyers* also dealt with some of the community's material requirements. Regulated by the national government and coordinated on a departmental level, prefects and mayors requisitioned buildings and provided financial

---

[55] Comité Français de Service Social, *Le Travail Social auprès des Évacués dans les Départements d'Accueil*, p. 46.

aid to create individual *foyers*. The *foyer* in Limoges, established in December 1939, gave refugees access to social services, a meeting room, a library, a radio, a sewing machine, and rooms for unaccompanied women.[56] Annie Vallotton described a typical afternoon at the Limoges *foyer* where she also lived and worked: a "crowd" of people came "looking for a job, [...] to exchange housing for something closer to work, who want to find a couple capable of maintaining a garden, who quite simply want to find somewhere to live." In addition to these administrative tasks, she described, "Telephone calls without end, parcels, families for clothes and fittings, kids that must be entertained and fed, and besides, keeping an eye on the women who sew at the machine. I am exhausted."[57] The *foyer* did much to help Alsatians navigate problems in their daily lives, but it also helped segregate them from the native dwellers as it served the evacuees as a distinct group.

Thus by the Phony War's end in May 1940, the Alsatians were still not fully integrated into their host communities despite efforts made on the local level. Allocations, schooling, and Christmas traditions all marked the evacuees as outsiders despite the government's efforts to encourage acceptance. The refugees identified themselves – and were identified by others – as both an ethnic group (Alsatian–Lorrainers) and as forced evacuees. They faced both xenophobia and acts of kindness on a daily basis and on a local level. The government responded with a public relations campaign and relief programs. Local communities offered support, but with some trepidation. Divisions within society became more pronounced; there was no unanimous or spontaneous sense of a nation united in the face of a foreign enemy. And squarely at the heart of many of these issues were material concerns.

INTEGRATION AND SEGREGATION UNDER VICHY

Alsatian–Lorrainer experiences in the French interior did not end with the German invasion of France. If anything, the events of the summer of 1940

---

[56] An announcement advertising the services of the *foyer* appeared in *Le Courrier du Centre*. See "Pour les évacués du Bas-Rhin," *Le Courrier du Centre* number 4 (January 4, 1940): 4. *Foyers* functioned in Limoges, St.-Sulpice-Laurière, and St.-Yrieix by mid-December and were proposed for Bellac, Magnac-Laval, Le Dorat, Châteauponsac, Rochechouart, Ambazac, Mézières, Eymoutiers, Châteauneuf, St.-Junien, and Arnac-la-Poste. See AN F 23 225. Comité National des Activités Sociales. Création de Foyers Alsaciens-Lorrains dans les Départements d'Accueil (December 12, 1939).

[57] Gritou and Annie Vallotton, *C'était au jour le jour*, p. 62 (February 24, 1940).

reinforced the evacuees' status as outsiders and highlighted the material and cultural tensions between the communities. After the war began, the September 1939 evacuees were privileged in terms of housing, connections, and allocations having been in the Limousin longer than the new refugees fleeing the German army, but the sheer number of people in need put all future support at risk.

Even though the Third Republic officially ended on July 10, 1940, dealing with refugees was just beginning for the Vichy regime. In his radio address to the nation, Marshal Pétain invoked the refugees' suffering as a reason to ask the Germans for an armistice to end the fighting.[58] In theory, all refugees would be able to return to their homes once the hostilities ended. The armistice terms, the new government's agenda for the country's moral regeneration, and its commitment to collaboration would make the task of repatriation more difficult. The Vichy government attempted to walk a fine line between collaboration and maintaining its sovereignty during the Occupation; its repatriation policy was one opportunity for the new regime to demonstrate its efficiency and legitimacy to the French public while continuing power negotiations with the Germans, an effort that largely failed on both accounts.[59]

The complex reality of dividing France into zones after the armistice directly affected refugees' ability to repatriate. In addition to the occupied and unoccupied zones, Italy received some territory, the two northern-most departments of the Nord and Pas-de-Calais were attached administratively to Belgium, certain coastal and border areas were designated as "forbidden zones," and, most importantly for the evacuees, Germany effectively annexed the departments of Alsace-Lorraine. (See Map 1.) Complicating matters even further, the demarcation line between occupied and "free" France was sealed and controlled by German authorities making travel and communication nearly impossible. When repatriation finally began in August 1940, the Germans excluded foreigners, French communists, residents from the forbidden zones, Jews, and evacuees from Alsace-Lorraine refusing to swear allegiance to Hitler's Reich from the right to return. Many other refugees tried to remain in the unoccupied zone despite repatriation orders. When official repatriation ended on November 20, 1940, approximately one million refugees remained in southern France. Estimates suggest

---

[58] Philippe Pétain, *Discours aux Français 17 juin 1940–20 août 1944* (Paris: Albin Michel, 1989), 57.
[59] Dombrowski, "Beyond the Battlefield," pp. 317–18. Chapter 5, "Negotiating a Return: Vichy Officials and the German Occupying Authorities," traces the evolution of repatriation policy.

that only a minority of the original Alsatian evacuees remained in the interior.[60] However, the German presence in the border region led to the expulsion in the summer of 1940 of undesirables: Jews, strident Republicans, Gypsies, and other marginal members of society. Many found their way to the same interior departments as the evacuees from September 1939. As of June 1, 1941, the department of the Haute-Vienne, now part of the southern, unoccupied zone, reported that there were still 9,308 Alsatians and Lorrainers receiving aid in the area. Of this number, approximately 1,268 were Jewish.[61] Under Vichy, the remaining Alsatian refugees continued to be treated as a separate community of outsiders on both a local and a national level.

Despite the physical and psychological hardships all French residents – and especially refugees far from their homes – endured during the Occupation, the nation's experience of the war years cannot be described as simply a story of helpless victims.[62] Alsatian experiences after France's defeat demonstrate that community life continued although often in a different shape. The Haute-Vienne's local newspaper, *Le Courrier du Centre,* alerted Alsatians and Lorrainers to national radio programs directed specifically to audiences from the border region. The *Fusion* that sponsored the Christmas celebrations in 1939 also held weekly evening events (in well-heated rooms) featuring songs, dance, and other cultural exchanges with the locals. Dentists, pharmacies, opticians, and thrift shops, established for the express use of the refugees, served the evacuee community. A refugee from the city of Colmar opened an Alsatian charcuterie in Limoges, providing a small taste

---

[60] Boswell, "Franco-Alsatian Conflict," p. 575. He estimates that only 20,000–60,000 of the 600,000 original evacuees chose to stay in the French interior. Boswell argues that the treatment of Alsatians as *boches* and internal enemies was one factor that influenced the decision of many to return to their homes. Julian Jackson reports that two-thirds of the 410,000 refugees from Alsace-Lorraine returned to the German-annexed territories. See Jackson, *France: The Dark Years 1940–1944* (Oxford: Oxford University Press, 2001), 247.

[61] This does not include refugees not receiving aid from the French State, which would increase the overall number. The final statistics for the department report a total of 23,369 refugees in the department including 17,915 receiving aid and 5,454 not receiving aid. These numbers include refugees from Alsace-Lorraine, refugees from other departments in France, and foreign refugees. See ADHV 187 W 189 – États numériques par commune des réfugiés secourus (June 1, 1941). There were also 91 Jewish refugees from Alsace and Lorraine who were not receiving any aid, bringing the total to 1,359. ADHV 187 W 190 – États numériques par commune des réfugiés israélites secourus et non-secourus (June 1941).

[62] Robert Gildea outlines the three competing and misleading interpretations of the war years as the "good French," the "bad French," and the "poor French" in *Marianne in Chains: Daily Life in the Heart of France During the German Occupation* (New York: Picador, 2002).

of home. Church services on Sunday brought Christian evacuees dispersed in villages throughout the countryside around Limoges together on a regular basis as well. The French people proved to be resilient, creative, and hopeful in the face of authoritarianism, discrimination, and restrictions. Alsatians and Lorrainers throughout the unoccupied zone reaffirmed their identity and created imagined communities that proved resistant to assimilation and to Vichy's homogenizing moral agenda.[63]

A newspaper aimed specifically at the evacuees also helped to maintain a sense of community and identity while encouraging good relations with the local population. On March 2, 1941, the first edition of *L'Écho des Réfugiés* appeared. Advertised as an "aid organ for Alsatians and Lorrainers," the newspaper, available only by subscription, appeared weekly.[64] Claiming to be nonpolitical, the paper dealt with issues that particularly interested refugees, featured reports from communities in departments throughout France, ran a classified section, and served as a forum for locating friends and relatives separated by the evacuation. It also reveals the tensions between the refugee and native communities that persisted after the establishment of the Vichy government as well as continued concerns about shortages that affected daily interactions.

L'Écho des Réfugiés regularly addressed the practical matters of refugees' rights and obligations. Until the Vichy regime began withdrawing refugee allocations between May 1941 and May 1942, a refugee had a right to aid from the government, free medical assistance, as well as continued access to shoes and clothing, cooking utensils, bedding, and other essentials. In addition, each family had the right to plant a garden in the place where they lived. *L'Écho des Réfugiés* explained:

> [T]he plots of land will be given by municipalities and by individuals. The Refugee must use the loaned objects as if they belonged to him and keep them in good condition. By his propriety, he will win the sympathy of the authorities and the habitants of his place of refuge; many difficulties thus will be smoothed away, his conditions of existence much improved.[65]

Growing food was thus expected to be a tool in building relationships between refugees and locals. The newspaper reminded refugees that they

---

[63] The term "imagined communities" comes from Benedict Anderson, *Imagined Communities: Reflections on the Origin and Spread of Nationalism* (London and New York: Verso, 1983, 1991).

[64] The price of a subscription was 45 francs per year, payable by trimester. (Converting this price into modern terms, 45 francs in 1942 was approximately 67 francs in 2000 and 10 euros in 2002.)

[65] "Droits et devoirs des Réfugiés," *L'Écho des Réfugiés* number 2 (March 9, 1941): 1.

had the right to a garden in order to provide fresh vegetables for their family, but they also had the duty to maintain that garden in such a way that reflected respect and appreciation. The references to winning sympathy and smoothing away difficulties also suggest that there continued to be tensions between the evacuees and the local populations even two and a half years after the initial evacuation of Alsace and Lorraine. Officials' reports made explicit the tensions suggested in the article. The prefect of the Haute-Vienne reported that the region's natives expressed anxiety about the arrival of new waves of refugees after many of the original evacuees returned to their homes in Alsace with loaned items, and the General Bureau of Information (Renseignements généraux) reported in November 1941 that newly exiled refugees from Lorraine "live a little on the margins of the native population."[66] The daily experiences with the refugees influenced attitudes more than official reminders that the Alsatians and Lorrainers needed and deserved aid.

Despite having certain rights and privileges, the evacuees often found themselves with greater difficulties in obtaining food than their neighbors. By September 1940, the General Commissariat for Refugees had received so many questions concerning food issues that the general commissioner sent a circular to officials addressing supply distribution to refugees. Commissioner Cayrel reminded local authorities that refugees were to be "treated on absolutely equal footing" with the other commune inhabitants and that a percentage of rare goods should be set aside for the refugees. He placed particular emphasis on the fact that the "assisted who could not return to their homes due to the circumstances of the war will not be treated as 'poor relations' in their place of refuge."[67] Although the circular addressed the mechanics of provisioning the refugees, there was also a clear connection between provisioning and one's status as an outsider in the community. Furthermore, all rural inhabitants received reduced meat rations based on the assumption that they raised their own livestock and vegetables. Refugees living in rural communities faced the same restrictions even though they did not have the same access to farm products such as poultry, potatoes, eggs,

---

[66] For the prefect's remarks, see ADHV 185 W 1–45 – Rapports du préfet de la Haute-Vienne au ministère de l'Intérieur. Rapport mensuel (January 3, 1941), 4. On the new exiles, see ADHV 185 W 3–15 – Services départementaux des renseignements généraux – Haute-Vienne. Rapports mensuels du Commissariat spécial. Le Commissaire Principal, Chef de Service à Monsieur l'Intendant de Police à Limoges (Renseignements Généraux) (November 25, 1941), 2.

[67] AN F 23 234. Circulaire from Ministère de l'Intérieur, Commissariat Général aux Réfugiés. (September 18, 1940).

and pork. By February 1942, *L'Écho des Réfugiés* reported that complaints and pressure from the refugee community had forced the Service du Ravitaillement Général (General Supply Service responsible for rationing and distribution of foodstuffs) to consider a change in policy.[68] On March 1, 1942, refugees in rural areas would receive ration cards for meat and potatoes comparable to cities and towns. The newspaper viewed this as an equitable resolution to the problem and suggested that refugees express their gratitude to the public officials who had worked on their behalf.

Even with policy changes, many refugees continued to feel disadvantaged due to their status as displaced persons. A year after the promise of increased rations for refugees in rural areas, *L'Écho des Réfugiés* again returned to the subject of provisioning. Despite the best efforts of the *services du ravitaillement*, the problems of finding adequate amounts of food persisted, especially for the "secondhand rural" (*ruraux d'occasion*).[69] Tensions also existed between Alsatians and Lorrainers living in cities and their compatriots in rural areas. The wartime city dwellers assumed that the refugees in the countryside had increased access to food either through their access to land or through relations with their peasant neighbors. In reality, the paper reminded its readers, some former urban dwellers in Alsace and Lorraine now found themselves in rural areas where they were unaccustomed to cultivating the land or to raising animals de *basse-cour* such as chickens and rabbits.[70] Many did not have the time, the supplies, or the skills necessary for such work. With respect to relations with their neighbors, rural refugees still faced the issues of lingering language barriers, the necessity of rural families to take care of their own needs above the needs of others, and the often prohibitive costs of acquiring butter, eggs, and meat on the farm. Thus, they faced the double disadvantage of being discriminated against as refugees and as rural inhabitants.

Another group facing a double disadvantage was Alsatian Jews. Strangers in the Limousin due both to their status as refugees and to the local population's unfamiliarity with Jews, the Alsatian Jews' experience highlighted cultural differences while affirming their solidarity with other evacuees.

---

[68] "Une question angoissante reglée. Les expulsés et réfugiés des communes rurales sont assimilés aux réfugiés des villes pour leur ravitaillement en viande," *L'Écho des réfugiés* number 7 (February 28, 1942): 1.

[69] "Le ravitaillement des "ruraux d'occasion"! Ne pourrait-on pas les assimiler aux réfugiés des centres urbains?" *L'Écho des Réfugiés* number 8 (March 20, 1943): 1.

[70] The difference between farming methods in Alsace-Lorraine and the Limousin also created difficulty in adaptation. See ADHV 185 W1–45. Le Commissaire Spécial, Chef de Service à Monsieur le Préfet de la Haute-Vienne (February 12, 1941), 4.

Although dispersed throughout the Limousin, Jewish experience in Limoges gives the most evidence and provides a good example of daily life. Jews living in Limoges before September 1, 1939, numbered only 161.[71] In 1942, the housing office of Limoges, through the Refugee Service and the Prefecture of the Haute-Vienne, conducted a census of refugees living within the city.[72] According to the individual notices, approximately 676 French Jews from Alsace and Lorraine and 416 foreign Jews from the border region lived in the city. In order to accommodate the needs of the new Jewish population, Abraham Deutsch, a rabbi from Bischwiller (Alsace), installed his offices at 43, Boulevard Gambetta, on a main thoroughfare in the city. Rabbi Deutsch served as the focal point for the Jewish population (Alsatian and otherwise) in Limoges during the war, dealing with its material and spiritual needs. The city boasted a Jewish high school (under Rabbi Deutsch's direction), technical training facilities, aid organizations, and all the necessities of a practicing Jewish community including a kosher butcher and a synagogue.

Religious tensions in the Limousin during the Phony War centered on education, and the attempts to bring the native and refugee communities together presupposed the evacuees' Christianity. As the statistics demonstrate, however, Jews represented a sizeable percentage of the refugee population (13.6 percent of the refugees from Alsace-Lorraine receiving aid in the Haute-Vienne). The Jewish refugees from the border region faced the same material and cultural concerns as their Christian counterparts, but due to Vichy's legalized antisemitism, their situation was even more complex. The German directive of September 27, 1940, banning the repatriation of Jews to the northern, occupied zone or to the annexed territories of Alsace-Lorraine, precluded Jews from returning to their homes after the armistice. Antisemitism and the Jewish Statutes passed by the Vichy government in 1940 and 1941 further circumscribed the lives (materially, spiritually, and physically) of these refugees. After the first major roundup of foreign Jews in the unoccupied, southern zone on August 26, 1942, their situation became even more precarious. The Jews were also on the boundaries of multiple communities including the French national community, the evacuee community, and the foreign refugee community, which further complicated their standing in society.

---

[71] ADHV 993 W 221. Mesures gouvernementales prises à l'encontre des Juifs.
[72] See ADHV 993 W 608 and 609. Recensement (par l'office du logement des israëlites réfugiés à Limoges: notices individuelles avec indication de la profession, de la composition et des moyens d'existence de la famille, de l'adresse et de la description du logement), 1942. Israëlites français et étrangers.

Yet despite the tightening surveillance and increasing persecution, Jews appeared regularly, openly, and positively in the pages of *L'Écho des Réfugiés*. For the Vichy regime, their status as undesirable Jews took precedence over their status as Alsatians or Lorrainers. Viewed as inassimilable cultural outsiders, Jews lost their rights under Vichy although the laws and national officials often differentiated between French Jews with a record of service to the nation and foreign Jews. But for the refugees from Alsace and Lorraine, the Jews clearly constituted part of the community as reflected in the paper. Obituaries for Jews from Alsace and Lorraine appeared regularly in its pages. The funeral of Madame Camille Meyer was reported on December 20, 1942. Evacuated from Strasbourg, Madame Meyer continued her charity work with different religious groups in Limoges by working with needy refugees. Extending its sincere condolences, the paper described the large number of friends and refugees who went to the cemetery to pay their respects to "this model wife and mother, this incomparable benefactress, to the good friend of the poor and unhappy, to the woman with the generous heart and nothing but friends."[73] Published after two years of Jewish persecution and anti-Jewish propaganda and months after the first roundups of Jews, the sympathetic portrayal of Madame Meyer opposed Vichy's image of Jews and demonstrates, at least, the partial failure of its antisemitic program.

Despite the government's official stance on Jews, some Jewish evacuees willingly and explicitly identified their religious affiliation in classified advertisements in the paper. Items such as "Looking for a serious person, age 30 to 40, Jewish, who knows how to cook and run a small home for a single, Alsatian refugee man," or "Two Alsatian Jewish friends from good families, 23 and 30 years old, without relations would like to make the acquaintance of two men in hopes of marriage" appeared intermittently in the paper.[74] The Union Général des Israélites de France (UGIF), the state-created organization representing the "interests" of all Jews in France, also used the paper to help reunite family members separated by the relocation and expulsion by running ads with lists of names.

The presence of Jews in the newspaper for refugees from 1941 to 1944 demonstrates that they considered themselves to be members of the Alsatian–Lorrainer community. Even when it became more dangerous to be identified as a Jew, the evacuees from Alsace and Lorraine (like other French Jews) must have felt that this status afforded them a degree of protection against

---

[73] "Dans la Haute-Vienne," *L'Écho des Réfugiés* number 36 (December 20, 1942): 8.

[74] *L'Écho des Réfugiés* number 25 (August 30, 1942): 8 and number 31 (October 30, 1942): 8. Both advertisements ran after the August 26, 1942, roundup.

Vichy's antisemitic policies. They faced the same material and cultural concerns as their Catholic and Protestant neighbors from the evacuated region, but they did not have the same interactions with the community that their Christian neighbors did through Christmas celebrations or potential meetings in the school. As Vichy's agenda changed from the economic and social isolation of Jews to deportation, these connections would become vital for survival. Jewish aid organizations fulfilled some of these needs and became important for *all* refugees from Alsace-Lorraine who chose to remain in the unoccupied zone. The Israelite Social Aid Agency, constituted in November 1939 to aid Jewish refugees, extended their services to all Alsatians and Lorrainers in need after the German occupation of the border provinces.[75] The agency provided monetary assistance; ran an orphanage, apprenticeships, and hospices for the elderly; provided social services in hospitals; and worked with refugee youth. Even though anti-Jewish legislation sought to marginalize French and foreign Jews, the government relied on Jewish aid organizations to provide for all Alsatian–Lorrainer refugees regardless of their religion.

Confusion and ambiguity marked official government attitudes and policies toward the evacuees, refugees, and exiles from the border regions of Alsace and Lorraine during the Phony War and into the Vichy regime. Issues of identity, both local and national, played a role in attitudes. Some scholars have argued that the population of the French interior was unprepared for the reality of Alsatian–Lorrainer regional identity, leading many to treat the refugees as foreigners. Indeed, one observer suggested as late as 1943, "Since he [the refugee] is like a foreigner, he must rightly have the curious mind of a foreigner."[76] This writer intended to offer ideas that might aid in the refugees' adjustment and acclimation to his (or her) place of refuge, but others explicitly equated the language, religion, and culture of the evacuees with the enemy Germans. Many refugees understandably responded with indignation and found comfort by attempting to reconstruct their communities in the host departments. Despite the government's attempts to educate and form relationships between the evacuees and the Limousin natives, the reality of the situation and the changing policies made the endeavor more difficult.

---

[75] Centre de Documentation Juive Contemporaine (hereafter CDJC) CDXV – 34. Tableau de l'Organisation Administrative, Première Direction, Deuxième Section (anciennement "Les Oeuvres d'Aide Sociale Israélite") auprès des Populations Repliées (May 5, 1942?). See also CDJC CDXV – 22 UGIF Département des Oeuvres d'Alsace et de Lorraine. Compte-rendu pour la période du 10 octobre au 15 novembre 1942.

[76] "L'opinion des autres . . . Les devoirs des réfugiés et des non-réfugiés," *L'Écho des Réfugiés* number 5 (February 20, 1943): 1.

Cultural misunderstandings and material shortages were often related. Issues of language, housing, religion, and schooling reflected both concerns about what it meant to be French and local reactions to the difficult material situation. In his memoirs, Jean Orieux remembered the conflicts that arose over housing in his small southwestern village of Le Moustier (Haute-Vienne):

> Exhausted, bitter, some Alsatians were not happy with anything and always wanted more and better, they became violent. They had reasons, but this did not fix the situation; when they yelled in dialect or in German, the Limousins lost their heads. It was already the invasion; it was the Fifth Column![77]

In this case, the legitimate, material concerns of Alsatians in their daily life became explicitly linked with national issues such as fear of the Germans and potential invasion. Misunderstandings, however, occurred on both sides as the various problems led more than one Alsatian to ask about their hosts, "[W]hy did they not prepare anything here when they knew that we were coming?"[78] In fact, the Limousin population did not know that so many evacuees were coming nor were they prepared for the Alsatians' cultural differences.

The difficult integration of the evacuee populations – and the other refugees who eventually came to the region – cannot be explained solely by xenophobia or antisemitism. Indeed, the people of the Limousin accommodated outsider populations to varying degrees depending upon factors such as cultural assimilation, economic threat, and common stereotypes. This accommodation took place on an individual basis in daily interactions. The culture and material situation of the Alsatian refugees marked them as outsiders, and this status could not be changed by government initiatives. Though both communities were French, separate schools, *foyers*, and the payment of allocations only reinforced the differences and segregated the communities. The issues and concerns of daily life overrode national ideals as people learned from their own experiences and interactions rather than from the government's rhetoric. The primacy of individual concerns over national considerations established during the period of the Phony War and reinforced by evacuees' experiences in the Limousin continued throughout the war. Attitudes toward other refugees (French and foreign, Jewish and Christian) and the treatment of so-called undesirables were all shaped by the complex relationship between shortages, policy, concepts of identity, and individual experiences. The Alsatians in the Limousin were only the first to experience life on the margins of society.

---

[77] Jean Orieux, *Souvenirs de Campagnes* (Paris: Flammarion, 1978), 74–5.
[78] Gritou and Annie Vallotton, *C'était au jour le jour*, p. 54 (January 31, 1940).

3

"They are undesirables": Gypsies during World War II

On February 24, 1941, gendarmes in Limoges gathered information on "several tribes of undesirable nomads" parked on the city's northern outskirts after the prefect received a petition from neighboring residents. The local men and women living near the rue Descartes and the rue de Bellac complained that the thefts and damages in the area since the "bohemians'" arrival created an unpleasant living situation. The twenty-two inhabitants interviewed by the gendarmes all had similar opinions about the nomads: "The presence of bohemians in the street is undesirable. These people take no account of hygiene. They relieve themselves right in the middle of the street. They break the fences to heat themselves. They accost people to ask them for alms." The quarter's residents also expressed unanimity in their belief that the "nomads" (an administrative term synonymous with "Gypsies") were "undesirables and their departure [was] to be wished for."[1]

---

[1] Service Historique de la Gendarmerie Nationale (hereafter SHGN) Box 12701 – BT Limoges. Procès-verbal number 382 (February 24, 1941). The chapter's title also comes from this source. I use the terms "nomad" and "Gypsy" throughout the chapter, depending upon the circumstance. When the French word *"nomade"* is used, I use the direct translation of "nomad" to respect the vocabulary used at the time and to designate administrative references to this population. I use the term "Gypsy" to describe the perceived racial heritage of the people represented by the word "nomad," and when individuals are referring to the people as an undesirable group and not as an administrative category. Jean-Pierre Liégeois asserts that the use of the word "Gypsy" carries fewer derogatory connotations and is a legitimate term to describe a varied population, especially since many communities have no specific names for themselves. See Liégeois, *Gypsies and Travellers* (Strasbourg: Council of Europe, 1987), 25. In some cases, I employ the terms "Roma" or "Rom" to represent the linguistic, cultural, and ethnic communities believed to be descended from Indian ancestors. On the term's origins and the ancestry of present-day Gypsies, see especially Donald Kenrick and Grattan Puxon, *The Destiny of Europe's Gypsies* (New York: Basic Books, Inc., 1972), 13–7; and Isabel Fonseca, *Bury Me Standing: The Gypsies and Their Journey* (New York: Alfred A. Knopf, 1996), 83–112.

Despite the fact that the prefect instigated the investigation, the findings from the lengthy examination into the nomads' activities did not find their way into his monthly public opinion report for February 1941. In fact, Gypsies rarely appeared in official reports throughout the Second World War although they greatly occupied local residents as evidenced by petitions and gendarmes' *procès-verbaux*. The prefect instead described the growing material shortages during the month that prompted residents to focus on their own personal situation rather than the hardships facing the entire country. Claiming that the majority of the population still venerated Marshal Pétain and had confidence in his government, the prefect nonetheless noted that the presence of "too many" Jews – not Gypsies – in Limoges had influenced public opinion by creating residents' hope for a return to the past.[2] By the time these Limoges residents made their official complaint about the undesirable nomads in early 1941, the Vichy government's concerted propaganda efforts on behalf of the National Revolution were already failing to produce the desired results, and the French were also engaging in widespread illegal activities.[3]

These conditions eroded the regime's legitimacy, but attitudes toward the Gypsies remained the one area where the French State and the public agreed on most counts. Both the government and the local population held the same low opinion of the traveling bands and expressed this attitude through common stereotypes: Gypsies were dirty beggars and thieves, posing a danger to the health and welfare of society. The combination of ideological and material issues unique to the war years created an environment in which Gypsies were particularly vulnerable to repressive measures. When it came to the Gypsies, many French people embraced the same tenets of the National Revolution that they often ignored in their own lives. The government and individuals justified the exclusion of some Gypsies from the national community due to the nomads' failure to embody the values represented in the National Revolution's motto "Work, Family, Homeland," as well as by citing the material inconveniences created by the undesirables in local communities. But natives' treatment of Gypsies did not reflect a total commitment to Vichy's ideology; rather, it reveals an area in which individuals displayed their complicity with the regime's

---

[2] Archives Départementales de la Haute-Vienne (hereafter ADHV) 185 W1–45. Rapports du préfet de la Haute-Vienne au ministère de l'Intérieur. Rapport mensuel du 4 mars 1941.
[3] For a concise discussion of Vichy's propaganda agenda, see Denis Peschanski, "Control or Integration? Information and Propaganda under Vichy" in *War & Society in Twentieth-Century France* edited by Michael Scriven and Peter Wagstaff (New York: Berg, 1991), 201–18.

actions further complicating our ideas about the nature and specificity of Vichy's popular acceptance.

THE "GYPSY PROBLEM" IN FRANCE

The discrimination against and marginalization of Gypsies has a long history in France. Pushed to the edges of society in medieval Europe due to their dark skin, strange language, indifference to established religion, and perceived threat to guilds, the first anti-Gypsy legislation in France appeared in 1539.[4] In modern times, the Third Republic's battle against vagrancy, which began in the 1880s, ultimately resulted in the law of July 16, 1912. The law provided the government with a legal means to control traveling professions, defined various categories of itinerant merchants, and introduced a new identity card aimed specifically at Gypsies.[5] The French government, drawing upon the traditions of revolutionary republicanism, was careful to avoid defining Gypsies in racial terms in the new law.[6] Instead, the law separated mobile traders into three groups: traveling salesmen (*marchands ambulants*), traders at markets and fairs (*forains*), and nomads (*nomades*). The first article of the law defined traveling salesmen as anyone (French or foreign) having a fixed residence in France and practicing an itinerant trade. The second article required *forains* – French nationals who had no fixed residence and lived by selling items at markets and fairs – to carry a special identity card with a picture, stating their personal information, profession, and last address. The third article defined nomads, "regardless of nationality," as "all individuals

---

[4] On the origins of discrimination in Europe, see Kenrick and Puxon, *The Destiny of Europe's Gypsies*.

[5] On the battle against vagrancy and evolution of identity cards in France, see Pierre Piazza, *Histoire de la Carte nationale d'identité* (Paris: Odile Jacob, 2004). For the full text of the July 16, 1912, law, see Denis Peschanski with Marie-Christine Hubert and Emmanuel Philippon, *Les Tsiganes en France 1939–1946* (Paris: CNRS Editions, 1994), 125–30. The law remained in effect in France until 1969.

[6] See Hubert, "Les réglementations anti-tsiganes en France et en Allemagne, avant et pendant l'occupation" in *Revue d'histoire de la Shoah: le monde juif* 167 (1999): 20–52, for a discussion of the differences in French and German policies, especially in terms of racial aspects. See also Christophe Delclitte, "La catégorie juridique 'nomade' dans la loi de 1912," *Hommes & Migrations* 1188–89 (June–July 1995), 26. Drawing on Enlightenment and French revolutionary principles, the Third Republic distinguished between race and nation with priority going to shared culture and heritage. See Gérard Noiriel, *The French Melting Pot: Immigration, Citizenship, and National Identity* translated by Geoffroy de Laforcade (Minneapolis and London: University of Minnesota Press, 1996), 10–1.

circulating in France without a home or fixed residence and not falling into any of the above categories, even if they have resources or claim to exercise a profession."[7] The law also required individuals in this third category to carry anthropometric identity cards documenting their physical characteristics.

Article three of the July 16, 1912, law thus introduced both a new administrative category and a new identity card without clearly defining who was a "nomad." The ethnically based words *Tsigane, Gitan, Bohémien, Romanichel,* or *Manouche* appear nowhere in the text, but according to Marie-Christine Hubert, "it is exactly Gypsies (*Tsiganes*) that the legislator meant to designate by the term 'nomad.'"[8] The categories' vagueness also meant that some families of Gypsy (Roma/Sinti) descent were classified as *forains*. Although officials avoided using the language of race in the laws, the daily determination of who was a *nomade* took place on a local level and did, in fact, depend upon certain undefined characteristics that can best be labeled as racial.[9] Required to present the anthropometric cards upon arrival and departure in any commune, nomads used the cards as a kind of travel visa, which allowed officials to track their movements.

The establishment of anthropometric cards also demonstrated the lawmakers' association of nomadic Gypsies with criminality. In 1913, the government officially outlined the information to be included on the cards: name, date and place of birth, height, chest measurement, size of head, length of right ear, length of left middle and little fingers, length of left arm from elbow to middle fingertip, eye color, all ten fingerprints, and two photographs (full face and profile). Such physical descriptions had been recorded only for criminals previously. Biological determinism and environmental factors as explanations for criminality thoroughly permeated medical and political thinking about deviance by 1912.[10] Many believed that the

---

[7] Peschanski, *Les Tsiganes en France*, p. 126.

[8] Hubert, "Les réglementations anti-tsiganes," p. 25. Delclitte makes the same argument by tracing parliamentary and journalistic debates in "La catégorie juridique 'nomade'."

[9] The exact number of Gypsies in France remains unknown as censuses with ethnicity questions do not exist. See Hubert, "Les réglementations anti-tsiganes en France et en Allemagne," p. 28. Kenrick and Puxon estimated the number to be 40,000, although this is probably an overestimation. See *The Destiny of Europe's Gypsies*, p. 183.

[10] Robert A. Nye, *Crime, Madness, and Politics in Modern France: The Medical Concept of National Decline* (Princeton, New Jersey: Princeton University Press, 1984). See also Sarah Fishman, *The Battle for Children: World War II, Youth Crime, and Juvenile Justice in Twentieth-Century France* (Cambridge, Massachusetts, and London, England: Harvard University Press, 2002), 19–21.

"criminal" behavior of Gypsies – begging, stealing, and vagabondage – was passed on to future generations. Modifying the criminal's social environment, however, could rectify this behavior.

Indeed, one goal of the 1912 law was to make the itinerating Gypsy population sedentary, thereby eliminating the threat from dangerous vagrants on French roads and simultaneously encouraging assimilation. Lawmakers believed that those who chose to conform to French cultural norms, including having a permanent residence, could be integrated into society. However, Gérard Noiriel has noted an important aspect of the French assimilatory process that early-twentieth-century politicians overlooked: "the nation-state did not assimilate individuals of immigrant origin. On the contrary, it is they who assimilated national norms."[11] Many immigrants proved willing to adapt to French culture, but Gypsies throughout Europe have remained remarkably hesitant to adopt the dominant culture's norms. Economic, linguistic, and educational marginalization limited Roma social contact with Europeans as did Romani culture, which prohibits close association with *Gadje* (the Rom word for non-Gypsies) in order to protect ritual purity. This separation has also preserved Romani society, culture, and tradition despite centuries of persecution.[12] Some nomads did become sedentary after 1912; however, others continued to travel the roads of France.

With the start of the Great War in 1914, fear of all foreigners and the government's desire to control foreign populations increased. Foreign nationals from enemy states – including Gypsies – faced internment and surveillance throughout the war. Gypsies from Alsace-Lorraine (considered foreign after the loss of the provinces in the Franco-Prussian War) were interned in a concentration camp in the Drôme after 1915 due to their "uncertain attitude and dubious feelings" toward France.[13] Internment measures rarely touched French nomads although they were often viewed as potential spies and therefore faced severe limitations on their mobility during the war. Fear of espionage, desertion, subversive activities, and

---

[11] Noiriel, *The French Melting Pot*, p. xx.
[12] Ian Hancock, "Romani Americans ('Gypsies')" in *Roma and Sinti: Under-Studied Victims of Nazism*, Symposium Proceedings (Washington, D.C.: Center for Advanced Holocaust Studies, United States Holocaust Memorial Museum, 2002), 3–4. See also Fonseca, *Bury Me Standing*.
[13] Emmanuel Filhol, *Un camp de concentration français: Les Tsiganes alsaciens-lorrains à Crest 1915–1919* (Grenoble: Presses Universitaires de Grenoble, 2004), 24. On average, 160 Gypsies were interned in a former monastery in Crest throughout the war in abominable living conditions. See ibid., 50. Unlike other interned civilians, Gypsies were rarely allowed to leave the camp.

shortages led to the extension of identity cards from undesirable nomads to immigrants in general in 1917, when cards became mandatory for every foreign resident over the age of fifteen.[14]

The continuing codification of a Nationality Code in the 1920s and 1930s set the stage for the Vichy regime's exclusionary politics between 1940 and 1945. Immediately following the Great War, politicians called for identity cards for French nationals. These calls intensified in the 1930s as waves of refugees flooded France, and officials wanted to be able to control the movement of all French residents, identify citizens, and create a sense of national belonging. While not explicitly intended to "stigmatize certain categories," the cards, a result of a 1935 decree and first appearing in 1939, were meant "to delimit more rigorously the contours [of the national community] and to better locate those who did not make up part of it."[15] What had begun as a means of identifying and controlling nomads would now apply to everyone living in France, although anthropometric cards for nomads continued to distinguish them from the rest of the population. The concurrent evolution of specialized police forces to deal with foreigners during the interwar period made surveillance of non-nationals even easier.[16] Antinomad measures also continued to appear between the wars. A decree issued on July 7, 1926, required prefects to retain a copy of nomads' anthropometric cards in their archives and to forward an additional copy to the Ministry of the Interior, thus creating a centralized, national registry. The same year, a decree required nomads to renew their cards biennially, bringing them into regular contact with authorities. After the Kristallnacht pogroms in November 1938 and the subsequent arrival of thousands of foreigners fleeing persecution, French decree-laws established "special centers" for illegal, undesirable refugees, allowed the government to strip naturalized citizens of French nationality, and effectively closed France's borders to all legal immigration. The difference between French and foreign was thus crystallized and codified under the Third Republic and could be readily used against foreign, undesirable nomads.

These laws could be applied to nomads, but the law of 1912 and subsequent decrees and circulars concerning nomads laid the legal foundation for the French response to Gypsies after the declaration of war in September

---

[14] Piazza, *Histoire de la carte nationale d'identité*, pp. 119–21.
[15] Ibid., p. 127.
[16] On policing and immigrants, see Clifford Rosenberg, *Policing Paris: The Origins of Modern Immigration Control between the Wars* (Ithaca, New York, and London: Cornell University Press, 2006).

1939. The law of April 6, 1940, promulgated by the French Third Republic and later perpetuated by the Vichy regime, forbade the circulation of nomads in France for the war's duration and forced nomads to reside in an assigned area under police surveillance. The introduction to the 1940 anti-Gypsy decree-law included a letter to the president of the republic, explaining the need for such restrictive measures:

> In wartime, the movement of nomads, wandering individuals generally without a home, a homeland, or an actual profession, constitutes a danger to the national defense and the safeguarding of secrets that must be removed.
>
> The nomads' incessant displacements – which must not be confused with *forains*, industrial or commercial, for the most part honorably known – permit them to discover troops' movements, units' campgrounds, defense locations and systems, [and] important intelligence information that they are likely to communicate to enemy agents.[17]

Accused of potential spying for foreign enemies, nomads were among the first groups to be singled out for repressive measures after the war began. By focusing surveillance on the predominantly foreign *nomades* and allowing French *forains* to continue their migrations, the authors of the law demonstrated the degree of prewar xenophobia in France.[18] However, the accusation of Gypsy spying also reflected a longstanding cliché in French society. The wave of Gypsies crossing the Rhine around the time of the Franco-Prussian War in 1870 gave rise to suspicions of spying, and the government interned nomads during World War I for the same reasons.[19] Increased xenophobia thus does not fully explain the law or the treatment of nomads with the outbreak of World War II.

Gendarmes in the Creuse wasted no time putting the April 6, 1940, law into effect in their department under the prefect's instructions. Although waiting for more detailed information concerning the law's application, authorities knew that nomads were to be immobilized immediately in their current locations. The prefect, however, feared that "bordering departments might evacuate their territories of these undesirables and send

---

[17] Peschanski, *Les Tsiganes en France*, p. 131.
[18] On xenophobia, see Eugen Weber's chapter "Foreigners" in *The Hollow Years: France in the 1930s* (New York and London: W. W. Norton & Company, 1994) and Ralph Schor, *L'Opinion française et les étrangers 1919–1939* (Paris: Publications de la Sorbonne, 1985).
[19] On the war of 1870, see Jacques Sigot, "La longue marche vers l'internement des Tsiganes en France pendant la seconde guerre mondiale," *Etudes tsiganes* 13:1 (1999): 20. On World War I, see Hubert, "Les réglementations anti-tsiganes," pp. 29–30 and Filhol, *Un camp de concentration français*. Guenter Lewy notes a similar phenomenon in Germany in *The Nazi Persecution of the Gypsies* (Oxford and New York: Oxford University Press, 2000), 65–6.

them to the Creuse."[20] As a result, the platoon leader of the gendarmerie in the Creuse instructed his brigades to turn away any new nomads trying to set up camp in their district. The memo to the section leaders made no mention of the nomads' potentially traitorous actions, nor did it instruct the gendarmes to monitor the population and report any suspicious activities. Rather, officials sought only to prevent a larger, undesirable Gypsy population from staying in the department, which would create additional policing responsibilities and require attention for the remainder of the hostilities. Local, pragmatic concerns appeared more important to these departmental officials than the potential military threat that nomads posed to the native population.

The minister of the interior (via General Director of National Security A. Bussière) provided prefects with a more detailed explanation of the new law in a circular dated April 29, 1940. Prefects had the responsibility of determining the exact location for the assigned residence areas for the Gypsies in their department, though Bussière advised against the creation of "concentration camps," noting the inconveniences created by such a solution.[21] Not only would camps group nomads that authorities had long worked to separate, but they would also create a financial burden for the locality in terms of lodging, feeding, and guarding the inmates. Instead, the circular suggested that smaller groups of nomads remain dispersed throughout the department in distinct zones outside large cities yet within close proximity of gendarmerie posts. The law permitted nomads to move about freely within the zone designated by the prefect; in exceptional cases (such as the death or illness of a close relative or the need to attend legal proceedings), individuals could apply for passes to travel outside their assigned area. Under no circumstances were nomads allowed to exchange their anthropometric identity cards for other forms of identification that would exempt them from the current measure, nor were they to receive any funds from the state to ensure their subsistence.

Just three months after the April 1940 law, the Third Republic voted itself out of existence and on September 3, 1940, the Vichy government upheld the application of the law under the new regime. Although the Vichy

---

[20] SHGN Box 12536 – Grpt Guéret, R/2, Le Chef d'Escadron Chapaux à Messieurs les Commandants de Section (April 15, 1940). A military decree issued on October 22, 1939, had already forbidden nomads in eight Western departments, including the Haute-Vienne, from circulating in the region. Cited in Hubert, "Les réglementations anti-tsiganes" p. 29.

[21] Archives Nationales (hereafter AN) F7–16044. Letter from le Ministre de l'Intérieur à Messieurs les Préfets (April 29, 1940).

regime promised to recreate a renovated civilization free from undesirable elements and fundamentally different from the degenerate society of the interwar years, the regime remained committed to the idea of nomad assimilability throughout the war years. Like Third Republic legislators, the new government avoided racially defining nomads; neither settled Gypsies nor *forains* of Roma heritage faced sanctions nor the threats reserved for nomads. Vichy claimed the restrictions placed upon nomads during the war provided them with a path to social reintegration. To become part of the national community, nomads had to fit within the National Revolution's tenets of "Work, Family, Homeland." The best way to encourage this assimilation, according to the Vichy regime, was through internment.

Although the April 29, 1940, circular restricting nomadic movement during the war advised against creating concentration camps, this policy quickly changed following the French defeat. After the armistice, Nazi officials requested the establishment of concentration camps for Gypsies throughout France under French administration. Over forty such camps (mainly in the northern zone) existed during the war, housing somewhere between 3,000 and 6,500 nomads (90 percent with French nationality.)[22] In March 1942, the Vichy government decided to move all nomads assigned residence in the free zone to a new camp in the town of Saliers (Bouches-du-Rhône). The camp in the Camargue had a specific political agenda: "Above all, the Saliers camp must be a governmental propaganda argument. This argument consisted of giving a concentration camp the look of a village and of allowing family life there and respecting the customs and beliefs of the internees."[23] Yet nothing within the camp system coincided with the traditional Gypsy way of life. Internment and the National Revolution did, however, provide sedentary Limousin residents with easily accessible justifications for the exclusion of Gypsies from local communities.

GYPSIES, THE LIMOUSIN, AND WORLD WAR II

Nomads found themselves under a kind of house arrest by the spring of 1940, though some movement continued, especially after German troops began their assault on France in May. Gypsies joined the millions of other

---

[22] See Donald Kenrick and Grattan Puxon, *Gypsies under the Swastika* (Hatfield, United Kingdom: Gypsy Research Centre, University of Hertfordshire Press, 1995), 66–7, and Hubert, "L'internement des Tsiganes en France 1940–1946," *Etudes tsiganes* 13:1 (1999): 14. On French camps for nomads, see especially Peschanski, *Les Tsiganes en France*.

[23] Quoted in Mathieu Pernot, ed., *Un Camp pour les Bohémiens: Mémoires du camp d'internement pour nomades de Saliers* (Arles: Actes Sud, 2001), 5.

French men and women attempting to flee the Nazi advance by heading south during the *exode*. The de facto annexation of Alsace and Lorraine to the Third Reich prompted German authorities to expel some undesirable nomads from the territories in the fall of the same year, putting more Gypsies on the roads to the southern zone. The ancestors of many of the Gypsies assigned residence in the Limousin in 1940 likely arrived in the region during the late nineteenth or early twentieth century. Most *Manouche* in the Limousin had been wandering the region for generations, staying largely within two or three of the area's departments. Like many refugees during the Second World War, the nomads stayed due to the region's material advantages: "because there was brush, because there were hedgehogs, because there was pasture for the horses, because there were rivers with trout, because the peasants were giving them hay, bacon and milk, because there were springs on the mountainsides and fountains in the villages."[24] Thus, the nomads immobilized in the region by the April laws included refugees, expellees, and regular travelers.

By the end of September 1940, citizens in the Limousin began to complain about the nomads forced to reside in the region. These complaints coincided with the start of official rationing and the growing competition and cooperation between residents in their daily search for food over the course of 1940–1. Gendarmes reported that, as of October 22, fifty-eight nomads (all French) resided under surveillance in the Haute-Vienne. By mid-November, the number forced to live in the department had reached 163.[25] Despite the small numbers (significantly less than any other refugee group in the area), the nomads' presence engendered considerable grumbling from the local population. There was no concerted government-sponsored propaganda campaign on behalf of the nomads as there had been following the arrival of Alsatian evacuees the previous year. Facing complaints, letters, and petitions from permanent residents, local gendarmerie brigades searched for solutions to the disagreeable living situation. The Limousins' primary complaints stemmed from "inconveniences" such as the theft of poultry and vegetables that resulted from the prolonged stay of Gypsies in any particular commune.[26] Petitioners felt it was only fair that other areas

---

[24] Patrick Williams, *Gypsy World: The Silence of the Living and the Voices of the Dead* translated by Catherine Tihanyi (Chicago and London: University of Chicago Press, 2003), 3.
[25] SHGN Box 12640 – BT Limoges, R/2, Etat des Nomades astreints à résider dans le département de la Haute-Vienne (October 22, 1940, and November 14, 1940).
[26] SHGN Box 12753 – BT Saint-Léonard-de-Noblat. Procès-verbal number 365 (August 10, 1941). The procès-verbal uses the term *"forain"* to describe the people stationed near the village though they had been there for over a year.

share equitably in the hardship of living near the unwanted population.[27] Authorities promised the fair and equitable distribution of food, clothing, and heating materials, and locals living in proximity to nomads also wanted the fair and equitable dispersion of Gypsies throughout the department.

Residents throughout the Creuse and the Haute-Vienne pointed to both the material and more intangible burdens created by their new neighbors in the petitions and complaints. Despite the reminder in the preface to the April 6, 1940, law that *nomades* and *forains* should not be confused, the region's residents used the terms interchangeably and often also complained about *forains* without fixed residences. To Limousin residents, the appearance of being a nomad or being of Gypsy descent counted more than the official designation. People officially classified as *forains* retained the right to practice their trades and move about freely; yet in daily interactions with the region's natives, the traders were often viewed as *nomades*. Rural inhabitants blamed the theft of precious items, such as wood and farm products, on "nomads," whether the culprits were nomads, *forains*, or perhaps neither. On the outskirts of towns, residents complained about the human waste, about empty cans and bottles, and about the general dirtiness of the people parked in neighboring fields. By failing to conform to the accepted ideals espoused by French society and by creating further material difficulties through their thefts and littering, nomads faced increased marginalization, which ultimately led to the incarceration of thousands in concentration camps.

Gypsy Thieves

Thefts motivated by both necessity and opportunity became a regular aspect of daily life in France during the second phase of shortages between September 1940 and March 1942. As residents experienced the first extreme shortages, an unguarded vegetable field or a stray chicken proved too tempting for many hungry and frustrated French men and women to resist. Nomads, forced to reside within a specific area and with limited opportunities to earn a living, were no exception. What was exceptional was the regularity with which native residents blamed nomads for the thefts. Ingrained stereotypes meant many people in law enforcement and on the street believed that while the laws "[said] 'nomads' [they] think 'gypsies,' spies, thieves."[28] Paying no mind to administrative designations, sedentary

---

[27] SHGN Box 12640 – BT Limoges, R/2, Le Chef d'Escadron à Monsieur le Préfet de la Haute-Vienne (October 26, 1940, and November 15, 1940).
[28] Peschanski, *Les Tsiganes en France*, p. 17.

residents in the Limousin blamed Gypsies for stealing wood, vegetables, chickens, and rabbits.

Although often greatly exaggerated, Gypsy thefts were a reality of daily life. Gypsy thievery, exacerbated by the shortages of the war years and the inability to move to new markets, reflected a long-standing practice in the community. The stereotype of the sneaky, stealing Gypsy existed long before the Second World War and was a reaction to the nomadic population's lifestyle.[29] Gypsies' willingness to steal from their non-Gypsy neighbors reflected both material need and part of their belief system. Jan Yoors, a Belgian who spent much of his adolescence in the late 1930s and early 1940s living with Gypsies wandering throughout Western Europe, learned much about such practices from his adoptive family. The differences between Rom and *Gadje* attitudes toward nature helped explain the practice of subsistence thieving. Yoors asserts, "In a general way they [Gypsies] consider the entire Gajo [non-Gypsy] world a public domain," thus picking up wood for fires or hay for horses did not constitute a crime in their eyes.[30] Yoors's friend Putzina explained the Gypsy's position: "[S]tealing from the Gaje was not really a misdeed as long as it was limited to the taking of basic necessities, and not in larger quantities than were needed at that moment. It was the intrusion of a sense of greed, in itself, that made stealing wrong, for it made men slaves to unnecessary appetites or to their desire for possessions."[31] Gypsy custom also prohibited Gypsies from stealing from one another and as a Gajo, Yoors was forbidden from taking anything that was not his. The difference in worldviews meant that Gypsies considered the occasional theft of a chicken or a rabbit from a farmer for family consumption legitimate, while the region's natives, believing in private property and facing extreme shortages, viewed it as nothing more than illegal activity.

As more town residents ventured into the countryside in search of food and fewer peasants brought their goods to markets during 1941, the livelihood of *forains* and *nomades* who relied on local markets and fairs as places of business also suffered. Like other French men and women, nomads ventured into the countryside in order to find food and materials. Neighbors reported that the nomad Madame Loustalot and her children spent their days "covering the countryside to find some supplies," while

---

[29] See Lewy, *The Nazi Persecution of the Gypsies*, pp. 11–2.
[30] Jan Yoors, *The Gypsies* (New York: Simon and Schuster, 1967), 7. Fonseca also addresses the Gypsy attitude toward stealing in *Bury Me Standing*.
[31] Yoors, *The Gypsies*, p. 34.

the male members of the *forain* families in Sauviat-sur-Vige went out in search of rabbit skins to purchase.[32] Unlike most other residents, however, nomads and *forains* also went door to door in order to sell items and services rather than solely purchasing farm products. Some women sold buttons or stationery; other nomads or *forains* offered to "re-seat chairs, sharpen razors, and repair umbrellas."[33] The daily trips replicated the phenomenon of the city venturing into the countryside that became ubiquitous during the war years, but reversed the economic relationship because peasants were supposed to purchase items rather than sell them.

Visiting farms not only provided *forains* or *nomades* with the opportunity to make money but also brought them into contact with scarce food items. All French residents found it difficult to make ends meet during the war and often resorted to extra-legal or illegal means for survival. However, the migratory outsiders lacked many of the connections, finances, and other resources required to participate in bartering or the black market. Traveling and living in family groups without any kind of fixed address also meant that nomads could not easily turn to *colis familiaux* for additional food. Gypsies – like their sedentary counterparts – yielded to temptation on occasion and were probably aided by previous experience in stealing. After having given two "nomad women" a couple of umbrellas to mend, Léonard Saulnier, a farmer in the village of Rouzeix just outside Limoges, noticed that three of his chickens were missing. A month later the women returned, and the suspicious farmer hid in his pigsty in order to watch them. Saulnier later claimed that they had dropped a trail of breadcrumbs and that when the chickens had begun to follow it, one of the women had grabbed two of the chickens. Both women – *foraines* – denied trying to trap the chickens and claimed that they had visited the farm only to deliver the repaired umbrellas. On finding the breadcrumb evidence in the yard, gendarmes arrested the women.[34] In another case, a farmwoman working in her cow pasture accused two women and two children "who appeared to me to be nomads" of killing and hiding a chicken. Overhearing one of the strangers saying, "We'll get it on the way back," Marie-Louise Paviot decided to investigate and discovered the still-warm chicken. On returning to her home, Paviot learned that the "two bohemians" had been

---

[32] On the Loustalot family, see SHGN Box 12724 – BT Nexon. Procès-verbal number 460 (November 18, 1941). On *forains* in Sauviat-sur-Vige, see SHGN Box 12754 – BT Saint-Léonard-de-Noblat. Procès-verbal number 115 (March 24, 1942).
[33] SHGN Box 12701 – BT Limoges. Procès-verbal (January 21, 1941).
[34] Ibid.

there selling lace and immediately filed a complaint with the gendarmerie.³⁵ In both cases, the "nomad" women allegedly committed the crimes while pursuing legitimate sales.

Complaints and accusations that *nomades* and *forains* stole wood appeared consistently. A general fuel shortage plagued French residents throughout the war; thus the disappearance of wood greatly affected daily life. With only 47 percent of the prewar amounts of coal available, people turned to wood for their heating, cooking, lighting, and transportation needs.³⁶ Converted cars ran on *gazogène*, a fuel derived from wood or charcoal. Increased demand for wood did not coincide, however, with increased production; France also faced a shortage of lumberjacks and lacked the transportation necessary to distribute the wood.³⁷ In the Creuse, the growing clandestine transport of wood out of the department prompted gendarmes to increase their surveillance of forests and logging trucks in early 1942.³⁸ In this context, wood thefts by nomads raised harsh criticism, and the thefts' destructive nature further angered the victims. Several residents of Saint-Léonard-de-Noblat (Haute-Vienne) and its surrounding communes complained that nomads and *forains* parked at the town's fairgrounds stole dead wood from hedges and fences.³⁹ After two years in the same location and numerous complaints, the mayor dispersed the thirty members of the four families to smaller villages near Saint-Léonard, hoping the problems would be solved. Instead, he received new petitions and individual complaints in November 1941 that the nomads "cut tree branches in the copses with hatchets" and "carry off the dead wood found in the hedges which serve to enclose ... meadows and fields." The same residents renewed their complaints four months later.⁴⁰ The Gypsies continued to steal wood and destroyed property in the process, furthering distancing themselves from local residents whose primary concerns centered on shortages in their daily lives. Gypsies' actions interfered with family supplies and were thus targeted for sanctions.

---

[35] SHGN Box 12753 – BT Saint-Léonard-de-Noblat. Procès-verbal number 376 (August 14, 1941).
[36] Statistic cited in Dominique Veillon, *Vivre et survivre en France 1939–1947* (Paris: Editions Payot & Rivages, 1995), 133.
[37] Sweets, *Choices in Vichy France*, p. 11, and Veillon, *Vivre et survivre,* pp. 137–8.
[38] SHGN Box 12538 – BT Guéret, R/2, Le Chef d'Escadron aux Commandants de Section de la Compagnie (February 20, 1942).
[39] SHGN Box 12753 – BT Saint-Léonard-de-Noblat. Procès-verbal number 384 (August 22, 1941).
[40] SHGN Box 12754 – BT Saint-Léonard-de-Noblat. Procès-verbal number 536 (November 28, 1941) and procès-verbal number 125 (March 31, 1942).

It often took little more than sighting someone who looked like a nomad to accuse him or her of a crime, although the entire country experienced a dramatic increase in thefts during the war.[41] The apogee of theft charges occurred in 1942, when over 26,000 juveniles and nearly 115,000 adults stood trial, with most defendants coming from the working class. Nearly all theft cases reported to the Gendarmerie Nationale in the Limousin cited an "unknown author" as the culprit, and investigations usually led to a non-Gypsy petty thief. But the Vichy regime's practice of stopping suspicious individuals to search for illegal activity combined with ingrained anti-Gypsyism made nomads more vulnerable than non-Gypsies. Gendarmes stopped individuals having a "nomadic allure," and the questioning process often demonstrated the prejudice prevalent in society.[42] Officer Hugonnaud of the La Souterraine Gendarmerie arrested Louis Lafleur in October 1941 on an outstanding battery charge. While searching Lafleur, Hugonnaud noted the *forain* was wearing a new leather jacket with a new hat, and was carrying 2354.25 francs and an automatic lighter. "Lafleur's tidy clothing [and] the possession of such a large amount of money," the gendarme noted, "appeared very suspicious for an individual from his class (*catégorie*), an illiterate, so-called chair reseater, but who in reality hardly seems to devote himself to any work and travels a lot." Lafleur "could not furnish any explanation for his trips," Hugonnaud concluded, "and there is every reason to assume that he is engaged in some illicit dealings and is likely to commit thefts." Furthermore, some unsolved robberies in an area Lafleur had visited during his travels could have been committed by *forains*, according to the locals.[43] Although Lafleur had been stopped for another reason, the mere appearance of material impropriety led the gendarme to assume he was a thief. Like Hugonnaud, permanent residents did not need to capture Gypsies in the act of committing a crime in order to accuse them of stealing. A widow living in a small village outside Limoges reported that someone had stolen eight rabbits from her farm. During the investigation, she told the

---

[41] Paul Sanders has called stealing even more prevalent in wartime society than the rampant black market, and Sarah Fishman's investigation of crime under Vichy reveals a remarkable increase in theft trials for both adolescents and adults during the war years. See Sanders, *Histoire du marché noir 1940–1946* (Paris: Perrin, 2001), 134–5. Fishman reports theft trials increased by 267 percent for juveniles and 245 percent for adults between 1937 and 1942. Fishman, *The Battle for Children*, p. 83. See also comparative charts on pp. 84–5.
[42] See for example SHGN Box 12708 – Haute Vienne, BT Limoges. Procès-verbal number 836 (May 7, 1943).
[43] SHGN Box 12631 – Grpt Creuse – Section de Guéret – BT La Souterraine, R/2, Rapport de l'Adjudant Hugonnaud, cmdt la brigade de La Souterraine sur les agissements du forain Lafleur (Louis) (October 31, 1941).

gendarmes, "I have no suspicions; however, I must tell you that yesterday morning around eleven, two bohemians came to the house to sell some lace." To corroborate her story, a worker on the farm stepped forward to say that he had noticed a suspicious man on a bicycle who looked like a nomad.[44] On discovering the theft of her chickens, another farmwoman also contacted the gendarmes in Limoges to file a report. Like the widow, the woman could not name a suspect but made a point of mentioning that two young women who she thought were nomads had recently visited her home in search of supplies. The women "stayed a fairly long time at the house and had the time to inspect the place. I cannot tell you if there is a correlation between the visit of these women and the theft."[45] Clearly, a correlation did exist between the nomads and the thefts in the minds of these women. Each victim implied that the Gypsies were the culprits. The mayor of Moissannes shared this attitude: "Since these *forains* have been in the commune, I have had frequent complaints about vegetable thefts. I cannot say if they are the authors of these thefts, but before their arrival in the village, such things did not happen."[46] We know, however, that at the time of his report in the fall of 1941, thefts were a regular part of daily life.

Theft victims never reported any suspicious "French-looking" or "Jewish types" in the area; the Gypsies bore the brunt of the accusations, which demonstrates the extent and specificity of antinomad sentiment in society. Although some farmers did suspect that urban residents traveling into the countryside for food were responsible for thefts, the stereotypical traits associated with Gypsies made them more likely suspects and more acceptable scapegoats. The frequent movement of nomads and *forains*, their lack of regular employment, and the general belief that they possessed large sums of money led to the conclusion that Gypsies must be involved in illegal activity. It did not cross the minds of most theft victims that Gypsies stole in order to provide for their families. With a limited potential for sales and without state aid, nomads turned to other options. But thievery was just one reason Limousin residents regularly applied Vichy's rhetoric about undesirables to their nomadic neighbors.

"Travail": Nomads and Work

Implicit in many local residents' complaints about nomads and in the government's attitude toward the population were ideas about work. Even

---

[44] SHGN Box 12702 – BT Limoges. Procès-verbal number 1058 (June 7, 1941).
[45] SHGN Box 12709 – BT Limoges. Procès-verbal number 2426 (November 19, 1943).
[46] SHGN Box 12753 – BT Saint-Léonard-de-Noblat. Procès-verbal number 365 (August 10, 1941).

before the establishment of the Vichy regime and Marshal Pétain's demands for a National Revolution, French officials concerned themselves with nomads' work ethic. The minister of the interior, in his April 29, 1940, letter to the prefects, expressed his hope that by requiring nomads to provide for themselves and denying all state aid, a few of them would acquire "if not the taste for, at least the habits of regular work."[47] The prerequisite for sustained employment was a sedentary lifestyle, and the wartime law tried to force Gypsies into immobility. Officials in the Haute-Vienne specified that nomads had to report weekly to the gendarmerie station in the area where they were assigned residence. Additionally, they had to have all travel itineraries approved before they could leave the district. To ensure that nomads returned to their place of assigned residence, gendarmes held the nomads' family identification cards and anthropometric cards and provided travelers with a receipt to be traded for the cards once they came back. Nomads who left their assigned areas without permission faced fines, arrest, and imprisonment. The laws concerning the movement of non-Gypsy French and foreigners during the war required these populations to remain within the zone where they resided (occupied or unoccupied, etc.). Infractions carried a fine of between 11 and 15 francs and up to five days in prison for repeat offenders. Nomads, forced to remain within certain communes, faced prison terms of one to five years for the first infraction.[48] The constant threat of reassignment to another area also added to the uncertainty of nomads' daily lives. For example, during the spring of 1941, the minister of the interior ordered all nomads expelled from the department of the Allier where the new government had established itself at Vichy.[49] Over one hundred nomads thus ended up in the neighboring department of the Creuse. Nomads were also moved from commune to commune after residents complained to local authorities.

The inability to practice traditional occupations that required mobility, such as bringing in seasonal crops or selling wares at markets and fairs, brought nomads into conflict with the surrounding population. Though permitted to move about within a prescribed area, nomads, like many other French residents, could no longer meet all their material needs. It soon became apparent that rather than forcing Gypsies to find regular employment, the circumscribed areas only further encouraged them to turn to

---

[47] AN F7 – 16044. Letter from le Ministre de l'Intérieur à Messieurs les Préfets (April 29, 1940), 6.
[48] See Joseph Valet, "Gitans et Voyageurs d'Auvergne durant la guerre 1939–45," *Etudes tsiganes* 6:2 (1995): 212.
[49] SHGN Box 12537 – BT Guéret, R/2, Le Chef d'Escadron aux Commandants de Section (April 23, 1941).

illegal activities such as begging and stealing or to abandon their areas of assigned residence. In November 1940, the gendarmes warned, "one must not place too much hope on changing the nomads' wandering mentality; their work remains, in all likelihood, limited to basket making, knickknacks, or lace making."[50] Numerous subsequent petitions and investigations made reference to the begging of nomads or their children, and gendarmes arrested nomads asking residents for food, claiming they had been "caught red-handed begging."[51] Gendarmes in the Haute-Vienne arrested a *"romanichel* tribe composed of a woman and five children" for leaving its area of assigned residence in the Creuse in early December 1943. On questioning, Marie Wiss explained that she had left the town of Pontarion two weeks earlier in order to sell some lace: "I left my assigned residence because I could no longer find anything to eat for my children. I knew that I should not leave; it is destitution that pushed me." She also acknowledged that the tribunal in Guéret had already condemned her once for the same infraction the previous year.[52] Thus for many, assigned residence did not lead to stable employment, and the inability to provide for oneself and one's family led to behavior that only worsened relationships with other residents.

Farmers facing labor shortages and daily thefts found the unemployed "nomads" in their communities troublesome. In the fall of 1941, the mayor of Moissannes reported that the local population resented the refugee *forains* that had been living in the commune since the previous summer. "These people, not engaged in any steady work," wrote Mayor Léonard Dumoulard, "are the object of criticism from the commune's population that lacks labor due to the large number of prisoners of war."[53] By the next spring, two of the families previously living in Moissannes had moved to Sauviat-sur-Vige, just five kilometers farther east in the rural Limousin. The mayor in Sauviat argued that all three of the families of *forains* in his community should be reclassified as *nomades* and interned in "special camps" because they did not practice an identifiable profession. The apparent wealth of the families, despite their inactivity, led many residents to believe that the

---

[50] SHGN Box 12640 – BT Limoges, R/2, Le Chef d'Escadron à Monsieur le Préfet de la Haute-Vienne (November 15, 1940).

[51] On begging, see SHGN Box 12701 – BT Limoges. Procès-verbal number 382 (February 24, 1941) and Box 12724 – BT Nexon. Procès-verbal number 460 (November 18, 1941). On the arrests, see SHGN Box 12754 – BT Saint-Léonard-de-Noblat. Procès-verbaux numbers 188 and 189 (May 16, 1942).

[52] SHGN Box 12710 – BT Limoges. Procès-verbal number 2554 (December 2, 1943).

[53] SHGN Box 12753 – BT Saint-Léonard-de-Noblat. Procès-verbal number 365 (August 10, 1941).

forains thrived by illegal activities, fostering discontent among the native population. In addition to the mayor, the gendarmes interviewed at least four other people who critically noted that none of the men – "nomad types" – worked.[54] For the residents of Moissannes and Sauviat-sur-Vige, the solution to the problem was not to find regular jobs for the men on farms but to place them and their families in centers under surveillance. The call for internments reflected not only the usual anti-Gypsy sentiments but also local frustrations about labor shortages, perceived economic inequalities, and the *forains'* refusal to participate in new forms of employment.

Despite the stereotype that nomads were lazy and never worked, some did find regular employment. Joseph Vingerder, forced to reside in Saint-Alpinien in the central Creuse, remembered: "When my father saw that we had nothing to eat, he placed all of us to work with peasants. I was twelve at the time." Tsigane Coussantien's father and brothers worked in the forests near Felletin in the southern part of the Creuse, making charcoal to be used in *gazogène* vehicles. After the German troops' arrival in the unoccupied zone in late 1942, the family moved farther south to the Corrèze to continue their work.[55] The government succeeded in forcing these men into jobs in areas in which labor was greatly needed but not, unsurprisingly, in converting them into supporters of the new regime or of "Work, Family, Homeland."

"Famille": Internment and the Family

Gypsies' failure to conform to the accepted ideas of family – the centerpiece of the National Revolution – became another reason for the government and for ordinary citizens to exclude them from society. The twelve members of the Loustalot family, assigned residence in Janailhac (a rural town twenty-six kilometers due south of Limoges) moved to an isolated house in the countryside after previous neighbors in town had complained about their drinking and nightly fights. According to gendarmes' reports, the ten children begged for food from neighbors, destroyed hedges, and were often left hungry and alone. Neighbors observed that Georges Loustalot and his wife, "when they have some money, indulge themselves in drinking and leave their children in an appalling state. [The children] are dressed in rags and never have anything to put on their feet. These poor children are to be pitied." Others agreed that "the Loustalot parents raise their children in a deplorable

---

[54] SHGN Box 12754 – BT Saint-Léonard-de-Noblat. Procès-verbal number 115 (March 24, 1942).
[55] Valet, "Gitans et Voyageurs d'Auvergne," pp. 214, 217.

manner and are incapable of meeting their needs," and more than one neighboring resident went so far as to say that the pair were "unworthy of raising their children." The mayor, like many other residents, concluded: "It would be desirable, as much for the region's inhabitants as for the Loustalot children, who are completely destitute, that an internment measure be pronounced against them."[56] For sedentary neighbors, poor parenting skills as demonstrated by the pitiable material condition of the children, warranted the whole family's internment. Such action would also remove begging, undesirable Gypsies from the community.

While the children appeared destitute to neighbors, it is possible that this assessment represented only an outsider's interpretation. The Loustalot family's downstairs neighbor, Jean Latouille, reported that each time one of the ten children came to ask for a little salt or some garlic, they offered him a one-franc piece. The farmer never accepted the money, believing it was just part of the children's begging routine.[57] In Gypsy culture, children's begging does not always stem from necessity. It not only allows children "to pick up a little pocket money," but it also encourages a distancing between Gypsies and *Gadje*. Isabel Fonseca explains, "This attitude – though not necessarily the begging – is widely encouraged by adult Gypsies, who are understandably anxious that their children should neither mix with *gadje* nor be thin-skinned."[58] In any case, it created further distance between the two communities during the war.

The children's torn clothing also reflected Gypsy customs and may have served as a strategy to gain additional food items, especially useful in a time of extreme shortage. Children throughout France often helped supplement

---

[56] SHGN Box 12724 – BT Nexon. Procès-verbal number 460 (November 18, 1941). Despite the complaints, apparently no action was taken against the family. On June 1, 1942, gendarmes returned to Janailhac, and the mayor reported that the family had left its assigned residence without permission. The family returned sometime in 1943 because the gendarmes questioned the father and his brother multiple times that year. See SHGN Box 12725 – BT Nexon. Procès-verbal number 196 (June 1, 1942).

[57] SHGN Box 12724 – BT Nexon. Procès-verbal number 460 (November 18, 1941). Another man interviewed in Janailhac also reported that the children always offered to pay, but he considered this to be evidence of their skill at begging.

[58] Fonseca, *Bury Me Standing*, p. 51. Fonseca focuses on modern, Eastern European Gypsies in her anthropological study. Despite the difference in time and place, Gypsy culture has maintained some central tenets, just as European stereotypes draw upon remarkably similar themes. Hancock notes the continuity of culture among the Roma in "Romani Americans," including the fact that "Romani culture itself (called *rromanipé*) does not permit involvement with the non-Gypsy world beyond the minimum required for business." See p. 3. In *The Gypsies*, Yoors notes similar attitudes among the Western European Gypsies with whom he lived and traveled in the 1930s and 1940s (including in France). Kenrick and Puxon also note continuities in *The Destiny of Europe's Gypsies*.

FIGURE 2. Gypsy children. Four Gypsy children pose for a photograph in unoccupied France during the war. Photo credit: USHMM, courtesy of Elizabeth Eidenbenz.

the family's food supply during the war by visiting neighboring farms to purchase goods or by tending garden plots. The Loustalot children also went from house to house in the area, and Mayor Barrette reported (six months after the initial complaints against the family) that the people of the countryside gave the Gypsy children "lots of provisions (*beaucoup de vivres*)" out of pity.[59] Dressed in "rags" and without shoes, the children aroused sympathy in some neighbors. (See Figure 2.) But their clothing also reflected Gypsy cultural attitudes: Adults expected children to get dirty as they played, and adults saw no need to mend torn garments. The appearance

[59] SHGN Box 12725 – BT Nexon. Procès-verbal number 196 (June 1, 1942).

of poverty also had several uses: It could scare non-Gypsies into keeping their distance from the "dirty" Gypsies or it could inspire *Gadje* to give alms to the "poor" Gypsies.[60] Judging by the local residents' statements given to the gendarmes, the Loustalot children appeared successful in getting food for their family, and the mayor reported that the children, despite being dirty, were "robust and in good health."[61] The "advantages" of Gypsy attitudes toward clothing and cleanliness proved detrimental in times of heightened xenophobia, when the "filth" of Gypsies became associated with disease and contamination.[62] Furthermore, many in French society viewed outward appearances as indicative of one's worth. Under Vichy, "moral hygiene was inseparable from social hygiene."[63] Dirty, begging, tattered Gypsy children thus fit with preconceived notions about nomadic criminality and loose family morals, both undesirable traits in the New France under construction. In daily practice in towns like Janailhac, the "mistreatment" of the children thus led some residents to believe that the Loustalot children would be better off in the care of a charitable organization or in a government-run internment camp.

For other Limousin residents, the moral and material filth in which nomads raised their children also demanded some form of administrative action. Many people residing near the Gypsies deplored the tendency of the nomads and *forains* to drink, as well as the lurid scenes that resulted. Firmin Delaire, a neighbor of the Mayer family of *forains* stationed in Sauviat-sur-Vige, complained about living next to the family of eleven: "From time to time, domestic scenes erupt between the husband and wife, during which indecent remarks are exchanged, to such a point that I had to forbid my children from going near their home. Moreover, the Mayer children are repulsively dirty."[64] The fields, roads, and neighbor's yards around the Gypsies' wagons, littered with human excrement and garbage, engendered fears of epidemics. Residents of Saint-Léonard-de-Noblat complained that the nomads and *forains* using the fairgrounds as a campsite "drink daily at the public fountain and leave all kinds of filth around the faucet." With dozens of people refusing to use the "toilets located fifty meters from their

---

[60] Fonseca, *Bury Me Standing*, pp. 50–1.
[61] SHGN Box 12725 – BT Nexon. Procès-verbal number 196 (June 1, 1942).
[62] Fonseca, *Bury Me Standing*, p. 50.
[63] Julian Jackson, *France: The Dark Years 1940–1945* (Oxford and New York: Oxford University Press, 2001), 329. Sarah Fishman notes that social workers investigating juvenile delinquents regularly viewed "an adolescent's level of hygiene within the limits of the situation" as "an external manifestation of the family's internal order." See Fishman, *The Battle for Children*, p. 97.
[64] SHGN Box 12754 – BT Saint-Léonard-de-Noblat. Procès-verbal number 115 (March 24, 1942).

wagons," Saint-Léonard's mayor viewed the nomads as a serious threat to the public health of the entire surrounding community.[65] "Real" French families faced danger from living in proximity to the Gypsies, and the danger needed to be removed.

Justifying internment as being "for the good of the family" gave residents a legitimate reason to call for the removal of undesirables from the area. No longer just a material nuisance, nomads and *forains* constituted a threat to future generations, and the government's duty was to protect all children – Gypsy and non-Gypsy alike. Vichy actively promoted the family as a central element of the National Revolution, but even if one did not fully support the Vichy regime, it was easy to find other advocates who promoted a return to traditional family values.[66] Therefore, one could reject the legitimacy of the Vichy government while remaining complicit with some of its ideas about the family, especially in the case of Gypsies. Even though overall support for the regime was eroding, it is clear that the government still had enough authority for local residents to turn to the administrative system in the attempt to rid themselves of the Gypsy "nuisance." Both the government and ordinary citizens supported the internment of nomads: In camps, Gypsy children would be educated, parents would be forced to work in productive enterprises, and everyone would be closely monitored, thereby preventing future crimes that affected the material situation of "true" French men and women.

Ironically, the strong familial tendencies of the Gypsies, forged through years of discrimination and persecution, became evident once they were interned in camps. The Gypsies ate together, slept together, and always remained within the family unit. A visitor to the nomad camp at Montreuil-Bellay, established in the occupied zone after the armistice, wrote in the weekly *Toute la Vie* that, "above all things, the Gypsies [*les Gitans*] have basically the family feeling."[67] Scholars' assessments of Gypsy culture echo

---

[65] SHGN Box 12753 – BT Saint-Léonard-de-Noblat. Procès-verbal number 384 (August 22, 1941). Traditions and taboos concerning cleanliness and ritual purity were, in fact, often stricter among Gypsies than among non-Gypsies. See Kenrick and Puxon, *The Destiny of Europe's Gypsies*, pp. 36–7. See also Lewy, *The Nazi Persecution of the Gypsies*, p. 13, and Fonseca, *Bury Me Standing*. Kenrick and Puxon report that Gypsies "regard the indoor lavatory with suspicion as a source of infection, and its use by both men and women as most undesirable if not immoral," p. 38.

[66] During the Third Republic, politicians, scientists, demographers, and Catholic leaders all called for stronger families. See Miranda Pollard's chapter, "'We Are Beaten': Women, Natalism, and Familialism from the Third Republic to Vichy" in *Reign of Virtue: Mobilizing Gender in Vichy France* (Chicago and London: The University of Chicago Press, 1998) and Jackson's chapter, "Reconstructing Mankind" in *France: The Dark Years*.

[67] Cited in Christian Bernadac, *L'Holocauste oublié: Le massacre des tsiganes* (Paris: Editions France-Empire, 1979), 47.

the visitor's observations: "In the life of Gypsies [...] everything revolves around the family, the basic unit in social organization, the system of family groups, the economic unit in which work is carried out and working solidarity exercised, the educational unit which ensures social reproduction and security, and protection of the individual."[68] Yet the Gypsies' understanding of family did not have a place in the moral order of the New France being developed under Vichy.

According to the regime, authorities in Gypsy camps had a "moral and social obligation" to alter the existing Gypsy family culture. The camp experience should "inculcate then develop family feeling," but it was to be a different kind of family feeling than Gypsies had experienced in the past. To change attitudes and bring nomads more in line with other French families, officials needed to

> keep in check parents' habit of exploiting [...] their children (especially the youngest) for their profit; to require that parents treat their children humanely and that children respect their parents; to see to indoor cleanliness and create emulation [... and] improvement by rewarding the families that keep things cleanest with special meals; to make families feel solidarity in good and bad times.[69]

Cleanliness, the external manifestation of internal moral worth, would be rewarded with food, a strong incentive in this period of increasing scarcity. Yet the government often did not live up to its promises because it could not adequately supply the camps. The difficult living conditions and shortages in the camps then became a justification for removing children from the camps and placing them with nonnomadic families or aid organizations. Such placements aided in Vichy's goal to socialize, sedentarize, and assimilate nomads into French culture by destroying traditional family bonds and reshaping impressionable children. Ordinary citizens supported such activities because it removed a threat to their material situation.

"Patrie": Homeland and Assimilation

For Vichy officials, the assimilation of Gypsy culture into the French mainstream still remained the ultimate goal. By conforming to accepted ideals, domiciled Gypsies avoided persecution; the Vichy government's ideals disseminated in internment camps urged other Gypsies to follow suit. The desire to instill nomads with a particular sense of community was also made

---

[68] Liégeois, *Gypsies and Travellers*, pp. 54–5.
[69] Cited in Bernadac, *L'Holocauste oublié*, p. 71.

explicit in camp instructions. Officials were to "inculcate and then develop the idea of the possibility and the necessity of society by organizing the camp like a civilized hamlet [...] where each person contributes as much as possible to the improvement of the community's fate, by making it felt in practice that all efforts are worthwhile, not only for the general interest, but above all for the individual."[70] Theoretically, when nomads changed their work habits and acquired a new idea of family and society, they could reenter the French national community.

Though conditions in the camps were difficult, living behind barbed wire in France was preferable to being deported to the death camps in Poland. The French camps, often without running water or bedding, provided inadequate amounts of food and fuel for the internees. Suffering from cold, hunger, and isolation, most nomads did not receive outside assistance, unlike other internees whose relatives sent packages or visited the camps. A few charitable organizations did try to ameliorate the poor living conditions for nomads, but overall, the privations did little to encourage assimilation.[71] In fact nomads like Berthe Lafleur, Irène Blanvin, and François Reinhardt all told the arresting gendarmes in the Haute-Vienne that they had illegally fled Saliers because of food shortages.[72] Other Gypsies cited their "Frenchness" and their patriotism, demonstrated by their willingness to fight and die for France, in letters asking for their release from internment camps.[73]

While local residents called for the internment of Gypsies, many nomads in the Limousin continued to live with their neighbors in their areas of assigned residence rather than adjusting to life in camps. Even after the German invasion of the southern zone in 1942 and the creation of Saliers, most did not face the mass internment experienced by their counterparts in the occupied zone. Instead, nomads felt daily discrimination because they did not look or act like other French men and women, and the Vichy regime's commitment to the ideals of "Work, Family, Homeland" provided ample justifications for exclusion.

[70] Ibid.
[71] On conditions in the Gypsy internment camps, see especially Hubert, "L'internement des Tsiganes," pp. 14–15; Guy Hantarrède, "Les Tsiganes au camp des Alliers (novembre 1940–mars 1946)," *Etudes Tsiganes* 13:1 (1999); and Kenrick and Puxon, *The Destiny of Europe's Gypsies*, pp. 103–7.
[72] Extracts from procès-verbaux reprinted in Pernot, *Un Camp pour les Bohémiens*, pp. 75–7.
[73] See for example the letter from Paul Reinhardt to Philippe Pétain cited in Emmanuel Filhol, "L'internement et la déportation de Tsiganes français sous l'Occupation: Mérignac-Poitiers-Sachsenhausen, 1940–1945," *Revue d'histoire de la Shoah: le monde juif* 170 (September–December 2000): 148.

The National Revolution clearly contributed to the exclusion of nomads from French society during the Second World War, but quotidian concerns dominated attitudes and reactions. Citing the material difficulties created by living in proximity to the Gypsies and pointing to the moral shortcomings of the community as a whole, petitions and complaints called for the removal of the undesirable population from towns and villages. Individuals expressed this desire clearly and explicitly. One man commented to gendarmes, "I wish with all my heart that the administrative authorities rid us of [the nomads] as soon as possible" while another stated, "I would be especially happy to be rid of their presence."[74] Public support for the removal of the nomadic population assigned permanent residence in the Limousin as a consequence of the hostilities with Germany coincided with the Vichy government's willingness to intern the Gypsies. Locals' own references to "special camps" or "centers under surveillance" demonstrate their knowledge and approval of the internment camp system within France. The Vichy regime claimed internment would lead to the assimilation of nomads, but the native population of the Limousin just wanted to be rid of a group of people that contributed to the hardships of daily life. Respecting the administrative definitions established by the Third Republic, Vichy maintained a distinction between *forains* and nomads, and never applied racial criteria in determining which members of these populations to intern. Nomads remained the only peripatetic group subject to confinement, and the French State even worked to free itinerants not subject to Article Three of July 16, 1912, law regardless of whether or not the individual was of Gypsy heritage.[75] Ordinary citizens, however, usually failed to make the same distinction between nomads and *forains*, underlining the fact that exclusion and inclusion occurred on a local level and on a daily basis. The treatment of so-called undesirables during the Vichy period cannot be explained fully by the intensification and codification of latent French racism or xenophobia. Poverty, living conditions, and thievery became central issues in ordinary citizens' treatment of Gypsies during the war, reminding us that shortages became a political issue that directly affected outsiders.

---

[74] SHGN Box 12754 – BT Saint-Léonard-de-Noblat. Procès-verbal number 115 (March 24, 1942) and procès-verbal number 125 (March 31, 1942).
[75] Hubert, "L'internement des Tsiganes en France," p. 17.

4

"At any price":
Housing, the Black Market, and Jewish Daily Life

In January 1943, the department of the Creuse accepted 692 foreign Jews evacuated from France's southern coastal regions. Officials provided each Jew leaving the train with a flyer "welcoming" them to the department and reminding them of their duties. Signed by Prefect Jacques-Henry, the flyer outlined six regulations authorities deemed important as a result of experience with the thousands of French and foreign Jewish refugees already in the Creuse. Most of the points reflected concerns about Jews' living arrangements and provisioning practices: Under no circumstances could the new arrivals leave their assigned commune without proper documentation; all food had to be purchased at shops and markets with the appropriate ration tickets; officials forbid all direct purchases on farms; and ration and identity cards had to be stamped "JUIF."[1] By restricting Jews' movements to the commune where they lived and warning against illegal purchases, the prefect hoped to prevent black market activity resulting from Jews residing in his department. The prefect also notified the Jews that any infractions of these rules would result in "serious sanctions." Concerns about refugees, politics, and daily life intersected yet again.

At this point, France had been under Vichy rule for two and a half years. Inhabitants of the southern half of the country were still adjusting to direct occupation after the arrival of German troops in November 1942. Vichy's antisemitism as codified in the National Revolution was well established, and the first massive roundup of foreign Jews had taken place the previous fall. All residents were suffering through their fourth

---

[1] Archives Nationales (hereafter AN) F1c III – 1150. Rapport Mensuel d'Information du 1er Décembre 1942 à 31 Janvier 1943 (January 31, 1943). The other points required Jews to register for jobs and to enroll their children in school.

winter at war and dealing with extreme shortages of foodstuffs and heating materials. A general atmosphere of fear, violence animated by the Resistance, and increasing thefts reigned. But food was not the only commodity in short supply during the Second World War. A dire housing shortage still existed in areas that received thousands of refugees as a result of the hostilities like the Limousin. Many blamed the arrival of refugee Jews for both food and housing problems – issues that some government officials (like Prefect Jacques-Henry) and locals saw as intimately related.

Prefect Jacques-Henry's focus on food in his flyer's main points demonstrates the issue's centrality in official perceptions of Jews during the war. The belief that Jews animated the black market also reflected cultural stereotypes that the Vichy regime perpetuated. The emphasis officials placed on prohibited activities as opposed to permitted ones suggests a decidedly negative overall attitude toward Jews. Yet, examining life in the Limousin complicates the debate over whether the French were generally sympathetic or hostile to Jews during the war. For some scholars, the day-to-day concerns of life in the war's early years meant that the French population paid little attention to Vichy's attack on the Jews.[2] Before the imposition in the northern zone of the requirement that Jews wear a yellow Star of David and the subsequent mass deportations in July and August 1942 in both zones, they argue, the French were indifferent or ambivalent to the plight of Jews in France.[3]

Although many Limousin inhabitants expressed antisemitic sentiments in the war's early years or identified themselves as antisemitic, their daily actions were more pragmatic. The population was not in "total ignorance" of the "Jewish Question" as the head of the Limoges region's Police for Jewish Affairs (PQJ) – the new organization charged with gathering information on anti-Jewish law infractions and often participating in the arrest of Jews – complained in May 1942, nor were they indifferent to the arrival

---

[2] Vicki Caron notes this interpretation in her synthesis of the historiographical debates surrounding public opinion in "French Public Opinion and the 'Jewish Question,' 1930–1942: The Role of Middle-Class Professional Associations" in *Nazi Europe and the Final Solution* edited by David Bankier and Israel Gutman (Jerusalem: Yad Vashem, 2003), 376. See also Michael R. Marrus and Robert O. Paxton, *Vichy France and the Jews* (Stanford, California: Stanford University Press, 1981), 16.

[3] See for example John F. Sweets, "Jews and Non-Jews in France During the Second World War" in *Nazi Europe and the Final Solution*, pp. 370–1 and Susan Zuccotti, *The Holocaust, the French, and the Jews* (Lincoln and London: University of Nebraska Press, 1993), 40 for the term "indifferent." On "ambivalence," see Caron, "French Public Opinion," p. 409. On public opinion's evolution, see also Pierre Laborie, *L'Opinion française sous Vichy: Les Français et la crise d'identité nationale 1936–1944* (Paris: Editions du Seuil, 2001).

of thousands of Jewish refugees.[4] What this police statement reveals, however, is that the regime's antisemitic ideology did not permeate Limousins' daily lives nor had it achieved the desired effects by the time the government was preparing more drastic measures. Local concerns – economic, material, or moral – often triumphed over national calls for a country purged of undesirable elements. The PQJ's regional head perhaps summarized the public's attitude more accurately at the beginning of September 1942, just weeks after the first roundup of Jews in the southern, unoccupied zone: "individual interest and egotism still count for a large number of the French, the general interest is still often neglected. In reality, the Aryan does not complain about the Jew except when the latter bothers his material existence, but he tolerates the Jew very well when his individual interest is satisfied."[5]

If Jewish refugees impinged on a native's food supply, housing situation, or other personal interests, an administrative structure and set of laws existed that could facilitate their removal. The interests of non-Jewish French citizens could also include personal financial gain, perhaps supplemented by Jewish purchases, or considerations of the private relationships they had established with refugees. Tensions clearly existed between the native population and the Jewish refugees, but they were the same as many of the problems that existed between urban and rural dwellers and for other refugees/evacuees. A close examination of the rural Limousin reveals that while the region's natives may not have publicly reacted to Vichy's discriminatory anti-Jewish legislation before 1942, they were not indifferent to the material consequences created by the Jewish refugees living in their midst.

JEWS IN FRANCE DURING WORLD WAR II

In 1940, France had a population of 43 million. Of the approximately 300,000 Jews in France at the beginning of the war, about half were French citizens and the other half were foreigners; 90,000 of the French citizens came from old, established families and the remaining 60,000 had been recently naturalized. Overall foreign Jews constituted less than 0.4 percent

---

[4] Archives Départementales de la Haute-Vienne (hereafter ADHV) 185 W 1–148 – Rapports du chef de la police des questions Juives, Délégué pour la Région de Limoges. Le Chef de la Police des Questions Juives, Délégué pour la Région de Limoges à Monsieur le Chef de la Police des Questions Juives en Zone Non Occupée (May 26, 1942), 6.

[5] ADHV 185 W 1–73. Rapports mensuels du chef de la police aux questions juives. Rapport No. 9 du 1er au 31 août 1942 (September 5, 1942).

of France's total population.⁶ Vichy's legislation, individual citizens, and French Jews all made distinctions between Israelites long established in French society and newly arrived Jewish immigrants. Before the war, the term "*Israélite*" denoted acculturated, assimilated people who practiced the Jewish faith as opposed to "Jews," which carried a more pejorative connotation and was often applied to recent Jewish immigrants from Eastern Europe.⁷ Like Catholics or Protestants, Israelites represented a religious affiliation rather than a "race." Historians have noted the divisions within the Jewish community between French men and women of the Israelite confession and the unassimilated Jewish immigrants. The regional prefect for Limoges noted the tension between the two communities as well, claiming the French Jews sought to distance themselves from foreign Jews in the Limousin due to the latter's participation in antigovernmental activities and the black market.⁸ In legal terms, assimilated Jews who had faithfully served France in the past could receive exemptions from some of the provisions of the new Jewish Statutes while a large number of naturalized foreigners saw their citizenship revoked.

The "Jewish Question" often conflated xenophobia and antisemitism as many Jewish refugees were of foreign origin. The 1930s and the Second World War greatly tested France's reputation as a country accepting of immigrants and as a place of asylum. The active recruitment of foreign labor to replace losses after World War I gave way to increasing restrictions after major waves of immigration in the years following Hitler's rise to power in Germany.⁹ During the late 1930s, between 400,000 and 600,000 new refugees arrived

---

⁶ Statistics in François and Renée Bédarida, "La Persécution des Juifs" in *La France des années noires*, vol. 2, edited by Jean-Pierre Azéma and François Bédarida (Paris: Seuil, 1993), 130. Others place the number of Jews in France between 300,000 and 330,000. For example, Renée Poznanski, *Jews in France during World War II* translated by Nathan Bracher (Hanover and London: University Press of New England, Brandeis University Press in association with the United States Holocaust Memorial Museum, 2001), 1, and Michael R. Marrus, "Coming to Terms with Vichy," *Holocaust and Genocide Studies* 9:1 (Spring 1995): 24.

⁷ On the differences between "Israelite" and "Jew" see André Kaspi, *Les Juifs pendant l'Occupation* (Paris: Editions du Seuil, 1991, 1997), 32–7, and Phyllis Cohen Albert, "Israelite and Jew: How Did Nineteenth-Century French Jews Understand Assimilation?" in *Assimilation and Community: The Jews in Nineteenth-Century Europe* edited by Jonathan Frankel and Steven J. Zipperstein (Cambridge: Cambridge University Press, 1992), 92.

⁸ See especially Poznanski, *Jews in France during World War II*, Chapter 1: "1940: Jews and Israelites in France," and Kaspi, *Les Juifs pendant l'Occupation*, Chapter 1: "A la recherche de la communauté juive." AN F 1c III – 1200. Rapports du Préfet Régional (July 11, 1942).

⁹ For an examination of French refugee policy in the 1930s with specific reference to Jewish refugees, see Vicki Caron, *Uneasy Asylum: France and the Jewish Refugee Crisis, 1933–1942* (Stanford, California: Stanford University Press, 1999). See also Pierre Guillaume, "Du Bon usage des immigrés en temps de crise et de guerre, 1932–1940," *Vingtième Siècle: Revue d'histoire* 7 (July–September 1985): 117–26.

in France, bringing the total number of foreigners in the country to approximately three million.[10] On May 2, 1938, under Prime Minister Daladier, France officially shifted its refugee policy with a decree-law that distinguished between "old" and "new" refugees. Coming on the heels of the German takeover of Austria and the wave of emigration it inspired, the law made it more difficult for refugees to find even temporary haven in France. Following the Kristallnacht pogroms in November 1938, immigration restrictions became even harsher with new decree-laws that established "special centers" for illegal, undesirable refugees, that allowed the government to strip naturalized citizens of French nationality, and that effectively closed France's borders to all legal immigration. In the interest of public order and national security, foreigners could be forced to live in certain areas or in centers created for the express purpose of housing suspects. They were subject to close observation by police forces, and any infractions concerning residence were punishable by six months to three years imprisonment. By the end of 1940, between 35,000 and 40,000 foreigners found themselves in French internment camps.[11] Required to carry and regularly renew special identity cards, foreigners were also subject to random controls for merely "appearing foreign" during the war years.[12] The difference between French and foreign was thus crystallized and codified.

Antiforeign measures thus touched many Jewish refugees, but specifically anti-Jewish laws proliferated under the Vichy regime as part of the National Revolution's agenda to economically, socially, and physically isolate Jews from the rest of the national community. The National Revolution engendered more than 1,500 new laws by the end of 1941, hundreds of which were directly related to Jews.[13] The law of October 4, 1940, following on the heels of the first Jewish Statute issued the previous day, gave prefects the authority to intern foreign Jews in "special camps" or to assign them to forced residence at any time; a law passed on June 2, 1941, ordered a census of all Jews in France,

---

[10] See Timothy P. Maga, "Closing the Door: The French Government and Refugee Policy, 1933–1939," *French Historical Studies* 12:3 (Spring 1982): 426, and Vicki Caron, "Prelude to Vichy: France and the Jewish Refugees in the Era of Appeasement," *Journal of Contemporary History* 20 (1985): 157.

[11] Christian Eggers, "L'internement sous toutes ses formes: approche d'une vue d'ensemble du système d'internement dans la zone de Vichy," *Le Monde juif* (January–April 1995): 60–1.

[12] See for example Service Historique de la Gendarmerie Nationale (hereafter SHGN) Box 12706 – Haute-Vienne, BT Limoges. Procès-verbal number 1744 (August 12, 1942). Gendarmes in Limoges stopped "an individual appearing foreign" and discovered he was a Polish Jew who had fled Paris to avoid arrest. Without the proper paperwork for circulation or permission to enter the free zone, the rabbi was "invited" to join a foreign labor battalion. The renewal of work permits and identity cards could cost around 400 francs for each renewal. See Guillaume, "Du Bon usage des immigrés."

[13] See Marrus and Paxton, *Vichy France and the Jews*, p. 138.

creating a centralized record of Jews, their addresses, and their possessions; the Second Jewish Statute of the same day allowed prefects to order the internment of French Jews as well as foreign Jews; as of January 2, 1942, foreign and naturalized Jews who arrived in France after January 1, 1936, could be ordered to Foreign Workers' Units (*Groupement de Travailleurs Etrangers*, or GTE) or to "Special Centers"; on November 9, 1942, all foreign Jews were effectively assigned residence, since the law now forbid them to leave their place of residence without police authorization. The laws facilitated the marginalization of Jews in society and non-Jews' overwhelming silence on the restrictions demonstrated their complicity with the regime's actions, according to some historical interpretations.[14] The laws, besides isolating Jews from French society, also had material justifications and consequences. Placing Jews in internment camps meant more housing became available and more black marketeers were removed from the general population, but the concentration of Jews also aided in their deportation. Furthermore, the census of Jews, providing the address of each individual and family, also contributed to economic aryanization as well as to the arrest and deportation of 76,000 Jews from France during the war.

The Limousin region presented a combination of safety and threats for Jews during the war. For refugees fleeing the occupied zone, Limoges was the largest city near the demarcation line. Just seventy to eighty kilometers from the border between occupied and free France, the city saw its prewar population of 161 Jews grow to approximately 3,400 by the beginning of 1942.[15] In addition to geographical considerations, some Jewish survivors reported that the benevolence of local officials, including the prefects, ultimately assured the survival of many Jews.[16] The active, organized

---

[14] Caron, "French Public Opinion and the 'Jewish Question,'" p. 378. Denis Peschanski, *Vichy 1940–1944: Contrôle et exclusion* (Brussels: Editions Complexe, 1997): 179–82.

[15] For prewar statistics, see ADHV 993 W – 221 – Mesures gouvernementales prises à l'encontre des Juifs. Etat des Israélites établis à Limoges antérieurement au 1er Septembre 1939. For 1942, see AN AJ 38–259. Letter from Le Maire de la ville de Limoges à Monsieur le Colonel, Commandant le Département Militaire de la Haute-Vienne et de la Charente (January 12, 1942). The 1942 statistic does not reflect Jews who avoided the census. The number also likely increased in the summer of 1942 as the deportation of Jews in the occupied and unoccupied zones began.

[16] See for example Denise Baumann. Archives of the Oeuvre de Secours aux Enfants (hereafter OSE) – Box XXXIX, Dossier 1 – Témoignages Professionnels. See also Louis Aron, *Journal de Louis Aron, directeur de La Maison Israélite de Refuge pour l'enfance Neuilly-sur-Seine 1939 Crocq (Creuse) 1939–1942 Chaumont (Creuse) 1942–1944* edited and presented by Serge Klarsfeld with Annette Zaidman (Paris: Association Les Fils et Filles des Déportés Juifs de France and The Beate Klarsfeld Foundation, 1998), 194; and Mia Amalia Kanner and Eve Rosenzweig Kugler, *Shattered Crystals* (New York, London, Jerusalem: C.I.S. Publishers, 1997), 209, 212.

Resistance to the Vichy regime in the region also provided networks that could lead to life-saving contacts for Jews.

Yet despite the relative safety of the Limousin, Jews still faced antisemitic sentiment as well as considerable risks. In 1941, Xavier Vallat, the head of the Commissariat General for Jewish Affairs (CGQJ) – Vichy's new commission charged with administering anti-Jewish programs throughout France – complained that state prosecutors in Limoges were not strict enough in their determinations of who belonged to the Jewish "race" and ordered increased stringency in the application of the law in the region.[17] Joseph Antignac, remembered as the "particularly zealous" regional representative of the CGQJ for the Limousin, eventually served as the functioning head of the CGQJ for all of France in 1944.[18] Indigenous expressions of antisemitism in the region found their way into personal correspondence and in responses to a CGQJ opinion poll conducted in late 1942. More than 85 percent of the region's 300 residents questioned were "declared antisemites" and nearly 98 percent felt the anti-Jewish measures did not go far enough in solving the "Jewish problem."[19] Even though fear or the amateur nature of the poll-taking may have artificially inflated antisemitic responses, the conclusions do provide some insights. Many respondents in other regions chose the option "indifferent" to describe their attitude toward the Jews, unlike the residents of the Limoges region. Even with mitigating factors, historians

---

[17] Centre de Documentation Juive Contemporaine (hereafter CDJC) CXCIII – 83. Le Commissaire Général aux Questions Juives à Monsieur le Garde des Sceaux (November 21, 1941).

[18] Marrus and Paxton, *Vichy France and the Jews*, p. 188. Antignac became Commissioner Louis Darquier de Pellepoix's private secretary in November 1942 and chief of staff in January 1943. Marrus and Paxton assert that in the position of chief of staff, "Antignac in fact ran the CGQJ." In May 1944, Antignac was given the lesser title of secretary-general but was "commissioner in all but name." See pp. 288–9. Antignac's zeal was also outlined in a document prepared after the Liberation. Using specific examples, the author enumerated Antignac's "reprehensible, anti-national acts" against the Jews while he was the Limoges regional delegate. See AN AJ 38-253 "Rapport Antignac" (n.d.).

[19] AN AJ 38–5770. Enquête d'opinion en zone libre (position de l'opinion française devant 'le problème juif') effectué pour le service de la propagande du CGQJ 1er Trimestre 1943, pp. 43, 55. Marrus and Paxton believe that this poll "offers no real help" as it was not conducted by professionals and they believe fear influenced many of the responses. See Marrus and Paxton, *Vichy France and the Jews*, p. 181. However, other regions did poll substantially fewer "declared antisemites" and respondents could reply "indifferent." Renée Poznanski, while not taking the poll at "face value," does have a more forgiving view of the poll in light of the fact that "[t]he pollsters had been told that 'the General Commission's goal in conducting this survey is not to obtain a majority of antisemitic responses,' and so were accordingly instructed not to seek answers, but rather to interview people at random, guided only by the aforementioned socioprofessional and geographical quotas." See Poznanski, *Jews in France during World War II*, pp. 380–3.

must reconcile these 85 percent "declared antisemites" with the PQJ's complaint that the masses did not understand the "Jewish question" and Jews' own assertions that the region's residents facilitated their survival.

Furthermore foreigners – non-Jewish and Jewish – who violated the law or threatened public order faced restrictive measures in the Limousin. Internment camps such as Nexon in the Haute-Vienne or Evaux-les-Bains in the Creuse housed a mix of French and foreign undesirables throughout the war.[20] The 643rd GTE based in Oradour-sur-Glane (Haute-Vienne) incorporated unemployed foreign men without private resources, foreign Jews, and internees into its ranks.[21] Men assigned to the GTE provided labor on local farms or in factories, thus contributing to the economy rather than draining resources by receiving allocations from the state. Such groups also made the monitoring of foreign populations easier for officials and became the ultimate destination for many Jewish men who came to the area seeking refuge.

Despite the cultural differences between Jews and non-Jewish natives and Vichy's commitment to marginalizing the Jews, Limousin residents responded to the Jewish refugee population in complex and ambiguous ways. Jews' position as social outsiders combined with Vichy's antisemitic legislation affected their ability to navigate the period's material difficulties. With material shortages as most individuals' major concern, anything that affected provisioning had an impact on the local population. Thus even as Limousins could claim to be indifferent to the collective plight of the Jews under Vichy, they could not stay untouched by the arrival of thousands of Jewish refugees. Over 15,000 Jews from Alsace-Lorrane found themselves evacuated or expelled to the French interior in 1939 and 1940. Historians estimate that an additional 100,000 to 200,000 Jews were among the four million people fleeing the German advance in May and June 1940.[22] The expulsion of thousands of Jews and other undesirables from the newly annexed territories of Alsace-Lorraine on July 16, 1940, combined with the German ordinance of September 27, 1940, forbidding Jews to return

---

[20] Internment facilities also existed in the Haute-Vienne towns of Saint-Paul-d'Eyjeaux, Saint-Germain-les-Belles, La Meyze, and Sereilhac. In the Creuse, there was also a facility in Boussac. For a basic chronology and understanding of internment camps in the region, see Yves Soulignac, *Les Camps d'Internement en Limousin 1939–1945* (Saint-Paul: La Briderie, 1995).

[21] For a more extended discussion of the 643rd GTE and its relationship to Jews, see Sarah Farmer, "Out of the Picture: Foreign Labor in Wartime France" in *France at War: Vichy and the Historians* edited by Sarah Fishman et al. (Oxford and New York: Berg, 2000), 249–60. See also Eggers, "L'internement sous toutes ses formes."

[22] Alsace-Lorraine statistics in Poznanski, *Jews in France during World War II*, p. 27. On the exodus, see Zuccotti, *The Holocaust, the French, and the Jews*, p. 37.

to the occupied zone contributed to the enduring Jewish refugee "problem" in the free zone. Thus the necessity of meeting the basic housing and provisioning requirements of the refugee population forced the native and transplanted populations to interact, building alliances and tensions that were often expressed in material terms.

JEWS, THE HOUSING CRISIS, AND INTERETHNIC RELATIONS

One place where Jewish refugees and Limousin natives met was in locals' homes and apartment buildings. While the severe shortage of housing brought refugees and natives into close contact, it also provided locals with a justification for the removal of Jews from their communities. Housing shortages have not received the same attention as the shortages of foodstuffs in historians' exploration of the war years; however, restricted housing directly affected French residents' ability to negotiate the everyday.[23] For example, officials in the Limousin used requisitions and expulsions as a means to provide accommodations for workers, civil servants, and their families. The delegate prefect of the Haute-Vienne questioned the legality of such actions, yet acknowledged their necessity in the circumstances. He did, however, order an investigation in order to ensure that property owners' lawsuits to evict renters were legitimate rather than merely a ruse allowing landlords to re-rent rooms at higher prices.[24] The need to evict residents and provide more housing resulted from drastic population changes. In Limoges, the prewar population of approximately 92,000 increased dramatically during the war, finally leveling out at around 120,000 inhabitants.[25] The issue of housing remained critical in the city and in many towns and villages all over the Limousin throughout the war, and rents skyrocketed as a result. The combination of legal housing requisitions and Vichy's conservative and exclusionary vision made Jews particularly vulnerable to expulsions. Since the government viewed Jews as foreigners and/or undesirables outside the organic national family, the appropriation of Jewish apartments became standard practice, as did the transfer of these refugees from cities to rural areas.

---

[23] A notable exception is Danièle Voldman, "Le logement: crise, pénurie ou restrictions?" in "Le temps des restrictions en France (1939–1949)," special edition of *Les Cahiers de l'Institut d'histoire du temps présent* edited by Dominique Veillon and Jean-Marie Flonneau 32–33 (May 1996): 377–88.

[24] AN F 1c III – 1197. Rapport Mensuel d'Information du 1er mai au 31 mai 1942 (June 5, 1942).

[25] See "Lorsque la population de la Haute-Vienne avait triplé," *Le Courrier du Centre* number 236 (August 24, 1940): 2 and ADHV 185 W 1–71 – Rapports mensuel du Délégué régional à la Famille (September 1941) for population numbers.

In this atmosphere of shortages and high prices, finding a place to live proved difficult for Jewish refugees. Many of the available residences did not live up to the refugees' expectations or even to simple health standards. Jewish refugees remember the dire situation and the difficult living conditions in the city. Frederick and Liane Reif both recall spending six weeks in the spring of 1940 with other refugees in Limoges' amphitheater, sleeping on straw mattresses between rows and eating their meals at public kitchens before moving with their mother to a room on the westernmost edge of Limoges. On the rue d'Aixe, the family lived in a single room furnished with straw-filled mattresses and tables and chairs made from crates in a building they shared with other refugees. Water came from an outdoor pump on the corner, and the toilet, located down the hall, consisted of a hole in the floor.[26] This "Turkish toilet" would have seemed normal to most rural French residents, but for the Reifs it represented a significant change in their lifestyle. The family had come from Vienna where their father had had a thriving dentist's practice, a large apartment, and servants to cook and clean. The converted tavern on the outskirts of Limoges with its leaky, mildew-covered ceiling and the stinking bathroom with its feces-covered floor bore no resemblance to their previous middle class, urban life. Gerda Freund also remembers the difficulties of refugee life in Limoges during the war. Born and educated in Vienna, Gerda fled to France in January 1939. After getting married in 1941, she and her husband shared a room in a working-class neighborhood in Limoges, across the Vienne River from Saint-Etienne Cathedral. In 1943, the couple had a daughter, and Mrs Freund remembers the difficulty of caring for a baby in a second-floor room with no running water and no toilet. She had to "fetch water on the street" and travel up and downstairs with dirty water and dirty diapers.[27] Other inhabitants of the city also faced difficult living conditions, prompting the delegate prefect of the Haute-Vienne to remark on numerous occasions that the housing situation in Limoges constituted "a very serious crisis."[28]

[26] Frederick Reif, interview with author (August 1, 2000), and Liane Reif-Lehrer, interview with author (August 7, 2000). Information concerning the family's physical address comes from ADHV 993 W – 609 – Recensement (par l'office du logement des israëlites réfugiés à Limoges: notices individuelles avec indication de la profession, de la composition et des moyens d'existence de la famille, de l'adresse et de la description du logement) 1942. Israëlites étrangers.

[27] Gerda Freund, questionnaire responses and interview with author (August 15, 2000). Address information from ADHV 993 W – 609.

[28] AN F 1c III – 1197. Rapport Mensuel d'Information du 1er mai au 31 mai 1942 (June 5, 1942). See also the reports for January 1942, July 1942, and September 1942.

More likely to have family connections and relationships with non-Jews, French Jews often fared better than their recently arrived foreign counterparts in their day-to-day lives. In 1942, the Refugee Service and the Prefecture of the Haute-Vienne conducted a census of Jewish refugees in Limoges presumably to locate Jews and to determine the living conditions and citizenship status of the new arrivals. Each individual filled out a half-sheet of paper providing personal information including his or her present and former addresses, present and former occupations, date and place of birth, nationality, financial status, and a description of the housing. These declarations reveal that French Jews averaged 1.63 people per room inhabited. For foreign Jews the administration deemed "good workers," the number increases to 1.73 people per room. The figure jumps to 1.94 people to every room for those Jewish refugees simply labeled "Foreign Workers." Foreigners without any form of employment were more likely to be alone in the city yet still averaged 1.92 people in each room occupied.[29] The statistics do not include those individuals who failed to provide the requested information nor those living in dormitory-like arrangements in the city. While the numbers provide an idea of the crowded living conditions, they do not reflect other difficulties such as living in a hotel room, the small size of rooms, the necessity of sharing a kitchen or bathroom facilities with other residents, or living with improvised furnishings.

Timing partially explains the differences between living conditions for French and foreign Jews. The overwhelming majority of French Jews seeking refuge in Limoges before 1942 came from Alsace-Lorraine and other portions of eastern France affected by evacuations in September 1939. Many came in the fall of 1939, but for those who followed in 1940 and 1941, there was already an established community of Alsatian Jews including the well-connected Rabbi Abraham Deutsch and refugee organizations such as the Israelite Social Aid Agency. Suzanne Dortort-Glantz recalls fleeing Paris to join her father in Limoges after the roundup of Jews in Paris in July 1942. For the young Suzanne Dortort, the living conditions were "just like medieval times": she lived with her mother and younger brother in one room on the third floor with no plumbing and a wood stove for cooking while her father occupied a separate room. She distinctly remembers the refugees from Strasbourg who also lived in the building, but in much better conditions. To Suzanne it seemed that the people from Alsace had better

---

[29] Estimates based on my own calculations drawn from notices found in ADHV 993 W – 608 (Israélites français) and 609 (Israélites étrangers). Many of the Jews considered to be "Foreign good workers" were naturalized French citizens.

places to stay because they had been there longer.³⁰ While timing provides one possible explanation for the differences in living conditions, exploring the "center" and "periphery" in Jewish communities provides another angle to investigate.³¹ As an established community with services, relationships, and an understanding of French culture, Alsatian Jews formed the center of the Jewish refugee population. Foreign Jews, lacking connections, financial resources, or any legal protections found themselves on the periphery, whereas naturalized citizens occupied a sort of middle ground. The housing situation in Limoges reflected this difference in status, and those Jews on the margins were also more susceptible to other troubles.

French and foreign refugees found accommodations throughout the city, from the centuries-old central shopping district to the newer, working-class suburbs. Jews lived in open-timbered buildings on the narrow, cobblestone streets around the market hall, in dark, medieval buildings near the Cathedral, in apartments on the main boulevards that cut across the city, in hotels near the Gare des Bénédictins, and in homes located on the major routes leaving Limoges. There was no pattern to the settlement, no major groupings of Jewish refugees, nor a specifically "Jewish quarter." In 1942, Jewish refugees in Limoges lived on no less than 280 different streets and at close to 650 different addresses.³² French and foreign Jews, employed and unemployed, lived on the same street and sometimes in the same building. Multiple families could occupy a building, although usually just one Jewish family lived at each address.

The size and condition of apartments and houses also covered a range. Micheline Castro's family lived for two years in two small rooms in the factory her father's employer rented in Limoges. The downstairs served as a warehouse for tailor's supplies and the four members of the Castro family lived upstairs along with the company's boss, a maid, and several other non-Jewish families.³³ Raymond-Pierre Kahn lived in two rooms "chez Madame Bernard" in Limoges with his family of three although he worked in Ambazac, over twenty kilometers away.³⁴ The Grand Rabbin Schwartz's sister and her family lived in two small attic rooms on a short street that ran between the Champ de Juillet and the Place Jourdan. On the rue Manigne, a Jew owned a building in which he rented apartments to three families: a middle-aged French couple with a prisoner-of-war

---

³⁰ Suzanne Dortort-Glantz interview with the author (August 2, 2000).
³¹ Ofer, "Everyday Life of Jews under Nazi Occupation," pp. 52, 54.
³² Information from ADHV 993 W – 608 (Israëlites français) and 609 (Israëlites étrangers).
³³ Micheline (Castro) Cohen interview with the author (August 9, 2000).
³⁴ ADHV 993 W – 609.

son; a French cobbler, his wife, and two of his three adolescent children; and an unemployed Polish Jew, his wife, and five children. The Jewish community from Strasbourg also used the ground floor of Monsieur Ab's building as a synagogue, holding services twice daily and late into the night on Saturday, much to the "great unhappiness of the renters and neighbors."[35]

With complaints like these and the general housing shortage, the government employed a variety of tactics in the attempt to provide more housing in cities for non-Jews. By targeting Jewish refugees, authorities hoped to improve the housing situation while simultaneously fulfilling its antisemitic agenda. In June 1941, the central police commissioner in Limoges suggested, in light of the near impossibility of finding anywhere to live in the city, that officials help hasten the departure of Jews seeking a haven in America.[36] For the most part, lodging restrictions and expulsions applied only to foreign Jews, and in November 1941, the General Information Bureau for the Haute-Vienne (Renseignements généraux) reported, "Foreign Jews, generally speaking, have been invited to leave Limoges."[37] Using the prefectoral authority to assign foreign Jews to residence instituted by the law of October 4, 1940, the "evacuation" of Jews from Limoges took place in several stages in 1941 and 1942. By May 1942, the regional prefect for Limoges had decided to rid Limoges of all foreign Jews and charged the PQJ with conducting the necessary investigations.[38] These actions against Jews in urban areas took place during the time period in which officials noted increasing animosity between all urban and rural populations. The first extreme shortages touched the relatively isolated Limousin residents, and they often expressed gratefulness for anything that could be perceived as ameliorating the food and housing shortages.

Police officials noted that the general population appreciated the increased availability of housing in Limoges after the removal of foreign

---

[35] ADHV 993 W – 223 – Commissariat aux affaires juives. Affaire Bloch (n.d.). Ab's information and quote found in Direction Générale de la Police Nationale. Le Commissaire Principal, chef de service à Monsieur le Préfet de la Haute-Vienne (July 4, 1942).
[36] ADHV 185 W 1–45 – Rapports du préfet de la Haute-Vienne au ministère de l'Intérieur. Letter from Le Commissaire Central à Monsieur le Préfet de la Haute-Vienne (June 26, 1941).
[37] ADHV 185 W 3–15 – Services départementaux des renseignements généraux – Haute-Vienne. Le Commissaire Principal, Chef de Service à Monsieur l'Intendant de Police à Limoges (Renseignements généraux) (November 25, 1941), 2.
[38] AN AJ 38–244. Le Chef de la Police des Questions Juives en zone non-occupée à Monsieur le Secrétaire Général pour la Police. Rapport d'activité de la Police des Questions Juives en Z.N.O. Mai 1942, p. 18.

Jews, but to say that public opinion generally supported these measures against Jews is an oversimplification. Joseph Antignac, in outlining the procedures for the "reassembly" of Jews in the department, emphasized that expulsions, internments, assigned residence, or assignment to a workers' unit did not apply to French Jews except if their occupations did not justify their presence in large cities and only in areas "where the housing crisis is acute."[39] Officials had to be careful to differentiate between French and foreign Jews in order to maintain the public's support for anti-Jewish measures. Such attention to possible repercussions contradicts interpretations of the population's indifference expressed in official reports. Explicitly linking persecution of the Jews to material concerns also demonstrates authorities' deliberate attempts to avoid criticism. It becomes clear that officials recognized that the public's major concerns were material as well as the importance of public opinion. Fearing a loss of support, Antignac emphasized that regrouping French and naturalized Jews "must not be interpreted as hazing [*une brimade*], but in the general interest, in order to solve the housing crisis."[40] Clearly, the regional representative of the CGQJ did not believe the non-Jewish population was indifferent to actions against some parts of the Jewish community.

Although the removal of Jews from major cities was supposed to ease the housing crisis, it did not always achieve the desired effect and emphasized the difference between the enactment of decrees and their daily enforcement. The task of notifying refugees of the prefectoral decrees assigning them to residences outside of Limoges fell to the Gendarmerie Nationale. Refugees usually acknowledged receipt of the notification and agreed to move to the designated town within the specified amount of time. Yet for some, the mere cost of moving prevented them from following the decree. For example, a decree issued on October 31, 1941, ordered the Polish refugee Antoinette Koslowska to move immediately from the Place de la République in Limoges to the town of Le Dorat, fifty-seven kilometers to the north. With only 2,000 francs, an interned husband, and a two-year-old daughter in her care, Madame Koslowska asked for an extension in order to borrow enough money from friends to complete the move. Due to her poor health, the Jewish refugee also asked that she be assigned to a town closer to Limoges in order to continue her medical treatment and to save money on transportation costs.[41] Rather than leaving

---

[39] AN AJ 38–258. "Projet de regroupement des juifs dans le cadre départemental basé sur les Circulaires en vigeur" (March 30, 1942), 3.
[40] Ibid.
[41] SHGN Box 12704 – BT Limoges. Procès-verbal number 2345 (November 7, 1941).

immediately, the refugee remained in Limoges until a solution could be found for her situation.

As the intelligence- and information-gathering arm of the CGQJ, the local agents of the PQJ also investigated cases of foreign Jews in Limoges in order to determine whether they could be expelled from their homes. The case of a German Jew, Sigmund Gerson, provides an example of the government's considerations in determining expulsions. PQJ Inspector Borde reported that Monsieur Gerson worked in receiving in a shoe factory, earning 2,000 francs per month – a sufficient amount to support his entire family without burdening the French State. As a man who had voluntarily joined the French army, the German refugee was exempt from the law of January 2, 1942, which allowed prefects to send foreign refugees to foreign worker units or assigned residence. Since the family lived in "two miniscule attic rooms (*mansardes*)," Inspector Borde concluded that "a special measure taken against the family would not resolve the lodging crisis."[42] Furthermore, deprived of Monsieur Gerson's income, the family would become dependent upon state charity. Given Monsieur Gerson's military status, the small size of the family's rooms, and the potential economic disadvantages for the French government, no action was taken. Even when authorities deemed an expulsion appropriate, lodging did not always become immediately available. Gendarmes complained that the expulsion of Jews from Limoges in the spring of 1942 did not free up a lot of additional residences. In fact, the expulsions further exacerbated housing shortages because the object of the decree moved, but left family members in the former apartment. Instead of one residence, the Jewish family now occupied two separate dwellings.[43]

Although Vichy's antisemitic laws allowed officials to initiate the expulsion of Jews, ordinary citizens also turned to overcrowding as justification for evicting their renters. The case of the conflict over the apartment at 5, avenue St Surin in Limoges illustrates the interplay between housing shortages, refugee status, and anti-Jewish legislation in everyday life. Before the war, Jean-Marie and Juliette Euzet lived with their two children in the five-room, third-floor apartment near the center of Limoges. The family used

---

[42] ADHV 993 W – 223 – Commissariat aux affaires juives. Affaire: Gerson, Sigmund (June 1, 1942).

[43] SHGN Box 12647 – BT Limoges. Rapport du Chef d'Escadron Rebour sur l'état d'esprit des populations (April 27, 1942). This was the case for Grand Rabbin Schwartz's sister's family in Limoges. His sister and her husband were assigned residence outside Limoges, but their children were allowed to stay in the family's rooms in the city. See ADHV 993 W – 223 – Commissariat aux affaires juives. Affaire Bloch (n.d.).

two rooms and the kitchen as their living quarters, while Jean-Marie utilized the remaining two rooms for his work as a music teacher. With her husband mobilized in 1939 and later taken prisoner of war, Juliette moved with her children into her parents' home. She sublet the three furnished rooms on the avenue St Surin in order to pay the rent, but left the lesson rooms unoccupied in case of future need. In 1940, Juliette rented the furnished rooms, previously let to Belgian refugees, to two Jewish families related by marriage and expelled from Alsace – the Kahns and the Kohns. After Jean-Marie's return from captivity in 1941, the Euzet family moved back into their apartment, occupying the still-empty lesson rooms. Jean-Marie Euzet then informed the Jewish refugees that they would have to leave and took the legal steps necessary to remove them. But after a year of searching for suitable housing in Limoges, the refugees were unable to find new accommodations.

Monsieur Euzet finally turned to the PQJ in January 1942. The police report contains no overtly antisemitic statements on the part either the plaintiff or the investigator. Both the Jewish and non-Jewish families registered at the departmental lodging office in the hope of finding suitable accommodations for the refugees. The police inspector reported that the Euzet family and the refugees remained on good terms, and that the Jewish renters had demonstrated their willingness to vacate the furnished rooms – provided they could find new lodgings. In order to facilitate the process, the PQJ recommended that the refugee families be split up: the ailing mother, Fernande Kohn, should be placed in a health-care facility, and her four-year-old daughter, Gabrielle, temporarily entrusted to a Jewish aid organization; her employed husband, Didier Kohn, could find lodgings for himself in Limoges. Citing various official circulars, the inspector decided that the four members of the Kahn family (unemployed French citizens and refugees from Alsace) could be assigned residence outside the city.[44] All three families involved had to cope with the city's housing shortage, but as non-Jews the Euzet family remained privileged. With the refugees out of the apartment, officials noted, Jean-Marie Euzet could fully practice his profession and the family's living situation would return to normal. In pursuit of this goal, however, a Jewish family was broken up. Though they were not indifferent to the plight of the Jewish renters, the Euzet family was not above using the anti-Jewish laws in effect to better its own material situation.

---

[44] ADHV 993 W – 225 – Commissariat aux affaires juives – SEC. Affaire: Euzet, Jean-Marie, Kahn, Robert, and Kohn, Didier-Jean (January 22, 1942).

Many Jewish families cited the lack of available housing options as the reason for their refusal to leave a house or an apartment, but the Vichy regime provided local authorities with the legal means to remove the Jews as well as the ideological justification for such an action. On January 1, 1942, Eugène Ardant informed the Polish Jews Moise and Gita Rother, residing with their two children in his house just outside Limoges, that they had to evacuate the premises by April 1. Monsieur Ardant lived and worked in Limoges, but in light of his circumstances, he had an "absolute need" for the building occupied by the refugees on the outskirts of town. As the father of eight in a society that valued and encouraged large families, Eugène Ardant enjoyed certain privileges. In addition, he was responsible for his three young grandchildren while their father remained a prisoner of war.[45] To enforce the eviction decision, he secured Antignac's approval. As justification for the decision, Antignac pointed out (among other facts) that the renters were Jews and that Moise Rother was unemployed. He also cited various circulars concerning foreigners to support his conclusion. Consequently, Antignac recommended that the four members of the refugee Rother family be placed in a "supervised residence" elsewhere in the department.[46] The material support and protection of the French family thus validated the removal of undesirable Jewish refugees from their homes.

The change in political regimes created such opportunities and heralded a transformation of daily relations. The arrival of refugees created a dire housing shortage, but it also forced native residents to interact with persecuted Jews, often for the first time. While some landlords enjoyed the economic benefits provided by these renters desperate to find lodging, the general overcrowding of cities forced authorities to seek solutions to the problem. Fully aware that the local population generally placed material concerns above all other considerations, including the Vichy regime's politics, government officials materially justified their actions against Jews. Such attention to public opinion refines our ideas about the extent of antisemitism and support for Vichy's anti-Jewish measures during the first half of the war. Complaints about Jewish neighbors, acquaintances, and renters over

---

[45] On the importance of large families as well as the central importance of prisoners of war in Vichy ideas, see Sarah Fishman, "Waiting for the Captive Sons of France: Prisoner of War Wives, 1940–1945" in *Behind the Lines: Gender and the Two World Wars* edited by Margaret Randolph Higonnet, Jane Jenson, Sonya Michel, and Margaret Collins Weitz (New Haven, Connecticut, and London: Yale University Press, 1987), 185–6.

[46] ADHV 993 W – 225 – Commissariat aux affaires juives – SEC. Affaire: Rother, Moise (March 17, 1942). The family was assigned residence in St Priest Taurion, eighteen kilometers away.

housing issues appeared rarely, but when a real problem presented itself, non-Jewish residents turned to the state's new exclusionary apparatus for aid. In addition to freeing up housing in cities, authorities hoped that removing undesirable Jews to the countryside would allow for closer surveillance. In small towns and villages, the foreign Jews were less likely to remain anonymous or to blend into the crowd. But Jewish residences in rural areas created new problems for locals, officials, and refugees.

JEWS, THE BLACK MARKET, AND LIFE IN THE COUNTRYSIDE

The expulsion of Jews from larger cities to rural areas led to two major concerns for officials in smaller towns and villages: overcrowding and provisioning. Like Prefect Jacques-Henry, mayors throughout the Limousin attempted to regulate Jews' movements and supplying practices. Official attention to these particular issues highlights both the continuity of economic antisemitism in France and assumptions about daily life and prejudices in rural areas. Vicki Caron has argued that historians must examine "the degree to which antisemitism is embedded in the socioeconomic structure and [...] that it must be understood in more than simply ideological terms."[47] As early as 1933, immigrant Jews were blamed for taking jobs and residences away from French citizens. Economic stereotypes of the rich Jew permeated even the isolated, rural Limousin by the war years. Finding their way into official reports, these attitudes have led some scholars to conclude that Jews faced more antisemitism in rural areas where residents were less habituated to outsiders. In some ways, this interpretation oversimplifies public opinion. By focusing on the living and provisioning situation of Jews in rural areas, we see the integration of Jews into local communities during a period of so-called indifference as well as the economic building blocks of native complicity with persecuted undesirables.

The decongestion of Limoges through expulsions led to the congestion of smaller towns in the surrounding countryside causing some tension between the native and refugee populations. In October 1941, the gendarmerie brigade in Saint-Léonard-de-Noblat, a town of fewer than six thousand residents, reported that approximately fifty Jews, mostly foreigners expelled from Limoges, lived in the canton. The brigade's commandant commented that the public, suspecting that the new residents were buying farm products "at any price," displayed ill will toward the Jews. He believed that the same

---

[47] Vicki Caron, "The Antisemitic Revival in France in the 1930s: The Socioeconomic Dimension Reconsidered." *The Journal of Modern History* 70:1 (March 1998): 28.

was true of lodging: "Apartments for rent are very rare in St-Léonard, yet despite this, the Jews are all adequately lodged. One assumes that they offer to pay more than the local inhabitants."[48] Based on the commandant's statements, one might conclude that public opinion toward the Jews was decidedly negative; at the very least, the people of Saint-Léonard were not indifferent to the new arrivals.

Micheline (Castro) Cohen, a teenager during the war, has different memories of the "adequate" lodging conditions in Saint-Léonard and the locals' reactions to refugees. She and her parents fled Paris in June 1940, ending up in Limoges where her father's employer had relocated his factory. Though her father had been in France since the age of seventeen and considered himself assimilated, Micheline's parents had never acquired French citizenship. In 1942, local officials expelled the Castros from Limoges because the parents were citizens of Spain and Greece. One of her father's business acquaintances lived in Saint-Léonard and helped the family of four (Micheline's mother gave birth to a son in October 1940) find an apartment in the town twenty kilometers east of Limoges. Cohen remembers: "In Saint Léonard we lived in a small apartment (one big room and a kitchen) – the bathroom was upstairs. We had no furniture and my mother covered crates with pink paper. That is where we stored our clothes. In the kitchen we had a wood stove that was used for heating and cooking and also an electric skillet."[49] Though the living situation was far from ideal, Cohen remembers the kindness of her neighbors and not hostility of the kind described in official gendarmerie reports.

Even small towns throughout the neighboring department of the Creuse faced overcrowding. The "shortage of housing" prompted Prefect Jacques-Henry to issue a decree regulating the access and stay of Jews in certain towns in his department. The decree stated that as of November 17, 1942, "no French or foreign Jews can come to reside temporarily or permanently in the cities and communes of Guéret, Aubusson, Boussac, Bourganeuf, La Souterraine, Evaux-les-Bains, Chambon-sur-Voueize, Bellegarde-en-Marche, Auzances, and Crocq."[50] Jews already residing in the specified communities could remain; however, the towns' mayors retained the right

---

[48] SHGN Box 12750 – BT Saint-Léonard-de-Noblat, R/4, Rapport de l'Adjudant Martin Commandant la brigade de St-Léonard sur l'activité des israélites (October 11, 1941).

[49] Quote from Micheline (Castro) Cohen's questionnaire response. Additional information provided in questionnaire as well as Mrs. Cohen's interview with the author (August 9, 2000).

[50] Archives Départementales de la Creuse (hereafter ADC) 7 W – 10 – Police. Arrêté du 17 Novembre 1942.

to remove the refugees at any time. Jews in smaller towns throughout the Haute-Vienne and the Creuse also saw their housing requisitioned in order to accommodate others. Upon the arrival of a Tunisian military battalion in Guéret, Jewish refugees living in the central part of town had their homes requisitioned for officers' use.[51] In Crocq (Creuse) and Ambazac (Haute-Vienne), officials requisitioned Jewish lodgings for the use of local gendarmerie brigades. After the occupation of the free zone in November 1942, Jewish residents also became the favored targets of evictions in order to provide housing for German officials. Towns, large or small, blamed Jewish refugees for the housing crisis and employed various measures to remedy the situation, which had the effect of marginalizing Jews and ultimately facilitating their eventual deportation from French soil.

Officials of smaller towns expressed concern about the effects of the refugees' arrival on their communities. Beyond housing issues, officials and locals expressed concerns about the "rich" and "lazy" Jews now in close proximity to rural agricultural products. Outside the city, Jews would have direct access to food supplies, which would facilitate their participation in the black market. By 1941, authorities began to complain that Jews in assigned residences paid high prices for items at the farm "to the detriment of the population in general"; the Jews' actions, the authorities claimed, resulted in egg shortages in Limoges and influenced peasants to remain at home rather than to deliver their goods to market.[52] Such accusations deliberately ignored the effects of non-Jewish urban residents searching the countryside for food and the effects of *colis familiaux* in limiting the food supply in markets. In April 1942, Saint-Léonard-de-Noblat's mayor

---

[51] AN F 1c III – 1150. Rapport Mensuel d'Information période du 1er au 31 octobre 1941 (November 2, 1941).

[52] Quote from ADHV 185 W 1–205 – Contrôle postal. Synthèse hebdomadaire du 6 Octobre. 12ième Division Militaire. Contrôle Technique (October 6, 1941). On eggs, see ADHV 185 W 3–15 – Services départementaux des renseignements généraux-Haute-Vienne. Le Commissaire Principal, Chef de Service à Monsieur l'Intendant de Police à Limoges (Renseignements généraux) (November 25, 1941), 4. For additional accusations concerning Jews in the countryside and black market activities, see ADHV 185 W 1–45 – Rapports du préfet de la Haute-Vienne au ministère de l'Intérieur. Le Commissaire Central à Monsieur le Préfet de la Haute-Vienne (August 25, 1941); AN AJ 38–242. Rapport sur le recensement, sur l'activité nuisible des juifs à la ville, à la campagne, et sur la création des camps de travail et d'hébergement dans la XIIème Région (October 1, 1941), 2; SHGN Box 12691 – BT Limoges, R/4, Rapport de l'Adjudant Boulesteix Commandant la brigade de Limoges sur l'activité des Israélites (October 13, 1941); CDJC CIX – 14 "Des Conséquences dangereuses de la présence des juifs réfugiés dans les petites localités" (November 1941); and ADHV 185 W 1–206 – Synthèses hebdomadaires du coordinateur du service civil des contrôles techniques (June 6, 1942, and November 7, 1942).

issued a decree limiting the circulation of Jews assigned residence in the town; in the decree he listed houses and farms on each road that the refugees were not allowed to pass. The prefect of the Haute-Vienne, reminding St-Léonard's mayor that the Jews were not interned in his village, demanded an explicit justification for the decree. In his response, the mayor listed "numerous complaints from the population" against the Jews: their "abnormal" unemployment made daily trips to the countryside possible (unlike French workers); they purchased goods "at any price" in order to feed their families as well as their friends in other regions; they attempted to purchase ration cards illegally; and their actions in general resulted in food shortages at markets.[53] Most of the activities the mayor described fell into the realm of illegal black marketeering. However, the belief that Jews were the principal actors in the black market, widely articulated in official reports, did not reflect accurately the wartime situation in France. Rather, the expression of this view defines the lengths to which authorities were willing to go in order to deflect criticism from their own failure to distribute goods effectively.

While local authorities expressed concern about the influx of Jewish refugees, some small-town residents welcomed the new consumers. In contrast to the assignment of Gypsies to residences in specific communes, which inspired a rash of popular complaints and petitions for internment, the arrival of Jewish refugees provoked no such expressions of popular anxiety. The stereotype of the rich Jew – as opposed to that of the thieving Gypsy – thus may have facilitated the acceptance of these refugees. Jews and non-Jews established mutually beneficial relationships that undermined Vichy's attempts to convince the public that there was a "Jewish problem." Shopkeepers, building owners, and farmers all profited from the influx of refugees who bought rations, paid rent, and searched for extra food. Moreover, refugees on occasion filled gaps in the local market. For example, in the town of Neuvic-Entier in the southwestern corner of the Haute-Vienne, a French-Jewish farmer received livestock from an "Aryan" in another department. Animals arrived regularly and apparently were sold on the black market. The PQJ asserted that the local population was enraged by the presence of the "true black market trafficker," yet the investigator acknowledged that the food supply administration was fully aware of this activity

---

[53] ADHV 993 W – 224 – Commissariat aux affaires juives – SEC. Mairie de St. Léonard-de-Noblat, Extrait du Registre des Arrêtés du Maire (April 4, 1942); Le Préfet de la Haute-Vienne à Monsieur le Maire de St Léonard (April 13, 1942); and Le Maire de St Léonard à Monsieur le Préfet de la Haute-Vienne (April 18, 1942).

and allowed it to continue.⁵⁴ Presumably, the acquisition of livestock benefited the community.

The officials' pragmatism helps to explain, in part, how a population that declared itself to be anti-Jewish tolerated, and even on occasion acted for the benefit of, Jews. Alain Giévis also aptly points out that one can be xenophobic and/or antisemitic, yet display compassion towards persecuted groups.⁵⁵ The difference is one of theory versus practice. The mayor of Saint Germain-les-Belles assured the regional prefect that a petition signed by ninety-six local inhabitants in support of a Jewish veterinarian in the fall of 1942 did not represent "a lack of loyalty, good sense, or devotion." Rather, the Romanian Jew in question had a good relationship with the local farmers, and they wanted him to continue to care for their animals – despite the fact that the Jewish Statutes forbade him to practice his profession. The mayor explained that Monsieur Kirmaier's "race and nationality" did not concern the rural residents and that any conflicts stemmed from urban interference in rural affairs.⁵⁶ After the prefect denied him an exemption, Monsieur Kirmaier continued to practice his profession clandestinely. Local farmers did not report him, but other veterinarians in the region whose practices suffered from the competition regularly denounced Monsieur Kirmaier – even going so far as to send letters to Marshal Pétain.

Although Jews could find some support in the Limousin, they often faced greater difficulties in satisfying their material needs than their non-Jewish counterparts due to the political atmosphere. The Jewish Statutes of October 3, 1940, and June 2, 1941, deprived increasing numbers of Jews of employment opportunities, and the economic aryanization of Jewish businesses further limited their revenues. By 1942, when urban–rural animosity was rampant and illegal means had become the most effective way to procure necessary items, over half of all Jews in France no longer had any source

---

⁵⁴ ADHV 993 W – 225 – Commissariat aux affaires juives – SEC. Affaire Blum, Jules. (February 23, 1943). The investigators requested an inquiry into the non-Jewish participant's activities as well. Jewish Jules Blum was assigned residence in another town in the Haute-Vienne in March 1943 and interned in June. For another example of the black market and relationships between Jews and "Aryans" see AN AJ 38–254. L'Intendant de Police de la Région de Limoges à Monsieur le Préfet Régional (December 5, 1942) and Le Commissaire Principal, Chef de Service à Monsieur le Préfet de la Haute-Vienne (December 9, 1942).

⁵⁵ Alain Giévis, "Les réfugiés juifs et l'opinion publique en Limousin (1940–1943)" in *Le Sauvetage des enfants juifs de France* (Guéret: Association pour la Recherche et la Sauvegarde de la Vérité Historique sur la Résistance en Creuse, 1996), 40.

⁵⁶ ADHV 185 W1–148 – Rapports du chef de la police aux questions juives pour la région de Limoges. Dossier Affaire Kirmaier, Lods, et Grador, vétérinaires de St. Germain-les-Belles et d'Uzerche. Letter from le Mairie de St Germain-les-Belles (October 3, 1942).

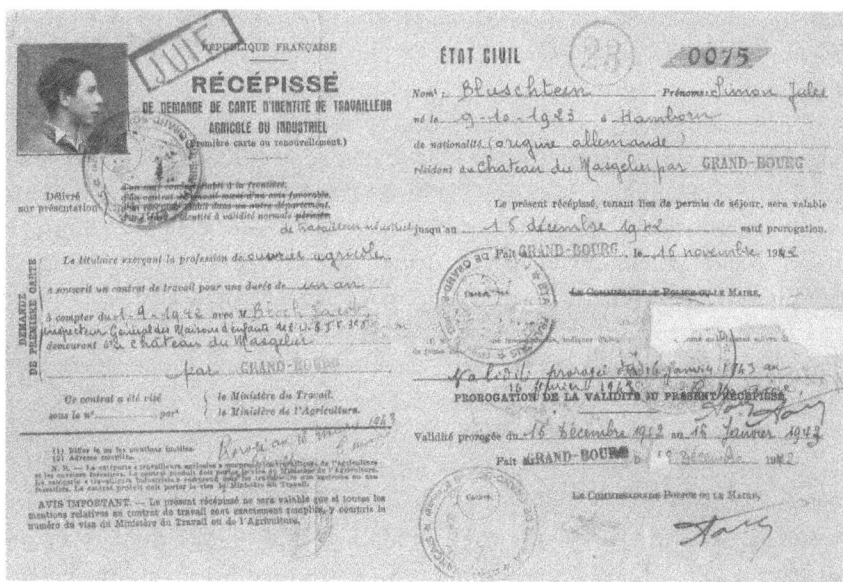

FIGURE 3. Receipt for worker's identity card stamped "JUIF." Issued to Julien Bluschtein on December 16, 1942, just days after the requirement for identity cards to be stamped "JUIF" went into effect. Photo credit: USHMM, courtesy of Julien Bluchetin [formerly Bluschtein].

of income.[57] On December 11, 1942, the Vichy government further circumscribed Jewish provisioning options when it issued a law requiring all Jews to have the word "JUIF" or "JUIVE" stamped on their identity card *and* their ration cards. (See Figure 3.) The stamp immediately identified the bearer as an undesirable to any official, including those who issued the monthly ration coupons.

In this atmosphere of increasing material, economic, and individual restrictions, assigned residence in rural areas had advantages and disadvantages for Jewish refugees. Even though the refugees were indeed closer to coveted products, they usually lacked the relationships with local peasants that some natives in the region enjoyed, and most Jews did not have the money necessary to purchase items directly on the farm in any case. Furthermore, rural communities offered fewer jobs still open to Jews than did larger cities. Unaware of the reality of Jews' economic situation, some non-Jews accepted the stereotype of the rich Jew further reinforced by their lack of employment. To some observers, such as the mayor of Saint-Léonard-de-Noblat, it appeared that the Jewish refugees had free time to spend combing the

[57] Dominique Veillon, *Vivre et survivre en France 1939–1947* (Paris: Editions Payot & Rivages, 1995), 237.

countryside in search of rare goods and the resources to pay exorbitant prices for the goods. In this way, it was alleged, Jews deprived hard-working French families of necessary supplies.

The media contributed to the image of the selfish Jew participating in black market activities in articles such as "The Jews in the Limousin," "Jewish Events in Haute-Vienne," and "Will We Let the Jewish Locusts Continue Their Devastation in the Unoccupied Zone?"[58] Each article touched on the housing and food shortages caused by the Jewish "invasion" and "raiding," but Gaston Derys' article "The Jewish Invasion of the Center" in the collaborationist paper *L'Appel* focused specifically on Jews' activities in the department of the Creuse. After describing the inherent beauty of the department where he spent several weeks each year, Derys turned to the changes created by the Jewish "infestation." Unlike other "modest, average" refugees who had visited the countryside to ensure their family's food supply, the wealthy Jews plundered villages for goods to sell in *"bédide gommerce"* [petite commerce or little business (i.e., black market sales) – note the association of Jews with a foreign accent]. The result, he asserted, was that "the inhabitants, the natives, the decent country folk settled in their village from father to son, no longer find anything to eat."[59] Even articles in the mainstream press alluded to Jewish black market activity. Philippe Henriot, a former deputy from Bordeaux and Vichy's propaganda minister in 1944, warned readers against any misplaced sympathy for Jews in the occupied zone forced to wear the yellow star in the summer of 1942. Rather than support the Jews, he argued, the French should condemn them for leading lives of leisure and for their active participation in the black market.[60]

Despite the propaganda, local officials in the Limousin found it very difficult to catch Jews participating in the black market. As refugees in assigned residences, Jews already received a great deal of official attention. Because of their obsession with the food supply and their convictions concerning Jewish participation in illegal activities, the authorities watched

---

[58] "Les Juifs dans le Limousin," *L'Appel* (August 6, 1942) microfilmed by YIVO Institute for Jewish Research (hereafter YIVO), Record Group 210, Microfilm 490 – Union Générale des Israélites de France, Records, 1940–4. Held by the United States Holocaust Memorial Museum (hereafter USHMM) Reel 99 Section 112.67, p. 1162; "Manifestations juives en Haute-Vienne," *Le Franciste* (September 19, 1942), YIVO, USHMM Reel 99 Section 112.67, p. 1138; and "Laissera-t-on les sauterelles juives poursuivre leurs ravages en Z.N.O?" *Le Matin* (October 9, 1942), YIVO, USHMM Reel 99 Section 112.67, p. 1128.

[59] Gaston Derys, "L'Invasion juive dans le Centre," *L'Appel* (December 17, 1942). YIVO, USHMM reel 99 Section 112.68, p. 1182.

[60] ADHV 993 W – 117 – Coupures du presse locale. Philippe Henriot, "La Romance de l'Etoile" (August 7, 1942). No publication information provided.

Jews especially closely. Gendarmes complained that, despite the constant monitoring, few Jews were caught at illegal activities and punished. Somehow, officials believed, Jews managed to monopolize the supplies that "should benefit the community."[61]

When performed by Jews, completely legal actions attracted official interest. Jewish refugees in rural areas, like millions of other French men and women, sent family packages to relatives in cities where shortages were more acute, yet authorities believed these packages contained goods in contravention of the law. Gendarmes investigated the mailing habits of Jews living in Sauviat-sur-Vige near Saint-Léonard-de-Noblat in the attempt to determine whether the refugees bought items at prices above the official tax and participated in the black market. Two of the men, refugees from Paris, regularly sent packages to their wives and children still living in the capital, while another sent occasional packages to family members in need of vegetables and other farm products, all in the intended spirit of *colis familiaux*. Despite interviews with six non-Jewish residents of Sauviat and the Jews themselves, the gendarmes did not uncover any illegal activity. A handwritten note on the official procès-verbal summarized the situation: "We must try to catch these individuals red-handed (at the moment when they buy). Your investigation proves nothing, and it is almost certain that there will not be legal proceedings."[62] In another instance, the Limoges gendarmerie investigated a case in which Henri Peiffer mailed two 500-gram pieces of cheese and some bread to his friend, Stern Wolf, interned at Noé (a Jewish internment camp in the Haute-Garonne). Both items were rationed and thus Monsieur Peiffer's package aroused suspicions of illegal activity. Peiffer explained that the skim milk cheese was not subject to rationing and that his two young children never ate all the bread allocated to them. Checking his story by visiting a baker and a cheese shop in Limoges, the gendarmes concluded that Peiffer provided plausible explanations.[63]

Jews ventured into the countryside in search of food items and probably paid more for the supplies than the government allowed, like many French residents. One survivor of the war in France remembers getting milk and produce from farmers around Bellac, forty kilometers northwest of Limoges.[64] Connections, however, remained important and as refugees, Jews often had

---

[61] SHGN Box 12557 – Cie Guéret, R/4, Rapport du Capitaine Chaumet sur la physionomie de la Section au cours du mois d'Octobre 1942 (October 24, 1942).

[62] SHGN Box 12754 – BT Saint-Léonard-de-Noblat. Procès-verbal number 349 (August 24, 1942).

[63] SHGN Box 12702 – BT Limoges. Procès-verbal number 484 (March 15, 1941).

[64] Ruth R. questionnaire responses.

fewer relationships to draw upon. Micheline Cohen believes that her friendly, talkative mother cultivated relationships with farmers surrounding Saint-Léonard-de-Noblat in order to supplement the family's food supply. In Cohen's memory, the family ventured into the countryside about once a week to get cheese and milk or maybe a chicken or some fruit in addition to the official rations.[65] Suzanne Dortort-Glantz remembers that her family did not visit the surroundings of Limoges in search of supplies because "you had to know someone." They did, however, have acquaintances in the rural town of Mézières, forty-seven kilometers north. The Dortort's Hungarian cousins had been assigned residence in the region and when Suzanne went to visit her family there, she always brought back precious items like eggs, butter, and oil.[66] The testimonies of Mrs Dortort-Glantz and Mrs Cohen support officials' accusations that Jews in forced residence in rural areas would use the proximity to farms in order supplement their food supply. But Jewish refugees' actions did not differ significantly from those of other residents living in cities or rural towns and villages. The difference came in official willingness to pursue such cases. Gendarmes generally agreed that when transgressions had to "do with the normal supplies of a family, it is good to close your eyes a little, because certain people are really in critical situations,"[67] but they did not apply the same standards to Jews who "due to their tendency to practice in the black market, . . . are the object of constant surveillance."[68]

Officials suspected Jews of participating in the black market on various levels. Not guilty of simply buying items at prices above the official tax, Jews almost certainly resold the goods at even higher prices; hence the authorities' concern with excessive trips to the countryside as well as the contents and frequency of Jewish family packages. Some of the stereotypes of the profiteering Jew probably stemmed from Jewish economic influence, role in business and finance, and association with capitalism that had existed in Europe for centuries as result of restrictive laws against them.[69] Vichy's antisemitic

---

[65] Micheline (Castro) Cohen interview with the author (August 9, 2000).
[66] Suzanne Dortort-Glantz interview with the author (August 2, 2000).
[67] SHGN Box 12721 – Grpt Haute-Vienne, BT Nexon, R/4, Rapport sur l'état d'esprit des populations (May 21, 1942).
[68] SHGN Box 12557 – Cie Guéret, R/4, Rapport du Capitaine Chaumet sur la physionomie de la Section, au cours du mois Juillet (July 24, 1942).
[69] On the role of Jews in economic affairs, see Howard M. Sachar, *The Course of Modern Jewish History,* new revised edition (New York: Vintage Books, 1990), especially Chapter 2 "The Glimmering of Dawn in the West" and Chapter 6 "Jewish Economic Life and the Frankfurt Tradition," and Paula E. Hyman, *The Jews of Modern France* (Berkeley, Los Angeles, and London: University of California Press, 1998). See also Caron, "The Antisemitic Revival in France in the 1930s."

measures, especially the systematic economic aryanization of Jewish businesses that began in 1941, were explicitly intended to "definitively eliminate Jewish influence in the French economy."[70] In this atmosphere of suspicion and economic repression, the most innocent actions acquired a potentially threatening dimension. Officials refused to accept that Jews could be concerned with their family's survival rather than with turning a profit. Gendarmes in Nexon demonstrated this attitude when they reported that they could not catch Jews participating in the black market because, they said, "[the Jews] transport the merchandise only in very small quantities."[71] Rather than recognize that the small quantities represented the amounts necessary to meet a family's daily needs, the gendarmes concluded that Jews made multiple trips to the countryside in order to conceal black market activities. In fact, Vichy's measures had separated many Jewish families as men, more vulnerable to arrest, fled the occupied zone or women were left alone when their husbands were interned. Individuals in the Limousin thus had legitimate reasons to send family packages to relatives in Paris or internment camps, justifying their purchases at the farm. But if the small purchases actually represented only a diversionary tactic, and not genuine attempts to meet family needs, the gendarmes could not muster the evidence to support their theory.

Even Jews with legal jobs faced black market investigations. One such investigation took place in the Haute-Vienne in July 1942, just a month before the mass arrest of Jews in the unoccupied zone. The PQJ in Limoges launched an inquiry into the activities of four French brothers whom locals suspected of black marketeering. Jewish refugees from Paris, the four brothers were legally employed in a perfume company in Limoges. Their occupations, however, required frequent travel to towns in the countryside around the city. According to the police inspector, "their numerous trips appear suspect in the eyes of residents in surrounding communes (Cieux, Javerdat, Oradour-sur-Glane) who do not know [the brothers'] professional activities and suppose that they, undoubtedly men of leisure, practice the black market on a large scale." Inspector Lathière's investigation revealed, conversely, that the men sent only small quantities of food to their parents,

---

[70] Quote from Commissariat Général aux Questions Juives, Service du Contrôle des Administrateurs Provisoires. Instruction générale et memento-guide à l'usage des Administrateurs Provisoires. Text in *Les Juifs sous l'Occupation*, p. 115. Vichy issued the law instituting economic aryanization on July 22, 1941.

[71] SHGN Box 12721 – BT Nexon, R/4, Maréchal des Logis Chef Magnol, Commandant la brigade de Nexon sur l'état d'esprit de la population (April 22, 1943). See also Magnol's report from June 18, 1943, for similar sentiments.

sister, and brother, all of whom had returned to Paris. The inspector acknowledged that the brothers were well placed to purchase hard-to-find items, but examinations of the family packages confirmed that the brothers were not "black market traffickers" looking for profit, but simply "sons seeking to help their parents."[72] Yet the mere appearance of Jews in some towns raised accusations, demonstrating the influence of antisemitic stereotypes and concerns about the food supply.

In order to catch Jews in black market activities, officials often relied on denunciations. Knowing that certain kinds of letters were more likely to elicit a response, individuals resorting to denunciation often accused others of material impropriety, and anonymous accusations of Jewish black market activity often triggered investigations. An inspector for the Special Police in the Haute-Vienne filed a detailed report with the sous-prefect of Bellac reporting the findings of a "discreet" investigation into the black market activities of foreign Jewish refugees from Paris initiated by an anonymous letter. In the course of the investigation, the inspector learned from a "trustworthy" neighbor that the members of the family purchased items from farms surrounding the town of Le Dorat, often returning late at night. Using the expedition information held by the head of the train station, Inspector Spiess determined that the family had sent thirty-two packages under false names over the course of October and the first week of November 1941. In his report, Spiess suggested that the explicitly fraudulent nature of the foreigners' actions did not warrant any leniency and that the population of Le Dorat would welcome the Jews' internment.[73]

Authorities' willingness to investigate anonymous denunciations of Jews implies a different attitude toward this method of information gathering for Jews and non-Jews. Throughout the war, government officials encouraged truthful, signed denunciations, while simultaneously discouraging anonymous letters in the belief that they tended to contain false information based on self-interest and the intent to harm others.[74] The Vichy government fought against *délation* (self-interested denunciations) because officials recognized that not all French could be trusted to act honorably. Even

---

[72] ADHV 993 W – 223 – Commissariat aux affaires juives. Le Chef de la Police des Questions Juives Délégué pour la Région de Limoges à Monsieur le Préfet Régional. Affaire: Lentschener, Simon, Isy, Léon, Jacques (July 31, 1942).

[73] ADC 976 W – 387. Letter from the Inspecteur de police spéciale Spiess to Monsieur le Sous-Préfet de Bellac (November 10, 1941).

[74] Vichy attempted to maintain a difference between *dénonciation* and *délation* during the war. For an extended discussion of denunciations in the Limousin, see Shannon L. Fogg, "Denunciations, Community Outsiders, and Material Shortages in Vichy France" *Proceedings of the Western Society for French History* 31 (2003): 271–89.

though false denunciations also targeted Jews, this reasoning did not apply when the accused were Jewish. The Special Police Inspector in the Creuse proceeded with a "meticulous investigation" of accusations against Jews in Bourganeuf contained in an anonymous letter mailed to the department's prefect in late 1941. He concluded that "the complaints contained in the previously cited letter are exaggerated as a whole." He found no evidence of antigovernment remarks, of "wallets full of food cards," or illegal packages containing rationed goods, as the letter had alleged.[75] The letter writer cited material concerns when the actual motivation probably stemmed from another source. In this case, the anonymous letter also cited common anti-Jewish stereotypes perpetuated by the Vichy regime. The willingness of officials to proceed with investigations despite the possibility of malicious intentions indicates that some government officials assumed that Jews were likely to be engaged in illegal activity (especially black market activities) that warranted investigation regardless of the source of the information.

Investigations often revealed information that contradicted official assertions about the role of Jews in the black market. For example, gendarmes investigating allegations that Jews were purchasing goods at higher than official prices in Sauviat-sur-Vige in August 1942 found not Jews but local peasants breaking the price laws. The gendarmes discovered that the Jews under investigation had sent modest three-kilogram packages to relatives, while local farmwomen admitted to having sold eggs to a French gardener from the region for 25 francs a dozen – well above the official price. The women also stated that they had never sold any eggs to Jews, but the gardener claimed he resold his eggs in Saint-Léonard – "principally to Jews living in this town" – for 35 francs a dozen.[76] The Jewish buyers were guilty of making purchases at illegal prices, but the peasants held greater responsibility as they profited from the sales.

Official propaganda continued to place most of the blame for shortages and the black market on Jews rather than on "virtuous" peasants. Jewish participation in the black market fit neatly into the propaganda and ideology of the National Revolution; peasant participation did not. Nevertheless, internal reports reveal that authorities were aware that non-Jewish citizens, and peasants in particular, bore the bulk of the responsibility for black market activities. While continuing to blame Jews for the "epidemic" ravaging the countryside, a monthly report based on intercepted letters declared

---

[75] ADC 95 W – 18 – Etranger juif – dossier individuels. Letter from the Inspecteur de Police Spéciale to Monsieur le Commissaire Principal des Renseignements Généraux de la Creuse (December 26, 1941).

[76] SHGN Box 12754 – BT Saint-Léonard-de-Noblat. Procès-verbaux numbers 349 and 352 (August 24, 1942).

that "the peasants are becoming more Jewish than the Jews and one must go kilometers in order find anything even at astronomical prices."[77] Another report stated that Jews allegedly bought goods directly from farmers at illegal prices in Saint-Germain-les-Belles, but noted that "one must recognize that the country people are the most responsible."[78]

An undated brochure (probably published in 1942) reminded peasants that they held "health of the homeland in their hands." The author called upon the peasants to renounce the black market in all its forms in order to ensure the nation's survival and to help reverse the divisions between urban and rural dwellers. Titled "The Black Market in the Countryside," the brochure explicitly implicated peasants as major players in the illegal economy. Jews were not mentioned.[79] Even the CGQJ conceded that despite the propaganda linking Jews to the black market, most French men and women did not make the same association. In their conclusions from the opinion poll conducted at the end of 1942, officials of the CGQJ elaborated on this contradiction:

It is curious, however, to note that the French do not seem to consider the Jews to be responsible for the black market, this reason coming only in sixth place with the small percentage of 4.73% of the entire investigation. This seems to prove that the propaganda that has already been circulated on this point has not had all the desirable results.

It is very evident, that if the Jews are at the root of the black market, they are not the only ones to participate in it and above all they are not the only ones to profit from it; the public knows this and each day sees non-Jews engaged in illicit trades; it is this that prevents our propaganda from yielding the expected results, and this demonstrates, moreover, that we must base our effort on more specifically Jewish arguments.[80]

It seems that despite the government's obsession with the Jews and the black market, most locals continued to view peasants – the producers of precious goods – as the principal perpetrators. While the government tried to stir up antisemitism and to associate it with material concerns, ordinary people based their opinions on what they observed in their daily lives – a fact not always reflected in official public opinion assessments.

Despite official recognition of the peasant's role in the black market, Jews remained the primary targets of invectives and investigations. Rather than

---

[77] ADHV 185 W 1–205 – Contrôle postal. Commission de Contrôle Postal de Limoges. Rapport Mensuel No. 67 (October 1942), 7.
[78] SHGN Box 12741 – BT Saint-Germain-les-Belles, R/4, Rapport du MDL Chef Defaye sur la Police Economique et l'état d'esprit des populations (May 21, 1942).
[79] "Le Marché Noir à la Campagne" par M. du Plessis de Grénédan, Doyen de la Faculté Libre de Droit d'Angers en collaboration avec le R.P. Boulanger, O.P. Professeur de Théologie morale à l'Université Catholique d'Angers. Collection "Mon Village." (Paris: Foyer Rural, n.d.).
[80] AN AJ 38–5770. Enquête d'opinion en zone libre p. 6. In the Limoges region, the percentage was significantly higher: 27.33 percent. See pp. 52–4.

"At any price" 141

publicly blaming peasants – the foundation of the new French society lauded in the National Revolution – for shortages and price increases, some people continued to hold Jews' corrupting influence responsible. Gaston Derys took this position in his *L'Appel* article when he asked readers, "When one offers a poor woman whose son is a prisoner eight or ten francs for an egg or a hundred francs for a pound of butter, how do you expect her to resist?"[81] Derys clearly implied that economic necessity pushed these women to accept the money, and that without the Jews' offers these suffering women would never have resorted to such sales. Officials charged with monitoring communications asserted, "One considers that the government made a big mistake in scattering Jews chased from big cities throughout the countryside. At the present time the infiltration of the countryside is complete; each village, each hamlet has its 'worm' that saps, eats away at, and perverts the healthiest element of the nation."[82] The goal of providing additional housing in cities through the assigned residence of Jews succeeded, but in the process the government undermined its moral agenda based on a "return to the soil" by introducing "unhealthy" elements into rural society.

Peasants and Jews, both implicated in black market activities, relied upon each other as sellers and buyers, although Limousin natives clearly remained in a position of power. Peasants maintained an economic advantage over all people in search of additional food, including Jewish refugees. As producers with items to sell, farmers could demand any price from buyers afraid of losing their source of agricultural products. Peasants wielded particular power over Jews due to Vichy's attention to the "Jewish problem" and the atmosphere of repression. Any hint of illegal activity on the part of Jewish refugees spawned investigations that could result in assigned residence or internment. Still, Jewish infractions remained difficult to uncover, due in part to the complicity and silence of the area's native residents. To officials, it was the "lure of gain" that pushed peasants into these clandestine dealings with the Jews.[83] Some locals in the region complained that sympathy for the "poor people mistreated by the government" only encouraged shop owners and others to sell their goods to Jews rather than the "real French."[84]

---

[81] Derys, "L'Invasion juive dans le Centre."
[82] ADHV 185 W 1–206 – Synthèses hebdomadaires du coordinateur du service civil des contrôles techniques. Période du 1er au 7 Novembre 1942 (November 7, 1942).
[83] SHGN Box 12557 – Cie Guéret, R/4, Rapport du Capitaine Chaumet sur la physionomie de la Section (January 24, 1943).
[84] AN AJ 38–265. Le Commissaire Général aux Questions Juives à Monsieur le Directeur Régional de la SEC Limoges (January 22, 1943). Letter requesting an investigation of allegations contained in a letter from Marie Bonnerot, Chenerailles (Creuse). Quote from Madame Bonnerot's letter.

Whatever the reasons, native producers and Jewish consumers formed relationships during the war years that could benefit both parties.

The case of a Czechoslovakian Jewish woman (a refugee from Paris) accused of participating in black market activities demonstrates the nature of personal interactions between Jews and non-Jews. Gendarmes in Limoges investigating the accusations interviewed the woman's neighbors as well as her present and former landlords, but no one claimed to have ever noticed any signs of black market activity nor did anyone have anything particularly negative to say about the foreigner with respect to her morality or political tendencies. The gendarmes, however, felt otherwise upon discovering a large stock of nondeclared rationed goods in the woman's possession.[85] While the hoarding of goods constituted an infraction that Vichy considered to be a black market activity, non-Jewish acquaintances apparently tried to protect the woman by denying noticing any suspicious activities. Either they did not see her illicit stockpile (unlikely at a time when the French were acutely aware of others' supply situation) or they may have been profiting from the situation. Another possibility is they were simply displaying social solidarity in the face of government interference.

In another instance in mid-1942, gendarmes in the Creuse received a letter denouncing a Jewish family for participating in the black market, traveling without the proper documentation, and trying to trade fabric for food. During the course of the investigation, not a single family acquaintance corroborated the accusations, and, conversely, the interviewees asserted that any trips to the countryside represented only honest attempts to feed the family. Either the non-Jews interviewed were trying to protect their Jewish neighbors or they were trying to protect their own interests as the family's arrest would mean fewer customers. It is also possible that the denunciation contained false information. Whatever the case, no one provided additional information to substantiate the claims in the anonymous letter.[86]

Economically based relationships confused authorities' assessments of antisemitism. Local reports assured higher-ups in the hierarchical political structure that rural Limousin residents blamed Jewish refugees for

---

[85] SHGN Box 12705 – Haute-Vienne, BT Limoges. Procès-verbaux numbers 525 and 526 (March 8, 1942) and number 660 (March 26, 1942). Gendarmes seized the goods on March 8, and on March 26 the woman and her children were assigned to a residence in the neighboring department of the Creuse.

[86] ADC 976 W – 279. Procès-verbal from mid-July 1942. Other examples include Louis Aron's statement in his wartime journal that he bought eggs from peasants in the middle of the night because the farmers feared denunciation. See *Journal de Louis Aron*, p. 70.

housing and food shortages in their communities. Economic antisemitism long ingrained in French society helped perpetuate the stereotype of Jewish black market activities, an attribute exploited in propaganda and used to justify restrictive measures against Jews. Despite the stereotypes, authorities found little evidence of Jewish black market activities and native residents based their interactions on the potential for personal gain rather than on the government's directives. Locals displayed both pragmatism and astuteness. They knew peasants, rather than refugees, animated the black market and controlled prices – a fact the government attempted to minimize and ignore. Between September 1939 and August 1942, Limousin residents often acted in a duplicitous manner. Largely keeping silent about Vichy's anti-Jewish legislation, they still interacted with undesirable Jews. Relationships and material contact patterns established during this period had important ramifications after 1942. Authorities' assessments of public opinion were often optimistic, misleading, or false; they cannot stand alone and must be reexamined in light of subsequent events.

FACILITATING AND THWARTING EXCLUSION: THE EFFECTS OF SHORTAGES AFTER 1942

August 26, 1942, marked a turning point in the unoccupied zone for Jews and, some scholars argue, for public opinion. The situation for Jews abruptly changed from inexcusable exclusion to life-threatening deportation. Persecution that had been managed through daily accommodations and new survival tactics moved into a realm that few could have imagined or predicted. Yet the early morning raids intended to capture undesirable foreign Jews was neither a major break with Vichy's previous anti-Jewish activity nor an isolated event. The visible and violent anti-Jewish activity provided an opportunity for non-Jews to voice their disapproval, but their quotidian interactions in the years before 1942 had already demonstrated their implicit rejection of politics in favor of their material well-being. Furthermore, some French residents continued to use the National Revolution's antisemitic legislation for material gain even after the events of August 26.

Before the German occupation of the southern zone in November 1942, Vichy officials participated in the roundup and deportation of thousands of foreign Jews who had arrived in France after January 1, 1936. Coming just a month after the massive police roundup of the *Vel d'hiv* in Paris, foreign Jews were feeling more vulnerable, yet many were unprepared for the arrival of gendarmes at their doors early on the morning of August 26. Gendarmes received detailed instructions for the roundup, including the composition of teams for the actions, the names of individuals to be arrested, the amount of time refugees had to leave their homes, and even information on what to wear.[87]

Despite the careful preparation and the insistence on secrecy, the operation in the Limoges region managed to arrest only 876 of the expected 1,308 foreign Jews: 446 of the 876 were deported (226 men, 200 women, and 20 children) to the occupied zone on August 29, while the others were released or remained interned in the region's concentration camp located in Nexon.[88] The action clearly demonstrated Vichy's willingness to participate fully in the Nazis' plan for deportation. Officials in the Limousin maintained that the public approved of Vichy's actions against the Jews, though at the same time, authorities noted expressions of pity and sympathy.[89] Despite the insistence on popular support, officials acknowledged that hundreds of the intended victims of the roundup had been warned in advance of the impending action.[90] After witnessing the arrests of August 26, indignant French citizens mailed letters to Marshal Pétain denouncing the "abominable scenes" they had seen, including the separation of families and suicides.[91] The Protestant and Catholic churches in Limoges also criticized

---

[87] See SHGN Box 12647 – BT Limoges, R/4, Note de Service relative à l'exécution de la CM No. 2675 P-Pol 9 du 5 Août 1942. (August 19, 1942) and SHGN Box 12557 – Cie Guéret, R/4, Le Capitaine Chaumet aux Commandants de brigade. Internements de Juifs (August 23, 1942).

[88] AN AJ 38–242. Le Directeur de la Section d'Enquête et de Contrôle, Délégué pour la Région de Limoges à Monsieur le Directeur de la Section d'Enquête et de Contrôle en Z.N.O. (September 2, 1942) and AN AJ 38–256. Le Commissaire Divisionnaire Chef du Service Régional des Renseignements Généraux à Monsieur le Conseiller d'Etat, Secrètaire [sic] Général à la Police Direction des Renseignements Généraux (September 1, 1942). For more details on the arrests, see also Gérard Gobitz, *Les Déportations de Réfugiés de Zone Libre en 1942. Récits et documents concernant les régions administratives de Toulouse, Nice, Lyon, Limoges, Clermont-Ferrand, Montpellier (Camp de Rivesaltes)* (Paris: L'Harmattan, 1996).

[89] ADHV 185 W 3–15 – Services départementaux des renseignements généraux – Haute-Vienne. Le Commissaire Spécial de Limoges à Monsieur l'Intendant de Police à Limoges (Renseignements Généraux) (September 25, 1942), 2–3.

[90] AN AJ 38–61, M 49. Direction des Renseignements Généraux, Note de Renseignements no. 3271/16B (August 18, 1942); AN AJ 38–256. Le Commissaire Divisionnaire Chef du Service Régional des Renseignements Généraux à Monsieur le Conseiller d'Etat, Secrètaire [sic] Général à la Police Direction des Renseignements Généraux (September 1, 1942); ADHV 185 W 1–73 – Rapports mensuels du chef de la police aux questions juives. Rapport No. 9 du 1er au 31 août 1942 (September 5, 1942), 3.

[91] CDJC CIX – 37 (September 1, 1942) and CIX – 43 (September 10, 1942). Both documents also in USHMM RG-43.024M reel 52.

the Vichy government in the wake of the arrests. In his sermon on September 13, 1942, the protestant Pastor Chaudier decried the "Dante-esque"[92] action against foreign Jews in the free zone, and Monsignor Rastouil, the bishop of Limoges, "disapprove[d] of these measures, [found] them barbarian, inhumane, and against the Catholic Church's doctrine of charity and aid."[93] For the first time, significant numbers of non-Jews spoke up in defense of the Jews, providing scholars with evidence that public opinion was shifting from indifference to support.

Some Jewish refugees found support through relationships that had grown over the course of the war's early years. The refugees now counted on their native acquaintances for more than just food. Suzanne Dortort's parents placed their youngest son with farmers in the countryside when the entire family went into hiding. Seven-year-old Marcel went to stay with a peasant family in Mézières after the Dortort's cousins, assigned residence in the town, provided the contact. Suzanne, placed in a convent, still attended public school and continued to move about freely, visiting her parents hidden in an attic and Marcel on the farm. While the farmers provided protection for the young boy, the Dortort family also benefited materially from Suzanne's trips to the countryside.[94] In Saint-Léonard-de-Noblat, Micheline Castro's father decided the family would not have their identity and ration cards stamped "JUIF" after the decree of December 1942, fearing the action was tantamount to a "death sentence."[95] Instead, other town residents gave them some of their ration coupons, shopkeepers sold them items without collecting coupons, and eventually the clerk at the town's city hall provided the family with the coupons they needed. Micheline's mother continued to draw upon her friendships with peasants to supplement the family's food supply. Food issues and survival were intimately connected as Jewish families drew upon relationships founded on material needs in order to circumvent Vichy's antisemitic legislation.

---

[92] ADHV 185 W 1–221 – Culte protestant. L'Inspecteur de Police des Renseignements Généraux Faure à Monsieur le Commissaire Divisionnaire Chef du Service Régional des Renseignements Généraux (September 14, 1942) and Le Préfet de la Haute-Vienne à Monsieur le Chef du Gouvernement, Ministre Secrétaire d'Etat à l'Intérieur Secrétariat Général pour la Police (September 18, 1942). Albert Chaudier would become the president of the Comité départemental de libération in August 1944.

[93] ADHV 185 W 1–220. Culte catholique. Le Préfet de la Haute-Vienne à Monsieur le Chef du Gouvernement, Ministre Secrétaire d'Etat à l'Intérieur. Secrétariat Général pour la Police (September 15, 1942).

[94] Suzanne Dortort-Glantz interview with the author (August 2, 2000).

[95] Micheline (Castro) Cohen questionnaire responses.

For some foreign Jews in the region, the networks they had established in their daily lives now helped save them from roundups, internment, and deportation. Ilan family connections with rural inhabitants throughout the war helped all but one member of the family survive. The family of German refugees illegally crossed the demarcation line separating occupied France from the free zone with the help of farmers that their son, Kurt, had befriended while working as an agricultural laborer. Turned in by hotel keepers shortly after their crossing, the family was temporarily interned in Limoges until they were assigned residence in Mézières, the same small town forty-eight kilometers northwest of Limoges where Marcel Dortort was hidden during the war. In the winter of 1942, the family settled into their new frugal lifestyle, and Kurt again found work on a nearby farm. Alice, the Ilan's daughter, worked as a dressmaker for farmwomen in the area and received payment in the form of "fresh eggs, milk, and smoked meat." She remembers, "Village people accepted them as an industrious family, simple folks who knew how to adapt themselves to their changed life."[96] Threatened with internment by the law of January 2, 1942, the local baker's assistant, a French Catholic, offered to marry 18-year-old Alice to protect her from deportation. After she turned down the man's proposal, police arrested the entire Ilan family in August 1942 and transported them to the transit camp at Nexon. However, the policeman who had arrested the family arranged for their release because Alice had saved his son from drowning. Alice's father and brother could not escape Vichy's second round of arrests and internments in February 1943, however. Following their arrest, Alice escaped from police surveillance in Mézières with the help of friends and survived the rest of the war under an assumed identity. The surrounding community's attitudes and courageous actions played a decisive role in the family's survival.

Good relationships with native residents between 1940 and 1942 led to warnings and protection when roundups began. Henry Wertheimer's family fled Germany in 1935 and joined the exodus from Paris in June 1940. They settled in Bellac in the northern Haute-Vienne, near his father's place of employment as a foreign worker. Henry was 13 in 1940 and has fond memories of the "comparatively good life" they led in Bellac.[97] A makeshift synagogue served the community of approximately twenty Jewish families, the Wertheimers used their bicycle to visit neighboring farms for supplies,

---

[96] USHMM RG – 02.195. "Dear Kurt" by Ruth Ilan. Section 30: "Mézières," p. 2. Alice changed her name to Ruth after immigrating to Israel.

[97] Henry Wertheimer interview with the author (August 7, 2000).

"At any price" 147

and Henry attended the public school where he never felt threatened or discriminated against. He also remembered "French friends" warning the family of possible police actions. With the faintest rumor, French inhabitants of the town contacted the family and they often hid in their neighbor's attic. Local residents of Saint-Léonard-de-Noblat also warned the Castro family of potential sweeps. Micheline Castro remembers sleeping in a barn for a few days after someone warned her family that the Germans would be coming through the town. The principal of the local girls' school also hid Micheline and other Jewish girls when the threat of arrest was particularly high.[98] While luck could play a role in one's ability to escape arrest, the aid of non-Jewish French men and women greatly increased the chances of survival.

The political decision to arrest, intern, and deport Jews was followed closely by official decrees that tightened the government's control over Jews through material means. Legally collecting food for daily consumption became increasingly difficult for Jews. The law of November 9, 1942, forbidding foreign Jews to leave their commune without police permission meant these refugees could not travel to neighboring towns to shop at other butchers, bakers, or grocery stores. The prefect of the Creuse and the department's head of supplies addressed this specific issue after the arrival of foreign Jews evacuated from coastal regions in 1943. Prefect Jacques-Henry made it clear to these Jews in his "welcome" letter that in no case were they to leave their towns of assigned residence, to buy goods outside official markets and shops, to visit surrounding farms, or to buy goods without ration tickets. Such expectations were unrealistic, however, in many towns where Jews were assigned residence. In Naillat, in the western part of the department, officials feared that the arrival of 150 Jews and an indigenous population of 1,512 meant local grocery stores would be unable to meet everyone's needs. The director of food supply hoped that wholesalers would be able to provide the grocers with adequate stocks. The director also suggested that heads of Jewish families in the small towns of Villard, Linard, and Villate in the northern Creuse be given authorization to travel to neighboring, larger towns each Thursday in order to buy meat because there were no butchers in their place of residence. In Champsanglard, there was neither a butcher nor anyone selling butter. To resolve the butter issue, Jewish

---

[98] Micheline (Castro) Cohen interview with the author (August 9, 2000). On the actions of Germaine Lalo, the school director, see also Limore Yagil, "Typologie de la Résistance sans armes et de l'aide aux juifs en Limousin," *Revue d'histoire de la Shoah: le monde juif* 172 (May–August 2001): 233.

families were to turn their ration coupons over to one member of the community who would get the corresponding amount of butter from the commune's wholesale supplier.[99]

For others, the simple act of picking up monthly ration coupons constituted a threat. Some Jews chose not to obey the law of December 11, 1942, requiring the word "JUIF" or "JUIVE" to be stamped on their identity and ration cards. These refugees risked arrest for noncompliance or for holding fake papers just by going to the mayor's office to pick up the month's coupons. Furthermore, by 1943, gendarmes increasingly guarded the distribution of coupons throughout the Limousin because Resistance groups attacked localities in order to obtain the all-important coupons.[100] In May 1944, the Vichy government made the mayor's role in monitoring Jews more explicit by requiring Jewish refugees to claim their ration coupons in their declared place of residence "in order to facilitate investigations concerning Israelites."[101] Even for Jews fulfilling all of Vichy's legal requirements, increased contact with government officials meant a greater chance of being caught for the slightest infraction.

In addition to the threats posed by interacting with the state, Jews still faced hostility from neighbors and acquaintances with access to Vichy's antisemitic bureaucratic system. One man complained that his German-Jewish upstairs neighbors made "life truly intolerable" for him and his ailing wife. Citing his family's "Frenchness" and the local gendarmes' inability to remedy the situation, the World War I veteran wrote directly to the Commissariat General for Jewish Questions in January 1943.[102] In another case sent to the CGQJ in December 1943, a 70-year-old veteran and his wife, who were living in a "shack" (*taudis*) on their own property, requested advice for ridding their home of Jewish refugees who refused to leave the

---

[99] The larger towns ranged from four to six kilometers away from the Jews' place of assigned residence. ADC 976 W – 353 – Hébergement des israélites (1943–1944). Réfugiés côtières. L'Intendant Directeur Départemental du Ravitaillement Général à Monsieur le Préfet de la Creuse (January 29, 1943) and L'Intendant de 3ième Classe, Directeur Départemental du Ravitaillement Général à Monsieur le Préfet de la Creuse (January 29, 1943).

[100] In the Haute-Vienne, gendarmes guarded distribution in the communes of Eymoutiers, St-Léonard, Châteauneuf-la-Fôret, and Châlus. In the Creuse, they defended La Souterraine. For instructions, see ADHV 185 W 1–63 – Rapports mensuels du directeur régional du ravitaillement général. Le Général de Brigade Bois, Commandant la 2ème Brigade de la Garde à Monsieur le Préfet Régional de Limoges (November 13, 1943).

[101] AN AJ 38–147. Le Secretaire Général au maintien de l'ordre à Messieurs les Préfets de la zone sud (May 22, 1944). The order also required mayors to create a central card catalog of all Jewish consumers in their districts.

[102] AN AJ 38–230. CGQJ – Demande d'enquête (January 5, 1943). Letter from A. P. Canu, Saint Sauver de Bellac.

"At any price" 149

farm at the end of their lease.[103] In both instances, officials initiated an investigation into the status of the offending Jews. Clearly, then, material concerns influenced locals' interactions with Jewish refugees not just before 1942, but after the roundups began as well.

Despite the range of weapons the public had at its disposal to use against Jews, authorities appear to have been fair in their investigations and to have applied Vichy's laws carefully. Some native non-Jewish residents turned to the CGQJ with complaints only when local authorities failed to "adequately" deal with Jews for their material infractions, suggesting that investigations conducted by local policing organizations, the principle enforcers of Vichy's anti-Jewish legislation, relied upon evidence of infractions rather than mere hearsay. Instead of rushing blindly to find Jews guilty of the accusations against them, police agents conducted investigations, searched for evidence, and even granted exemptions. In October 1942, police inspector Lathière conducted an investigation at the request of the prefect of the Haute-Vienne into the activities of a Jewish midwife in Châteauponsac. The Bulgarian-born woman had lived in the town forty-five kilometers north of Limoges since 1923. With her husband in a medical institution for over twenty years, the woman lived "conjugally" with a French man who owned a chemical factory and several homes in Châteauponsac. For about fifteen years, she had practiced medicine as a specialist in "women's illnesses" until forbidden to do so because she did not have the "necessary French diplomas." She then registered as a midwife and enjoyed a thriving practice and solid reputation in the commune and the surrounding area. Lathière noted that, aside from the fact that she lived with a man outside of marriage, the woman displayed proper conduct, morals, loyalty, and devotion to France. She "regularly attended all the patriotic events and charity evenings" and socialized with local officials including a former senator and the town's mayor. As to her religion, the inspector noted in his conclusion, "she has never been considered to be an Israelite in Châteauponsac, given that she practices the Catholic religion. Moreover, she does not frequent Jews and receives no suspect visits at home."[104] As a result of

---

[103] AN AJ 38–241. Le Directeur Adjoint de la Section d'Enquête et de Contrôle à Monsieur le Délégué Régional de la SEC de Limoges. Objet: Juifs indésirables à Nouzerolles (December 6, 1943).

[104] ADHV 993 W – 223 – Commissariat aux affaires juives. Direction Générale de la Police Nationale. Le Commissaire Principal, Chef de Service à Monsieur le Préfet de la Haute-Vienne (October 2, 1942). Lathière was also a "commissaire adjoint" for the Police des Questions Juives. See AN AJ 38–242. Ministère de l'Intérieur, Police des Questions Juives, Rapport numéro 569 (August 22, 1942).

Lathière's investigation and conclusions, a decree in December 1941 granted the Jewish woman a special dispensation to continue practicing her profession. The daily application of Vichy's ideals was indeed complicated.

The case of the rural Limousin raises important questions about the extent to which material issues affected relationships between Jews and non-Jews in other regions in France, as well as about the impact of shortages on public attitudes. Rhetoric about shortages could be used to prop up the anti-Jewish aspects of the National Revolution, or it could undermine them. The fact that few Jews were actually cited for black market activities, as compared to the propaganda, reflects the fact that the refugees and the natives formed alliances. Peasants interested in making money would sell to Jews, as to any other buyers, despite the government's prohibition of such sales. Jews weighed the risks and benefits of observing the law or turning to illegal activity in order to survive. While shortages persisted and even worsened after 1942, some non-Jewish French men and women set aside part of their precious food supply for Jews living in hiding or otherwise in contravention of Vichy's antisemitic legislation. But the difficult living conditions also left room for abuse. Ultimately, personal considerations – financial, material, and moral – prevailed over Vichy's agenda.

5

"The vast heart of mankind knows no boundaries": Refuge in Jewish Children's Homes

In July 1939, Stephan Lewy boarded a train in Germany bound for France. Born fourteen years earlier in Berlin to a Jewish father and a Protestant mother, Stephan had been living in an orphanage since 1932. Unable to care for his young son after his wife's death in 1931, Arthur Lewy placed the boy in the same orphanage that he had also lived in as a child. After Hitler's rise to power in 1933, the Nazis arrested the elder Lewy for his socialist political beliefs and he spent nine months in the Orianenburg concentration camp. In 1938, Herr Lewy remarried, and his new wife's relatives near Boston provided the affidavit necessary for the entire family to immigrate to the United States. In order to get their visas, the family had to pass a medical exam, but as a result of his time in detention, Arthur Lewy failed to meet the health requirements. Fearing a war in Germany and worried about their son's future, the Lewys allowed Stephan to leave the country on a transport that also included other children from the orphanage. Arthur Lewy knew the dangers of Nazism firsthand and hoped his son would be safer in France. Climbing onto the train, Stephan wondered when he would see his parents again.

The trip from Berlin to Paris marked the beginning of a harrowing journey that would lead Stephan, like hundreds of other Jewish refugee children, to the Limousin. After arriving in France, Stephan Lewy spent about ten months with forty other refugee children in an institution outside of Paris. When the Germans invaded the country in May 1940, the teachers decided to evacuate the home, and the children set off on foot for Paris. Once in the capital, they tried to head south via an inland barge, but the Seine was so congested with other refugees fleeing the city that advancing German soldiers soon overtook the children's boat. Mr Lewy remembers

FIGURE 4. Château de Chabannes. View of the OSE children's home in the rural Creuse (1941–2). Photo credit: USHMM, courtesy of Stephan H. Lewy.

huddling in a corner of the barge with the other German Jewish refugees when German soldiers opened the door to the hold and pointed a machine gun at them while someone said, "They all look like a bunch of Jews." The door closed without a shot being fired, but the frightened children gave up their attempt to escape Paris. Stephan spent the next six months in a Parisian apartment under the supervision of the American Friends' Service Committee (the Quakers) until the organization managed to get the forty children into the unoccupied zone. Once there, the children were transferred to the care of the Oeuvre de Secours aux Enfants (OSE), a Jewish children's aid agency that had established a handful of homes in the Limousin during the Phony War.[1]

Stephan Lewy thus found himself at the Château de Chabannes, a country home in the rural Creuse that had been converted into a temporary refuge for Jewish children. (See Figure 4.) By the time Stephan Lewy and the other refugee children arrived at the home located near Saint Pierre-de-Fursac,

---

[1] Information from Stephan Lewy interview with the author (August 14, 2000). Stephan Lewy's parents managed to escape Germany after his father passed the medical examination on his second try. They left Holland two days before the Germans invaded the country. With the help of the International Red Cross, Stephan Lewy located his parents in the United States and began the visa process. In 1942, Lewy was among the few children allowed to leave France for the United States.

just west of Guéret and south of La Souterraine, the staff had been caring for needy Jewish children for about a year. At the château, children received schooling, participated in sports, learned a trade, and found a sense of stability in uncertain times. When Vichy's policies toward Jews changed from exclusion to deportation in August 1942, the networks established by the daily functioning of the homes often provided life-saving assistance. Stephan Lewy was just one of the hundreds of Jewish children in institutions in the Limousin that represent a specific kind of refugee in the region during the war years. Living in legitimate, state-recognized, and well-financed homes, these children had certain advantages over children who arrived in the region in their families' care. In the period of wartime shortages, the economic compensation these institutions provided to the surrounding community often outweighed any antisemitic feelings, demonstrating the dependent, changing, and contingent nature of outsider status.

With the Vichy regime's emphasis on youth and its obsession with the regeneration of France, other scholars have addressed questions related to children and the war years. W. D. Halls has explored Vichy's policies toward youth and concludes: "the hardships of total war, bombing, food shortages, and forced labour dominated the lives of young people."[2] Sarah Fishman's work on juvenile crime provides important insights into how children experienced the war in general, including the material and economic effects on their daily lives. She convincingly concludes that rather than representing a breakdown in the family, "the behavior of delinquent minors was essentially shaped by economic circumstances."[3] Starting with the premise that the war's material conditions profoundly affected children's lives allows us to further examine their experiences and explore how natives viewed the youngest refugees in their midst.

Jewish children represented a significant portion of the Jewish population in France, and their experiences often differed from those of adults, especially for the children who spent part of the war years in the care of aid organizations or who were rescued. This difference has led many scholars to focus primarily on specific institutions, individual biographies, or particular rescue networks rather than the more banal events of the

---

[2] W. D. Halls, *The Youth of Vichy France* (Oxford: Clarendon Press, 1981), 400.

[3] Sarah Fishman, *The Battle for Children: World War II, Youth Crime, and Juvenile Justice in Twentieth-Century France* (Cambridge, Massachusetts, and London: Harvard University Press, 2002), 145.

everyday.[4] Children younger than age 15 comprised about 23 percent of the total Jewish population (70,000 out of 320,000), but only 11.5 percent (9,000) of Jews deported from France.[5] For some, this demonstrates the extent of child rescue in France as compared to other Nazi-occupied countries where the percentage of deported children was higher. But the attention focused on heroic rescue tends to obscure the more ordinary daily events that created an environment in which rescue could occur or which could facilitate arrests.

The arrival of young Jewish refugees in the Limousin cannot be separated from the arrival of other refugees and evacuees. Nor can any discussion of the daily lives of Jewish children and their rescue ignore the wartime material situation or the Vichy regime's ideological tenets. The first homes for Jewish children opened in the Creuse shortly after the evacuation of Alsace and Lorraine in 1939, and during the first difficult winter of 1940, aid organizations opened additional homes in the Haute-Vienne. Meeting the new arrivals' material needs could serve as a means of integrating the Jewish children into the community or could be viewed as an additional burden on an already strained provisioning system. In either case, rural communities could not be "indifferent" to the arrival of hundreds of children in their midst, nor did many

---

[4] See for example Sabine Zeitoun, *L'Oeuvre de secours aux enfants (O.S.E) sous l'Occupation en France, du légalisme à la résistance 1940–1944* preface by Serge Klarsfeld (Paris: Éditions L'Harmattan, 1990); Sabine Zeitoun, *Ces enfants qu'il fallait sauver* (Paris: France Loisirs, 1989); Vivette Samuel, *Sauver les enfants* (Paris: Liana Levi, 1995); *Au secours des enfants du siècle: Regards croisés sur l'OSE* edited by Martine Lemalet (Paris: Nil Editions, 1993); *Le Sauvetage des Enfants Juifs de France. Actes du Colloque de Guéret – 29 et 30 Mai 1996* (Guéret: Association pour la recherche et la sauvegarde de la vérité historique sur la Résistance en Creuse, n.d.); Hillel Kieval, "Legality and Resistance in Vichy France: The Rescue of Jewish Children," *Proceedings of the American Philosophical Society* 124:5 (October 1980); Isaac Levendel, *Not the Germans Alone: A Son's Search for the Truth of Vichy* (Evanston, Illinois: Northwestern University Press, 1999); Gaston Lévy, *Souvenirs d'un médecin d'enfants à l'OSE en France occupée et en Suisse, 1940–1945* (Paris, Jerusalem: Editions Le Manuscrit, 1974); Esther Kustanowitz, *The Hidden Children of the Holocaust: Teens who Hid from the Nazis* (New York: The Rosen Publishing Group, 1999); Stacy Cretzmeyer, *Your Name is Renée: Ruth Kapp Hartz's Story as a Hidden Child in Nazi-Occupied France* (New York: Oxford University Press, 1999); Sarah Kofman, *Rue Ordener, Rue Labat* translated by Ann Smock (Lincoln and London: University of Nebraska Press, 1996); Saul Friedländer, *When Memory Comes* translated by Helen R. Lane (New York: Farrar Straus Giroux, 1979). On the deportation of children, see Gérard Gobitz, *Les Déportations de Réfugiés de Zone Libre en 1942. Récits et documents concernant les régions administratives de Toulouse, Nice, Lyon, Limoges, Clermont-Ferrand, Montpellier (Camp de Rivesaltes)* (Paris: L'Harmattan, 1996) and Serge Klarsfeld, *French Children of the Holocaust: A Memorial* edited by Susan Cohen, Howard M. Epstein, and Serge Klarsfeld, translated by Glorianne Depondt and Howard M. Epstein (New York and London: New York University Press, 1996).

[5] Serge Klarsfeld, preface in Zeitoun, *L'Oeuvre de secours aux enfants*, p. 11.

residents express "ambivalent" feelings. They did, on occasion, express contradictory attitudes: Antisemitism appears regularly in official reports, yet personal interactions often belied the stated discrimination. Michael R. Marrus and Robert O. Paxton note in *Vichy France and the Jews*, "We have the impression that the most inhospitable areas for Jews were the villages and towns of rural areas, where highly visible conflicts of interest over food supply coincided with the least habituation to outsiders."[6] Examining Jewish children's experiences in the Limousin reveals that this statement needs greater qualification. The large Jewish communities that relocated to small, rural towns to care for children received support and aid from the local population both before and after the summer of 1942 due to the refugees' age and the material benefit the group homes provided to the communities.

The year 1942 did mark a turning point of sorts, however. The increased and more threatening persecution Jews faced created additional opportunities for aid from native communities. Children's homes established under the Third Republic during the Phony War continued their daily functions after the creation of the Vichy regime. Jewish leaders made accommodations in order to fit within the ideals of the National Revolution and to conform to the Jewish Statutes promulgated in 1940 and 1941. But the changes heralded by the arrests of August 26, 1942, required the Jewish aid organizations caring for children to reevaluate both their strategies and their position vis-à-vis the Vichy government. In some ways, the Jewish aid organizations, driven by ideological similarities, belief in legality, and a need for survival, became complicit in supporting the Vichy regime in 1940 and 1941. Their strategies changed in 1942 as they shifted from legal to clandestine activities on the children's behalf. As conditions for Jews in France deteriorated, Limousin natives demonstrated their own complicity with the young refugees by remaining silent, participating in illegal activities, and contributing to the rescue of Jewish children.

JEWISH CHILDREN REFUGEES, THE OSE, AND THE PHONY WAR

Many of the refugee children who found shelter in officially recognized homes, including Stephan Lewy, were not only Jewish but also foreign. The political situation in Central Europe created waves of Jewish refugees to France in the 1930s, many of whom needed the financial and material support of Jewish aid organizations. The OSE, the primary institution that provided for Jewish children during the war, had also fled persecution

---

[6] Michael R. Marrus and Robert O. Paxton, *Vichy France and the Jews* (Stanford, California: Stanford University Press, 1995), 186.

abroad. Created in 1912 by Jewish intellectuals as a medical-social welfare organization to aid Jewish victims of Tsarist Russia's antisemitism and pogroms, the Société pour la Protection sanitaire des populations juives (Society for the Health Protection of Jewish Populations) soon became the OSE. The organization provided health education and care for mothers and children in the Soviet Union until 1923 when it left the country after increasing political pressure. The OSE immediately reestablished its international offices in Berlin. But with the rise of National Socialism in Germany, the OSE again relocated, this time to Paris in 1933. Consistent with its commitment to aid Jewish populations in distress, the OSE soon opened *colonies de vacances* (vacation colonies) and children's homes in the Paris region to accommodate the influx of needy Jewish refugees from European countries touched by Nazism's antisemitic policies.[7] Some parents placed their children in OSE homes after the family's arrival in France; others tried to save their children from the Nazis by sending them to France on special trains while the adults remained behind. The OSE, working with the Alliance Israélite Universelle, had even managed to secure one thousand entry visas for Jewish children coming from Germany and Austria in December 1938 – no small feat in the atmosphere of prewar immigration restrictions.[8]

Fear of a Nazi invasion during the Phony War prompted the OSE to search for suitable locations for the relocation of its four homes located in the Paris region – two in Montmorency, one in Soissy, and one in Eaubonne. The homes provided shelter and aid to 276 refugee children from Central Europe in 1939. By November of the same year, the OSE had registered 1,105 children whose parents also wished to see their children evacuated from Paris and its environs. Even though the assumption that children would be safer in the provinces than near the nation's capital underlay the move, an OSE report noted, "It is essential to evacuate [the children] not only due to the present circumstances, but more to take them away from poverty, privations, [and] moral and physical decadence."[9] The report cited the cases of children left as virtual orphans with mothers in their country of origin and fathers enlisted in the Foreign Legion as well as children living in abject misery.

---

[7] For a summary of the organizational history of the OSE, see especially Sabine Zeitoun, "L'O.S.E. au secours des enfants juifs," in *Le Sauvetage des enfants juifs de France*, pp. 95–6 and Martine Lemalet, "Présentation," in *Au secours des enfants du siècle*, pp. 8–21.

[8] Vicki Caron, "The Politics of Frustration: French Jewry and the Refugee Crisis in the 1930s," *The Journal of Modern History* 65:2 (June 1993): 334.

[9] Archives Nationales (hereafter AN) F 1a 3706. "Rapport sur l'activité de l'Union OSE en Septembre-Octobre et jusqu'au 15 Novembre 1939," in *Revue "OSE." Organe mensuel de l'Union des Sociétés pour la protection de la santé des populations juives*. 14ème année (November 1939), 7.

"The vast heart of mankind knows no boundaries"   157

The decision to remove urban children from the physical and moral dangers of the city and into the safety of the provinces did not apply only to Jewish children and was not unique to the war years. Since the end of the nineteenth century, private and public charitable organizations funded rural summer camps and individual placements with farm families for working-class and lower-middle-class children throughout France. Based on the common belief that "the demographic future of France rested on the fragile bodies of urban, working-class children – delicate beings whose spiritual and material well-being were seen to be at constant risk, owing to overwork, undernourishment, tuberculosis, and the generally unhealthy climate that was held to prevail in the modern industrial city," the camps provided physical and spiritual nourishment for needy children throughout the years before the Second World War.[10] Catholics, Protestants, Jews, socialists, communists, individual communities, and Republican schools all offered summer programs in the provinces that focused on hygiene and education for urban children. For the OSE's doctors and educators, poor members of the Jewish community could be "emancipated" by changing their hygiene and their clothes, improving their diets, and participating in sports. OSE officials believed that the so-called racial traits of the Jews were really caused by societal factors and that by improving Jews' living conditions, one could also change the public's perception. Sending poor children to the countryside aided in this transformation.[11] Under the Popular Front in the mid-1930s, the various *colonies de vacances* rapidly expanded, and by 1939 nearly 700,000 children spent six to eight weeks in summer camp.[12] The idea of placing children in rural areas for their health and safety during the war thus seemed familiar and even desirable. Furthermore, on August 28, 1939, the prefect of the Seine ordered a meeting of primary school teachers in his department in order to organize the mass evacuation of all Parisian school children to rural districts. Like the evacuation of the residents of Alsace and Lorraine, the transfer of urban children lacked preparation and coordination, and many organizations decided to fend for themselves.

In the atmosphere of confusion and a general children's evacuation in September 1939, the OSE also moved its children in the Paris region to central France. Working in conjunction with the Eclaireurs Israélites (Jewish

---

[10] Laura Lee Downs, *Childhood in the Promised Land: Working-Class Movements and the Colonies de Vacances in France, 1880–1960* (Durham, North Carolina, and London: Duke University Press, 2002), 3.
[11] Ph. E. Landau, "L'Oeuvre de secours aux enfants ou les péripéties d'une organisation juive" in *Au secours des enfants du siècle*, pp. 48–52.
[12] Downs, *Childhood in the Promised Land*, p. 195. Statistics cited in footnote 3.

Scouts) and with the financial aid of Baron Robert de Rothschild and the American Joint Distribution Committee, the OSE first evacuated 230 older children.[13] Younger children, between the ages of 5 and 12, depended entirely upon the OSE for their health and welfare. In order to care for these children, the Jewish aid organization rented three châteaux in the Creuse during the fall of 1939. With a combined capability of housing over 450 children after extensive renovations, the Châteaux of Le Masgelier (in the commune of Grand-Bourg, west of Guéret), Chabannes (near Saint-Pierre-de-Fursac), and Chaumont (between La Serre-Bussière and Mainsat, southwest of Guéret) offered all the presumed physical and moral benefits of a rural location and received the support of local officials in the Creuse as well as the Ministry of Public Health.[14] (See Map 4.) Rural population decline in the 1930s combined with greater national support for *colonies de vacances* most likely contributed to the officials' welcome. Mainsat, a town less than twenty-five miles northwest of the tapestry-making city of Aubusson and near the Château de Chaumont, provides an example. The population decreased between the 1936 census and a 1942 count based on ration cards despite the arrival of refugees in the area, echoing the overall trend in rural areas.[15] The opening of a children's home represented both economic and demographic possibilities for the surrounding communities. Coming just two years after the minister of health passed the first nationwide, comprehensive state regulations for *colonies de vacances*, requests for temporary homes that would provide physical and moral aid for young urban populations also received the republican government's support.

The OSE was not the only Jewish organization to take advantage of the living conditions in the Limousin to create relative havens for children during the Phony War, though it was certainly the largest. In August 1939, La Maison israélite de refuge pour l'enfance (the Jewish Refuge Home for Youth) began searching for an appropriate place to relocate its home as the rumblings of war increased. Located in the Parisian suburb of Neuilly-sur-Seine, the Refuge was created in 1866 for troubled, orphaned, and illegitimate girls and was supported by private donations. After negotiations for a building in Normandy broke down, the Refuge's directors decided the home should be evacuated with the rest of Neuilly's public

[13] AN F 1a 3706. "Rapport sur l'activité de l'Union OSE en Septembre–Octobre et jusqu'au 15 Novembre 1939," p. 8.
[14] Ibid., 8–9.
[15] Archives Départementales de la Haute-Vienne (hereafter ADHV) 185 W 4–5 – Démographie. Dossier Creuse. Ministère des Finances, Service National des Statistiques, Direction Régionale de Limoges (n.d.).

and private schools. Upon learning of the "appalling conditions" in the official evacuation region, however, Refuge officials began looking for an alternative.[16] By chance, the director's wife, Madame Yvonne Aron, learned of an available building in the small Creusoise village of Crocq, approximately sixty kilometers southeast of Guéret. On August 30, Louis Aron left Neuilly for Crocq in order to inspect the property, and he immediately decided that "Les Granges" would be a suitable temporary locale for the Refuge. Formerly an agricultural school and later a convalescent home, the building could be easily converted to house the Jewish girls, and the neighboring town had all the essential shops and services needed to support the institution. As a result, the staff and ninety-six children boarded a train for the Creuse on the evening of September 1, the last day of unrestricted travel before the general military mobilization.

The departments of the Haute-Vienne and the Creuse offered Jewish aid organizations the same safety that government officials sought for the evacuees from Alsace and Lorraine. The French interior would be much safer for children than the industrial, populated, and strategically important Paris region in case of war. In addition, officials believed that the food supply in rural areas would remain more consistent than in urban areas due to close proximity to agricultural products. Empty estates that could be converted to house large groups of children also fit the organizations' needs. The OSE reported that the search for housing in other departments failed to yield results because buildings were either too small or reserved for evacuees from other departments. After all the homes in the Creuse and the Haute-Vienne were fully operational, they cared for an average of 750 children at any given time. The OSE also employed as many as 280 doctors, instructors, social workers, monitors, cooks, maids, gardeners, and other staff members (many of whom were also foreign refugees).[17]

The search for homes that could accommodate groups reflected both the OSE's ideology and pragmatic concerns. Unlike placing children individually with families, group homes allowed the OSE to fulfill its mandate to provide education (including religious education) to children in need. It also prevented

---

[16] *Journal de Louis Aron: Directeur de la Maison israélite de refuge pour l'enfance: Neuilly-sur-Seine 1939, Crocq (Creuse) 1939–1942, Chaumont (Creuse) 1942–1944* edited and presented by Serge Klarsfeld with the collaboration of Annette Zaidman (Paris: Fils et filles des déportés juifs de France and The Beate Klarsfeld Foundation, 1998), 1.

[17] Statistic from Renée Poznanski, *Jews in France during World War II* translated by Nathan Bracher (Hanover and London: University Press of New England for Brandeis University Press in association with the United States Holocaust Memorial Museum, 2001), 129.

the potential problem of affective bonds forming between children and surrogate parents. Furthermore, in the xenophobic atmosphere of the early 1940s, few French families were willing to welcome foreign, Jewish refugees into their homes.[18] Support from local and national authorities also played a role in the OSE's decision to move to the Creuse in 1939. Departmental and local authorities helped locate the three châteaux and demonstrated "great interest" in the organization's activities. With the help of the prefect of the Creuse and the minister of public health, the evacuated children also received free rail transportation from Paris to their new homes.[19]

In addition to authorities' support, the young Jewish refugees in the official homes felt welcomed by the local population who thought little about the children's religion. Lotte Schwartz, the director of the home established at the Château de Chaumont, remembers arriving with her young charges in the rain on the evening of November 7, 1939. After a long day of travel from Paris, two buses met the ninety children at the train station in Guéret, but deep mud prevented the buses from climbing the last hill to the château. Workmen leaving the château after a day of labor drove children by the carload or carried them individually on their shoulders up to the still-unfinished building. Schwartz discovered a building without glass in the windows, without doors and bathrooms, and without a working kitchen or any furniture. Rather than viewing the château's condition as a catastrophe, Schwartz remembers the benefits: "From our arrival, the locals were spontaneously mobilized to help us. Without any political consideration. Far from it. Simply. Humanely."[20] Rather than demonstrating xenophobia or antisemitism, local communities came to the aid of refugee children in need.

Louis Aron also recorded the kindness of strangers upon the Refuge's arrival in the Creuse in September 1939. Due to the military mobilization and requisitions, there were no buses to take the young girls the twelve kilometers from the train station at Létrade to Crocq. Monsieur Aron called the mayor and the gendarmerie in Crocq and shortly thereafter, individuals in cars, delivery trucks, and other small vehicles arrived to shuttle the girls and their belongings to Les Granges, all without accepting any form of payment. That afternoon, local residents appeared with food, mattresses,

---

[18] Renée Poznanski, "De l'action philanthropique à la résistance humanitaire," in *Au secours des enfants du siècle*, pp. 59–60.

[19] AN F 1a 3706. "Rapport sur l'activité de l'Union OSE en Septembre-Octobre et jusqu'au 15 Novembre 1939," *Revue "OSE"* (November 1939): 8.

[20] Archives of the Oeuvre de Secours aux Enfants (hereafter OSE) Box XXXIX – Lotte Schwartz, "La Résistance-autrement ou Pédagogie dans des miroirs," pp. 8–10. (In archival documents produced by French authorities, the director's last name is often spelled Schwarz.)

and blankets and three women prepared dinner that evening for all the new arrivals. In his journal, Aron noted, "all the personnel have tears in their eyes from this unimaginable welcome."[21] Reine (Irène) Paillassou, a schoolteacher in Chabannes, where another OSE home had been opened, recalled the arrival of the Jewish children as unremarkable:

> Throughout the Creuse, we received children from Paris. Because in 1939, when war was declared, many children were evacuated from Paris with their teachers into the provinces. And everywhere, new classrooms were opened to receive these children. So for us, none of this was surprising. We opened classes for refugee children. They were refugee children.[22]

Many inhabitants viewed the children as people in need of help – like many others at the time – and acted accordingly, without asking any questions. Yet there were two major differences between these refugees and the others that flooded the region in September 1939 and again in May 1940: They were children, and they brought significant new income into the region.

The initial preparation for the arrival of hundreds of children provided an economic boom for these rural communities. Louis Aron immediately contacted local artisans and workers to restore Les Granges, which had been uninhabited for three years. He ordered work on kitchen appliances, the installation and repair of toilet facilities, the reconnection of water and electricity, as well as straw for temporary bedding and various food items.[23] The OSE purchased construction material from different businesses in the Creuse in order to make its three châteaux inhabitable. For example, Félix Chevrier, the director at Chabannes, owed 555 francs for plaster purchased from a construction company in La Souterraine and paid Audie Perdon, a local painter from Fursac, 480 francs for his work. He owed an electrician in Guéret over 316 francs for his services.[24] A Monsieur Piscaglia sent a summary of the work he had overseen in the three OSE châteaux in the Creuse. The bill totaled almost 540,000 francs, including 350,000 francs for general repairs to restore proper living conditions, 26,200 francs for the installation of laundry facilities in each home, and 31,000 francs for the kitchens. Another

---

[21] *Journal de Louis Aron* (September 2, 1939), 2–3, quote from p. 5.
[22] *The Children of Chabannes* (New York: Perennial Pictures, 2000). Produced and directed by Lisa Gossels and Dean Weatherell. English translations in film subtitles.
[23] *Journal de Louis Aron* (August 31, 1939): 1.
[24] Some of the purchases were made before Chevrier became the director of Chabannes. A police report in 1940 noted that the former director, Monsieur Pichon, accumulated 60,000 francs of debt that Chevrier inherited. See Archives Départementales de la Creuse (hereafter ADC) 976 W – 65 – Etrangers. La Commissaire de Police Spéciale à Monsieur le Préfet de la Creuse à Guéret (September 20, 1940).

statement from Piscaglia dated November 8, 1939, gives an indication of the kind of work that had to be done. He detailed the purchases and installations done at Le Masgelier: plumbing work included the installation of a hot water heater, boilers, seven "Turkish" toilets, two "English" toilets, various sinks, faucets, and showers totaling almost 45,000 francs; 10,000 francs was spent on electrical needs; 14,000 francs for carpentry work; masonry supplies and workers totaled 29,500 francs; cleaning and painting the château cost 30,400 francs; and the purchase and installation of a brand-new coal-burning stove with two ovens cost the OSE 7,800 francs.[25] Some parents of evacuated children even took up residence in the neighboring small towns, providing additional income for local restaurants, hotels, and landlords.

Established and renovated during the relative calm of the Phony War, the homes had time to create daily routines and relationships before the French defeat in June 1940 and the creation of the Vichy regime. Like other refugees, the inhabitants of the group homes faced increasing shortages, restrictions, and prices for basic foodstuffs during the winter of 1939–40, and the urban dwellers had to adapt to their new rural communities. The sheer numbers of children (approximately a hundred in each home) that needed to be fed, kept warm, and clothed made securing the necessary goods even more difficult, but the material needs could be a source of rapprochement between the communities. Louis Aron began cultivating relationships with local farmers around Crocq the day after his arrival, and the staff frequented the weekly market to buy local farm products. The monthly fair, however, "disappoint[ed] our Parisian girls, expecting more bustle and boutiques."[26] Within a week, girls traveled two kilometers each way everyday to a neighboring village to collect the twenty liters of milk needed to meet daily needs. At the end of September, the girls helped farmers by collecting potatoes and watching cows and sheep while the farmers threshed their crops. Despite the growing relationships and local generosity, Director Aron noted the difficulty in acquiring adequate supplies from the three grocers in Crocq, only used to providing for the town's 800 residents. Aided by locals, Aron established contact with wholesalers and ordered three tons of potatoes, large quantities of dried vegetables and beans, 700 kilograms of pasta, and various canned goods.

[25] All these receipts can be found in Centre de Documentation Juive Contemporaine (hereafter CDJC) CCCLXXIV – 1. Fonds Félix Chevrier – factures. To put the prices in perspective, a cleaning woman at the Château de Chabannes earned 500 francs for a trimester's work, a washerwoman earned 510 francs, and a children's monitor earned almost 600 francs. See CDJC CCCLXXIV – 10. Fonds Félix Chevrier. Salaires Chabannes 3ème Trimestre 1943.

[26] *Journal de Louis Aron* (September 11, 1939): 6.

Yet the food supply remained uncertain because "it is impossible to know which part of the orders will be fulfilled, when they will be fulfilled, or how long it will take to be delivered."[27] Members of the staff also traveled to larger cities in the Creuse to find additional supplies.

While adults concentrated on assuring the food supply, many refugee children attended classes with local students in rural communal schools, setting the tone for wartime relationships and developing friendships. These first encounters also highlighted the differences between the city refugees and the rural natives. The girls at the Refuge attended Crocq's school for the first time on October 2, 1939. The urban refugees quickly recognized their educational superiority over their "country companions," creating a kind of "vanity" that compelled Madame Aron to insist on greater tolerance after overhearing many unkind comments from the Jewish girls.[28] At the Château de Chaumont, the home's director, Lotte Schwartz, also recognized the difference between the refugee and native children in their educational performance. The local schoolteachers considered the students to be "phenomenal," but Lotte Schwartz felt differently:

> They are neither more intelligent nor more gifted than their local friends. But they lived in cities, almost all of them speak two languages, and the adversity that they have endured – bullying [*brimades*], escapes, sometimes the destruction of families – taught them to react quickly. And then here, at the château, they are surrounded with books, we talk about all kinds of things. . . . How can peasant children who never leave their homes, who often miss school to help in the fields, how can these children have the same rate [of learning] as ours?[29]

Despite the differences in their educational development, the two groups of students soon became friends, and Schwartz recalled the young refugees staying in town for lunch with native families or helping to collect apples on a schoolmate's farm.

At Chabannes, it was the rural students who, at first, felt superior to the predominantly foreign refugees with their poor French. Renée Paillassou who, with her sister Irène, taught all the children in Chabannes, recorded the events of the first day of integrated classes, including the native students' laughter when a refugee struggled to express himself in the new language. Understanding the children's reaction but wishing to prevent a division between the two groups, Mademoiselle Paillassou responded sternly, creating a strong impression: "the children

---

[27] Ibid. (November 24, 1939), 12.
[28] Ibid. (October 2, 1939), 10.
[29] OSE Box XXXIX – Lotte Schwartz, p. 60. (Copy of letter written in October 1941.)

understood – At that precise minute, they felt their cruelty and the distress of their new schoolmates." She congratulated the new students on the remarkable accomplishment of learning French so quickly and asked the old students to imagine having to suddenly leave their homes for a foreign country or being laughed at by urban students. Her lecture worked: Instead of noticing differences, the students became friends who helped each other with their studies.[30] The refugee children soon performed well in their classes and one classmate from Chabannes remained impressed with "[the refugees'] way of studying . . . their seriousness" over fifty years later.[31]

Thus during the period of the Phony War, residents of the Creuse – both young and old – became habituated to life with the Jewish refugee children. The three OSE homes in the Creuse were operational by the end of November 1939, and the organization continued to open homes in the Limousin throughout the war. In Limoges, the OSE supported the Pouponnière, a nursery for infants, beginning in January 1940 (the everyday operation of the nursery was transferred to the OSE in March 1942) and opened the Internat (boarding school) for teenagers engaged in professional training in December 1940. In the rural Haute-Vienne, the aid organization also converted châteaux into children's homes including Montintin for boys (opened in June 1940 in the commune of Château-Chervix), Le Couret for girls (transferred from Mas-Jambost to La Jonchère in the summer of 1941), and Poulouzat for preschoolers, which opened in the commune of Condat-sur-Vienne, just outside Limoges, during the summer of 1942.[32]

Even though most of these homes were established during the Phony War under a republican government, it is important to remember that this period was one of the most inhospitable eras in French refugee policy. Although the majority of the children in these homes were foreign refugees, they were also children whose association with an aid organization brought income into small, rural communities plagued by depopulation. Familiarity with *colonies de vacances* also helped facilitate acceptance of temporary homes for children. The Phony War's end, the German Occupation of the northern zone, and Vichy's antisemitic National Revolution would all affect the Jewish children in the homes, but in ways that may be considered surprising.

---

[30] CDJC CCCLXXIV – 1. Fonds Félix Chevrier – Album.
[31] Collette Dony-Pascal in *The Children of Chabannes*.
[32] See the reports from June 1942 on each individual home in the Haute-Vienne found in ADHV 985 W–485 – Israélites français et étrangers.

THE HOMES UNDER VICHY: COMPLICITY WITH THE NATIONAL REVOLUTION

All French residents made accommodations in their daily lives in order to get by during the difficult war years, making them complicit with some of Vichy's actions and ideologies. Jews were no exception. Accommodation may mean an individual accepts the regime, or it may be employed as one of many survival tactics. Philippe Burrin's concept of accommodation helps explain why some French chose to associate with the Nazis during the Occupation. He argues that practical considerations, structural needs, political aspirations, and opportunism all influenced one's decision to make accommodations to the occupiers.[33] Most Jewish organizations in the Limousin had limited direct contact with the occupiers; however, they did make accommodations with the collaborating Vichy government, and their reasons for doing so varied. Marion A. Kaplan's study of Jewish daily life in Germany under the Nazi regime demonstrates how, "[i]n the pursuit of pragmatic solutions, even in extraordinary times, contemporaries may have missed or misread the danger signals in their daily lives."[34] The same may be said of organizations such as the OSE after the institution of the Vichy regime. These groups were complicit in that they were "participating in the consequences of actions that give rise to certain results."[35] By making accommodations to the tenets of the National Revolution, especially with regard to work, Jewish aid organizations helped uphold the regime's legitimacy and facilitated the marginalization of Jews until the dangers became manifestly clear in August 1942. Complicity, however, does not automatically imply intentionality or complete acceptance. Even though these aid organizations were passively supporting the Vichy regime, they were also actively participating in trying to protect Jewish communities caught in a no-win situation.

What was supposed to be a temporary evacuation to protect children from bombardments and fighting around Paris soon took on a more permanent aspect as German troops occupied the country's northern and coastal regions in the spring and summer of 1940. The Vichy government's promulgation of its own Jewish Statutes further changed the political

---

[33] Philippe Burrin, *France under the Germans: Collaboration and Compromise* translated by Janet Lloyd (New York: The New Press, 1996), 460–4.

[34] Marion A. Kaplan, *Between Dignity and Despair: Jewish Life in Nazi Germany* (New York and Oxford: Oxford University Press, 1998), 230.

[35] Gail Kligman, *The Politics of Duplicity: Controlling Reproduction in Ceausescu's Romania* (Berkeley, Los Angeles, and London: University of California Press, 1998), 14.

situation in France. Despite these changes, the OSE continued to open additional homes in the Limousin, but the goals and objectives of the homes in the unoccupied zone changed. No longer were the homes to be merely an expanded and extended *colonie de vacances*. In addition to housing, educating, and feeding the children, the OSE began to focus on preparing children "for the life of work that awaits them."[36] In order to achieve this goal, the OSE opened workshops in some of its children's homes and provided instruction in various artisanal trades starting in 1941. At Chabannes, students older than age 14 received three and a half hours of instruction in leather working every other day.[37] By the summer of 1942, Montintin had thirty-five student apprentices in its carpentry workshop, while another fourteen students learned how to mend shoes.[38] Furthermore, thirty girls at Le Couret learned sewing skills in order to prepare them for careers as seamstresses.

The children's preparation for these careers had both pragmatic and ideological justifications, but it also highlights the OSE's complicity in the marginalization of Jews under Vichy. First and foremost, the OSE wanted "to prepare children for life by giving them a trade [*métier*]."[39] Such goals were consistent with reformers' desires to integrate Jews into French society articulated during the interwar years. It also fit neatly with Vichy's emphasis on work as a cornerstone of the National Revolution. Aware of the increasing circumscription of Jewish participation in the French economy and the limited number of occupations still available to Jews after the promulgation of the Jewish Statutes, officials chose programs that fit within these restrictions.

The OSE worked with a Jewish professional education and retraining organization, the ORT (Organisation Reconstruction Travail), in order to

---

[36] OSE Box XXV – Dossier 1. "Rapport sur l'activité de l'Union OSE pour les mois de mars, avril et mai 1941," p. 3.

[37] CDJC CCCLXXIV – 10. Rapport Moral. Chabannes, St. Pierre-de-Fursac (October 31, 1942).

[38] ADHV 985 W–485 – Israélites français et étrangers. "Rapport sur le Centre d'apprentissage et d'éducation du Château de Montintin" (June 22, 1942). The OSE reported in early 1943 that it had space for sixty students in the carpentry workshop and thirty in the shoe mending shop at Le Masgelier and thirty places in the leather workshop at Chabannes. See microfilmed YIVO Record Group 210, Microfilm 490 – Union Générale des Israélites de France Records, 1940–1944. Held by the United States Holocaust Memorial Museum (hereafter USHMM) archives, reel 74 Section 98.1. "Rapport sur l'activité de la 3ème Direction durant le mois de Janvier 1943" and "Rapport sur l'activité de la 3ème Direction durant le mois de février 1943."

[39] OSE Box XXV – Dossier 1. "Rapport sur l'activité de l'Union OSE pour les mois de mars, avril et mai 1941," p. 3.

"The vast heart of mankind knows no boundaries" 167

establish workshops in the châteaux. Russian Jewish intellectuals and industrialists created the ORT in 1880 in St. Petersburg to aid their community. Restrictions on places of residence and professions left many Russian Jews in poverty. Designed to raise funds and retrain Jews for artisanal and agricultural jobs, the ORT created professional schools and model farms. After the First World War, the ORT expanded its work to include needy Jews in Eastern Europe, and the French branch of the international organization opened in 1921. The French ORT was originally intended to raise funds for projects in Eastern Europe, but after Hitler's rise to power and the subsequent wave of Jewish refugees in France, the organization started its own professional courses for adults in 1934. During the war, the ORT continued its work in training children and adults for farm work and manual labor.

The châteaux thus provided practical training for the children seeking refuge there, but with an ideological overtone. Joseph Koenig, the leather working instructor at Chabannes, explained his job in the following terms: "My goal is not only to form good leather workers, having fine taste, complete perfection, and a deep understanding of their craft, but also and above all, to form courageous and conscious workers, to inculcate in them a love and respect for Work, and the responsibility of their task."[40] In addition to preparing "thousands of children for a difficult life," OSE officials wanted "these workshops [to] contribute to the economic life of our Homes."[41] With monthly expenses totaling 1,200,000 francs, the OSE used the workshops to help meet their daily material needs.[42] For example, students in the advanced carpentry class at Montintin made desks, chairs, and tables for the homes' classrooms and workshops as well as armoires. A second group of students made beds destined for the OSE's nursery in Limoges, the Pouponnière, while beginners learned basic skills by constructing stools.[43] With the extreme

---

[40] CDJC CCCLXXIV – 1. Fonds Félix Chevrier – Album.
[41] OSE Box XXXIX – Ruth Lambert. "Note sur l'activité de l'OSE en France de juin 1940 à avril 1943 (zone non occupée)" (June 1943), 2, 4.
[42] This budget included all of OSE's activities and not only the children's homes. OSE Box XXV – Dossier 1. "Six mois de Travail Janvier–Juin 1942" (July 1942), 27. The money to cover the expenses came from the American Joint Distribution Committee, a subsidy from the Grand Rabbin de France, and aid from Switzerland. In 1941, the OSE reported that the American Joint Distribution Committee covered 90 percent of its costs. See OSE Box XXV – Dossier 1. "Rapport sur l'activité de l'Union OSE pour les mois de juin, juillet, et août 1941," p. 14.
[43] YIVO UGIF Records at the USHMM, reel 73 section 97.1, p. 916. Union Générale des Israélites de France, 2ème Direction "Travail" Section ORT, Rapport mensuel (July 1942), p. 14.

shortages of shoes, students in the shoe-mending workshop at Montintin provided the valuable service of resoling worn shoes from OSE homes while also learning to make made-to-order and orthopedic shoes.[44] When the necessary materials were available, the girls at Le Couret sewed clothes for themselves and other residents of OSE homes; they also mended items.[45] Leather goods manufactured at Chabannes were "known in all the surroundings" and the items also contributed to the well-being of the French nation as they were often sold at charity fundraisers or to raise money for prisoners of war.[46]

Children in all of the group homes in the Limousin helped garden plots of land, which had a practical, appreciable application in their daily lives as well as an ideological justification under Vichy's "return to the earth" program. First and foremost, the gardens provided fresh vegetables to supplement meals in the homes. Louis Aron described the meals at Crocq as sufficient, but consisting primarily of rice, pasta, and potatoes. Homegrown vegetables such as lettuce, radishes, and cabbage provided a little variety in the menu. Gardens supplied the OSE homes with food as well. Children at Le Masgelier, Montintin, and Le Couret each cultivated two hectares, while those at Chaumont had one and a half hectares under their responsibility.[47] Norbert Bikales, a refugee from Germany, remembers "a little garden in which we worked and we grew some vegetables and some fruits" at Chabannes, and the home's director reported that children usually spent two hours a day engaged in agricultural work.[48] Lotte Schwartz wrote of Chaumont's cook's pride in a typical meal: potatoes in a mushroom sauce, red beet salad, and *fromage blanc* with blueberry sauce for dessert. The potatoes and beets came from the home's garden while the children collected the mushrooms and blueberries in the surrounding forest, providing a homegrown and inexpensive meal.[49] While providing

---

[44] OSE Box XXV – Dossier 1. "Rapport sur l'activité de l'Union OSE pour les mois de mars, avril et mai 1941," p. 4.

[45] YIVO UGIF Records at the USHMM, reel 73 section 97.1, p. 916. UGIF, 2ème Direction "Travail" Section ORT, Rapport mensuel (July 1942), 14 and Mia Amalia Kanner and Eve Rosenzweig Kugler, *Shattered Crystals* (New York, London, Jerusalem: C.I.S. Publishers, 1997), 211.

[46] OSE Box XXV – Dossier 1. "Rapport sur l'activité de l'Union OSE pour les mois de juin, juillet et août 1941," p. 5.

[47] OSE Box XXV – Dossier 1. "Six Mois de Travail Janvier-Juin 1942" (July 1942), 6–8.

[48] Norbert Bikales quote from *The Children of Chabannes*. Félix Chevrier's report contained in ADC 976 W – 219 – Rapports moraux sur les maisons d'enfants israélites. "Rapport moral sur les TE et les enfants hébergés dans les centres de l'UGIF" (October 12, 1943).

[49] OSE Box XXXIX – Lotte Schwartz, p. 63.

"The vast heart of mankind knows no boundaries" 169

FIGURE 5. Jewish refugee children working at Le Masgelier. A group of children push wheelbarrows on the grounds of the OSE home at Le Masgelier (Creuse). Photo credit: USHMM, courtesy of Israel Lichtenstein.

much-needed additional food, the gardens also served the purpose of giving children "an agricultural apprenticeship," or at the very least fulfilled the goal of "habituating the children to working the earth."[50] As one of the younger children at Chaumont, Eric Thorn remembers being responsible for picking potato bugs off the plants.[51] Unlike the workshops reserved for older children, children of all ages could participate in aspects of maintaining the garden from planting to harvesting and everything in between. (See Figure 5.)

OSE officials explicitly linked refugee children's agricultural work to Vichy's moral agenda. A report from Le Masgelier in 1942 noted, "Considering that the return to the earth is one of the most important problems at the current time, the UGIF's Third Direction [the OSE] recommended in all of its children's homes, and particularly at Le Masgelier, the organization of large-scale gardening work." The report went on to say that the home's children had been responsible for clearing and planting two and a

---

[50] OSE Box III (reel 16). "Note sur le développement de l'activité de la 3ème Direction pendant la période avril-mi-mai," (May 12, 1942), 3 and OSE Box XXV – Dossier 1. "Rapport sur l'activité de l'Union OSE pour les mois de juin, juillet, et août 1941," p. 2.
[51] Eric P. Thorn, email to author, July 26, 2000.

half hectares and that their physical labor was supplemented with courses on botany, agricultural chemistry, and meteorology.[52] Agricultural training fit within the OSE's larger purpose of preparing children for a life of work, echoing Vichy's commitment to a National Revolution partially based on strong work ethics. "The cornerstone of the whole education system," explained an official OSE report, "was the preparation of children for a life of healthy labor. By starting with children's gardens, continuing with schools, and finishing with professional workshops for the oldest, the OSE created for the children, according to their age, the possibilities for work."[53] Thus the OSE was performing a vital function and contributing to the rebirth and regeneration of France. On a less abstract level, children in the homes also helped neighboring peasants with their farming chores. Félix Chevrier (the only non-Jewish director of a Jewish children's home) encouraged the children at Chabannes to spend their free time helping their neighbors, for which he "received daily the peasants' thanks, who are very grateful to me for the contribution of this volunteer labor."[54] With demands for increased agricultural production, requisitions, and labor shortages, the Jewish refugees provided valuable, tangible aid.

However, the OSE failed to fully recognize or acknowledge the incompatibility of *Jewish* labor with the ideals of the National Revolution. While "Work" formed an important part of the government's philosophy, so did antisemitism, including the exclusion of Jews from the French economy and culture. Although Jewish organizations rejected Vichy's antisemitism, by advocating preparation for a life of labor, the OSE seemed to accept the subordinate role of Jews in the "new" France, where they could only participate in menial jobs or manual labor. Hillel J. Kieval argues that the OSE and ORT's commitment to providing professional training for children demonstrated the organizations' internalization of "Vichy's traditionalist social critique."[55] Furthermore, according to Kieval, by working to train children for the new economic realities of Vichy's vision for France, aid organizations failed to recognize the Nazis' ultimate aim of a "Final Solution

---

[52] ADC 976 W – 118 – Maisons israélites de refuge. "Rapport Moral sur l'Activité de la Maison d'Enfants du Château du Masgelier" (November 5, 1942).

[53] OSE Box I (reel 15). "Rapport sur l'activité de l'OSE dans l'ancienne zone libre de 1940 à 1943," p. 3.

[54] ADC 976 W – 219 – Rapports moraux sur les maisons d'enfants israélites. "Rapport trimestriel sur les étrangers incorporés – 4e trimestre 1942" (March 22, 1943). I have found no complaints about the children's work on the farms although farmers did turn away other urban workers requisitioned to perform agricultural labor due to their lack of training.

[55] Kieval, "Legality and Resistance in Vichy France," p. 364.

to the Jewish Question."⁵⁶ In the end it took the deportation of men, women, and children (including children in OSE homes) in August 1942 to drastically change the views of many Jewish organizations. Renée Poznanski expresses a different point of view when she argues that the OSE recognized the dilemma, but as an apolitical philanthropic organization, it tried to ameliorate the living conditions of Jews faced with antisemitism and xenophobia without trying to understand the basis for anti-Jewish sentiment or to change the system. For Poznanski, the organization did not try to rebel against the government; it just tried to survive and when survival meant acting illegally, the OSE changed its tactics.⁵⁷ Whether the OSE accepted Vichy's ideals implicitly or made a conscious decision to make accommodations that fit the principles of the National Revolution, OSE officials believed in the rule of law and worked within the system for at least two years. Yet both interpretations do not fully explain why OSE reports continued to emphasize the importance of training the refugee children for a life of agricultural labor even after Vichy's policies clearly shifted from exclusion to deportation in August 1942.

To fully understand how Jewish aid organizations seemingly internalized the Vichy regime's work ideals requires placing their attitudes within broader contexts. Commitment to work was not a new concept for the aid associations. Dedication to retraining and teaching Jews "practical" skills predated the war years, as evidenced by the ORT's decades of existence and the OSE's stated goals for the children they helped. Emigration to Palestine, one way for Jews to escape European persecution, also required strong, healthy workers prepared for agricultural labor. Several French Jewish leaders and Third Republic government officials had also advocated agricultural settlements as a potential solution to the refugee crisis of the 1930s.⁵⁸ Psychologically, it was easier to adapt to the changed circumstances and maintain one's sense of dignity and worth than it was to grasp the implications of deportation. Jewish reluctance and inability to interpret the signs of genocide are well documented throughout Europe during the Second World War. Furthermore, the Vichy regime sent mixed messages about Jews' importance in supporting agriculture, which offered a glimmer of hope to people seeking any possible option for surviving the war years. The required, official reports also provided a cover for the OSE's active

---

⁵⁶ Ibid., 346, 354.
⁵⁷ Poznanski, "De l'action philanthropique à la résistance humanitaire," in *Au secours des enfants du siecle*, edited by Martine Lemalet (Paris: Nil Editions, 1993), 63.
⁵⁸ Caron, "The Politics of Frustration," pp. 336–9.

clandestine rescue work. Choosing to work within the system demonstrates organizations' simultaneous complicity and duplicity.

Despite the OSE's belief that the agricultural training of its children could provide them with a productive future, Jewish participation in agriculture in general raised concerns for Vichy officials. At the end of 1940, police surveillance of cafés and restaurants frequented by peasants in the Haute-Vienne revealed the "unhappiness" of the area's rural natives caused by Jewish purchases of farmland. The peasants resented the Jews who allegedly purchased land at exorbitant prices despite the fact that they had no farming knowledge or experience in running a farm.[59] A year later, Vichy officials also voiced their concerns about Jews practicing agricultural professions:

> It is not without peril, in the eyes of the Council, to disperse into the countryside under the guise of a "return to the earth," a population almost exclusively urban and commercial, who from its distant past until today, even in Palestine despite Zionists' efforts, and in eastern France where it has lived in certain villages for centuries, has always demonstrated itself to be radically inept at working in the fields.

In addition to contending that the "urban" Jews could never learn "rural" farming skills, officials believed Jews did not exhibit the proper national and moral traits essential for the nation's rebirth and feared that Jews on farms would contribute to black market activities.[60] Drawing almost exclusively on stereotypes, these officials sought to prevent more Jews from invading and corrupting rural areas.

Notwithstanding the government's antisemitic statements, the OSE's determination to provide agricultural training for children appears less peculiar when one examines Vichy's official stance as articulated in its laws. Despite some officials' concerns and objections, Vichy law did allow Jews to farm under certain conditions. Required to hold a special card authorizing them to practice an agricultural profession, Jews with five years previous agricultural experience or having completed an agricultural apprenticeship could work on farms. Under no conditions could they own property that they themselves did not directly maintain and inhabit.[61] Designed to prevent

---

[59] ADHV 185 W 1–45 – Rapports du préfet de la Haute-Vienne au ministère de l'Intérieur. Le Commissaire Central à Monsieur le Préfet de la Haute-Vienne (December 11, 1940), 2.

[60] AN AJ 38 122 dossier 33. Note. Séance du 6 décembre 1941. Signed by: Alfred Forche, Vice-Président du Conseil d'Etat, Président de la Commission; L. Canet, Conseiller d'Etat, Rapporteur; H. Giraudon, Secrétaire de la Commission.

[61] AN AJ 38 122 dossier 33. "Projet de décret en Conseil d'Etat pris en vertu de l'article 4 de la loi du 2/6/1941 réglementant l'accès des juifs aux professions agricoles et assimilées" and "Accès des juifs à la terre."

"*The vast heart of mankind knows no boundaries*" 173

Jews from economically benefiting from others' work on farms, the law left a clear opening for Jewish aid organizations that provided the necessary training. Again, the justification proved practical and ideological. The ORT hoped to place a thousand Jews between the ages of 18 and 40 on farms in order to "contribute to the supplying of the country" while also "aiding the largest possible number of needy Jews." Furthermore, these apprenticeships would "permit those involved to fulfill their legal work obligation with a large profit for themselves, for the professional stabilization [*assainissement*] of the Jewish Community, and for the country's economy." The ORT did not fail to mention the considerable aid that such internships would also provide for French peasants, hoping to make Jews invaluable assets.[62]

Beyond laws and the appeals of Jewish organizations, local governments required Jews to work in agriculture. In the Creuse, the Agricultural Labor Utilization Commission determined that farmers needed an additional 3,000 agricultural workers in 1942.[63] As a result of similar shortages throughout unoccupied France, René Bousquet, Vichy's chief of police, ordered that "inactive" Jews be "put at the disposal of rural service collective work bodies" that July.[64] Just days after Bousquet's requirement, the sous-prefect of Rochechouart (Haute-Vienne) reported that peasants dismissed many Jews conscripted to work on farms due to their inaptitude.[65] The work of the OSE and the ORT with Jewish children would prepare them for these agricultural jobs and hopefully prevent future dismissals of Jewish laborers.

Additionally, the legal status of Jewish aid organizations encouraged the development and maintenance of such programs. The Vichy government gave the OSE and other organizations little reason to believe that their work was ultimately futile. In the first year of the Nazi Occupation, Jewish social service agencies consolidated their efforts, a situation that was formalized by the establishment of the Union Générale des Israélites de France (UGIF) in November 1941. Intended to "assure Jewish representation to the authorities, notably for the questions of assistance, planning, and social rehabilitation," the UGIF reported to the General Commissariat for Jewish

---

[62] YIVO UGIF records held by the USHMM. Reel 73 section 97.4, p. 1025. "Les Travailleurs Juifs à la Terre."
[63] ADC 25 W – 44 – Réquisition de main d'oeuvre agricole. Commission d'Utilisation de la Main-d'œuvre agricole (March 28, 1942).
[64] Ibid., Le Secrétaire Général à la Police à Messieurs les Préfets zone sud (July 21, 1942).
[65] ADHV 185 W 1–58 – Sous-Préfecture de Rochechouart. Rapport Mensuel (July 24, 1942).

Questions and received orders from the government.[66] All Jews in France were required to belong to the UGIF, and a law passed in 1943 required Jews to pay a compulsory tax (360 francs per person in the southern zone) to the organization in order to cover the expenses incurred by its aid projects.[67] As of March 23, 1942, the ORT became the UGIF's Second Direction labeled "Work," while the OSE comprised the Third Direction, "Health."[68] No longer allowed to exist outside the authority of the UGIF, Louis Aron's Jewish Refuge was also assimilated into the Third Direction. The incorporated organizations remained largely autonomous although they legally ceased to exist as individual entities.

Despite divisions in Jewish circles concerning the institution of the UGIF and objections to such an organization, all Jews in France had little choice but to accept the new arrangement. Dependent upon the UGIF for official recognition and funding, the OSE conformed by sending detailed monthly reports and used the organization to work with the government to liberate Jewish children from internment camps and for emigration purposes. Jewish organizations worked within the structures created by the Vichy regime and had no way of knowing that the increasingly restrictive measures would facilitate the implementation of the Nazis' "Final Solution" in France. The OSE, like many other Jewish aid organizations, made concessions to the Vichy government that allowed them to exist and to fulfill their mandate of helping Jews in need.

When Vichy began rounding up Jews for deportation in August 1942, the group homes provided certain advantages and disadvantages for the children living there. The arrests of children in the early morning hours of August 26 marked the beginning of a shift from OSE's legal existence to a period of increasing clandestine and illegal activity. The organization's officials now saw the homes that had managed to shelter and protect the children by

---

[66] Text of law instituting the UGIF on November 29, 1941, can be found in *Les Juifs sous l'occupation: Recueil des textes officiels français et allemands 1940/1944* (Paris: CDJC, 1982), 102–3. On the creation and role of the UGIF in Vichy politics, see for example Jacques Adler, *The Jews of Paris and the Final Solution: Communal Response and Internal Conflicts, 1940–1944* (New York and Oxford: Oxford University Press, 1987), chapter 5: "The Establishment of the Union Générale des Israélites de France: September 1941 to January 1942"; Michael R. Marrus and Robert O. Paxton, *Vichy France and the Jews* (Stanford, California: Stanford University Press, 1995), 109–12; Poznanski, *Jews in France*, pp. 131–5; and Maurice Rajsfus, *Des Juifs dans la Collaboration: L'UGIF (1941–1944)* (Paris: Etudes et Documentation Internationales, 1980).

[67] See Poznanski, *Jews is France during World War II*, pp. 132–3, 338–40.

[68] UGIF in the southern zone was divided into seven sections: (1) "Family" for aid and assistance to Jews, (2) "Work," (3) "Health," (4) "Youth," (5) "Refugees," (6) "Emigration," and (7) "Schooling."

caring for their daily physical and psychological needs as a potential trap. The rescue of Jewish children from Nazi policies through emigration was always a stated goal of the organization, and over 250 children in OSE homes immigrated to the Americas in 1941 and 1942. The events of the summer of 1942 hastened other forms of rescue. Perhaps the organization's commitment to preparing children for a future in France through work and education lulled it into a false sense of security; perhaps it was the mixed signals received from the Vichy government itself. Yet it became clear after August 1942 that the hundred children in each home had become easy targets for raids and arrests.

Accordingly, the OSE decided to disperse the children gradually by placing them with local families, with non-Jewish organizations, or through illegal border crossings into Switzerland and Spain. At Chabannes, the Paillassou sisters enlisted the aid of their father, a former gendarme, to help prevent future arrests. The father asked a colleague to alert him of impending actions, which he did. When warnings came, the older children disappeared into the woods while village residents took in others.[69] Louis Aron procured extra ration cards for hidden children due to the local mayor's incompetence, remained informed of potential arrests from friends in the region, and asked the home's handyman to help find lodgings for the girls in case they were needed. Monsieur Marchand, the man who agreed to help, "is Aryan, known in the area, very resourceful, and will get along better with the owners than Israelites."[70] By the beginning of 1944, all but three of the OSE homes had been closed and all the homes disappeared by February with the exception of Louis Aron's Refuge at Chaumont. In little over a year, the stable daily lives of children in these homes lost all sense of normality.

When looking for people to fill deportation quotas, the Vichy government knew where the foreign Jewish refugees were supposed to be and often acted on this knowledge. After allowing the liberation of more than 500 children from French concentration camps between November 1941 and May 1942 (mainly through the work of the OSE), Vichy officials required families to be reunited for deportation in 1942. The prefect of the Haute-Vienne received specific instructions from Vichy on August 31: "In order to not separate parents and children, we inform you that it is advisable to send under escort

---

[69] Irène and Renée Paillassou, "L'école laïque protectrice des enfants juifs dans la Creuse: Chabannes," in *Le Sauvetage des Enfants Juifs de France*, pp. 143–4. Yad Vashem recognized the Paillassou sisters as "Righteous Gentiles."
[70] *Journal de Louis Aron* (April 23, 1944), 170.

before September 2 to the camp at Rivesaltes Jewish children currently in colonies in your department." An attached list demanded the immediate dispatch of sixteen girls from Le Couret, eleven children at Montintin, and five boys from the Pouponnière in Limoges.[71] After the arrest of dozens of foreign children older than age 16 and staff members in the OSE homes on August 26, the homes' directors tried their best to prevent the deportation of any more children. In the Creuse, thirty-three children in the homes were ordered to join their parents at Rivesaltes by September 2. Yet when the gendarmes came to take the children at Chabannes into custody, none of them could be found. A local doctor had provided the youngest children with medical certificates stating they were too sick to travel, two were sent to Limoges, Félix Chevrier denied any knowledge of students whose names had been misspelled, and another staff member had taken the remaining children for a walk in the woods.[72] The local gendarme's report found that Chevrier, who had been notified of the impending action, had done nothing to stop the escape of the children, but he had also done nothing to encourage it.[73] The children had been saved.

Between 1940 and 1942, Jewish aid organizations in the Limousin demonstrated passive complicity with the Vichy regime by making accommodations that assured their survival. Adherence to traditional ideas about work and Jewish labor continued even after Vichy police and gendarmes began arresting Jews for deportation in August 1942. This overlap in ideals should not be considered collaboration, however. Throughout the war, organizations like the OSE and the ORT saw the protection of children as their primary purpose. To that end, they took whatever steps they saw as necessary to ensure their continued existence and to try to prevent politics from overly intruding into the children's lives. Jewish leaders had no way of knowing that the ultimate goal of Jewish isolation would be deportation and extermination. Aid organizations remained outwardly complicit with Vichy's antisemitic policies; however, they were also developing duplicitous relationships with the region's natives. Built over a period of years, such relationships reveal the importance of material issues in creating bonds, the paradoxes inherent in assessing public opinion, and the extent of rural antisemitism during the war.

---

[71] ADHV 185 W1–149 – Instructions, reglementation à appliquer aux Israélites naturalisés et étrangers rentrés en France après le 1er janvier 1936. Intérieur Police 9e bureau à Préfets zone libre (August 31, 1942).

[72] *The Children of Chabannes* and Jean Michaud, "L'Administration creusoise et les Juifs," in *Le Sauvetage des Enfants Juifs de France*, p. 63.

[73] Michaud, "L'Administration creusoise," p. 63.

ANTISEMITISM, PUBLIC OPINION, AND MATERIAL SHORTAGES

In spite of changes such as the Vichy regime's establishment, the UGIF's creation, and the OSE's official dissolution, daily life in the homes stayed fairly constant for the children before the arrests in the summer of 1942. Children remained largely unaware of the details of Vichy's systematic persecution, often protected by the adults around them. Stephan Lewy believes that the rural town's isolation kept the students from receiving much political news or news about the extent of antisemitic measures in the northern, occupied zone. He remembers feeling protected while at Chabannes and focusing on the desire to survive the daily material battles with hunger and the cold rather than fighting antisemitism. It was not until he reestablished contact with his parents after they had immigrated to the United States that he began to understand the situation by reading his parents' concern and urgency in their letters.[74] Joseph Lerman also spent time in the OSE homes at Montintin and Chabannes and recalls, "As a child, you don't know what's going on. You know you were a Jew, but you couldn't fight back."[75] For Lerman, whose family had moved from town to town in occupied and unoccupied France before Joseph went to the OSE homes, the châteaux finally represented safety.[76] Very few children in the homes of the Creuse and Haute-Vienne remember overt displays of antisemitism on the part of the locals. Instead, they remember the daily routines of schooling, working in the gardens or workshops, and going in search of food supplies in the surrounding forests or neighboring farms.

The Vichy regime and its attitudes toward Jews did little to affect the relationships between the Limousin natives and the Jewish refugees living in homes in the area. State-sponsored antisemitism made few inroads in the rural Creuse and Haute-Vienne, and the anti-Jewish statutes did not prevent the group homes from receiving the support they needed to survive. Yvonne Labrousse, a native of Chabannes, and René Castille, a historian of the Creuse, believe that the welcome children received cannot be explained by the local population's religious convictions. There was no Jewish community in the Creuse before the war and, unlike other regions, there were no Protestants who felt a kind of kinship of persecution. In fact, Labrousse explains, "This part of the country is not religious. It's been that way for a long time since the masons of the Creuse went to Paris and brought back

---

[74] Stephan Lewy, interview with the author (August 14, 2000).
[75] Joseph Lerman, interview with the author (July 27, 2000).
[76] Joseph Lerman, videotaped testimony, USHMM RG-50.431*365. Oral History Collection of the Holocaust Documentation and Education Center, Inc. (March 7, 1996).

these ideas. We're not religious here."[77] Labrousse's opinion expresses a historical fact: At the end of the war, the Catholic Church sent missionaries to the Creuse where 214 of the department's 257 parishes had no resident priest and where less than 1 percent of men in nearly half of the department's cantons attended church.[78] Moral considerations inspired by Church teachings thus cannot explain the acceptance of young, persecuted Jewish refugees.

For Georges Loinger, an OSE educator, it was the locals' "republican" disposition that prompted them to reject Jewish persecution. A report commissioned by the Renseignements généraux (General Information Bureau) during the war examined the historical and contemporary political situation in the Creuse. In the 1936 election, 61 percent of voters in the department cast their ballots in favor of the Popular Front coalition of socialists and communists.[79] The investigators noted that despite the "moderately advanced ideas" of the people as demonstrated by their tendency to vote for leftist parties, the department remained calm. Peasants and civil servants did not agitate. In fact, many peasants supported Marshal Pétain and his revalorization of agricultural products.[80] Even with previously strong support of republicanism, most Creuse residents did not openly criticize the government for its treatment of Jews. The prefect noted occasional communist and Gaullist propaganda as well as *growing* expressions of antisemitism. The leftist tradition in the department may have encouraged some of the region's natives to act in opposition to the right-wing Vichy regime, but it cannot serve as a complete explanation for the treatment of young refugees collectively housed in the Limousin.

---

[77] Opinions expressed in *The Children of Chabannes*. Limore Yagil explores the role of religion, among other factors, in the rescue of Jews in the Limousin in "Typologie de la résistance sans armes et de l'aide aux juifs en Limousin," *Revue d'histoire de la Shoah: le monde juif* 172 (May–August 2001). On the role of Protestant regions in welcoming and rescuing Jews, see especially Philip Hallie, *Lest Innocent Blood Be Shed: The Story of the Village of Le Chambon and How Goodness Happened There* (New York: Harper and Row, 1979) and François Boulet, "Etrangers et Juifs en Haute-Loire de 1936 à 1944." *Cahiers de la Haute-Loire: Revue d'études locales* (1992): 301–50.

[78] See Laird Boswell, *Rural Communism in France, 1920–1939* (Ithaca, New York, and London: Cornell University Press, 1998), 94. The Church also sent missionaries to Limoges and other parts of the rural Limousin. For a discussion of the de-Christianization of the region in the nineteenth century, see Alain Corbin, *Archaisme et modernité en Limousin au XIXe siècle 1845–1880*, 2 vols. (Paris: Editions Marcel Rivière et Cie, 1975).

[79] ADC 7 W – 10. Police. Ministère de l'Intérieur, Direction générale de la police nationale (Direction des Renseignements généraux), Fichier départemental de la Creuse. (n.d. [after February 1942]). On communism in the Creuse, see Boswell, *Rural Communism in France*.

[80] ADC 7 W – 10. Police. Ministère de l'Intérieur, Direction générale de la police nationale (Direction des Renseignements généraux), Fichier départemental de la Creuse. (n.d. [after February 1942]) and AN F 1 c III – 1150. Prefect's report (March 1, 1941).

Jean Michaud, another historian of the Creuse, claims in an interview in the documentary *The Children of Chabannes* that the department's residents did not read the antisemitic newspapers produced in Paris; therefore, they did not internalize or express antisemitic sentiments. Yet there is convincing evidence that the people of the region could and did complain about Jews, sent denunciations, and blamed Jews for hardships.[81] Yet abstract antisemitism differed from the reaction of individuals who interacted with the children living in the homes of the Creuse and the Haute-Vienne. Personal relationships built on daily experiences directly influenced actions and cannot be overlooked or underestimated. Louis Aron noted the population's favorable response toward Jews just before the promulgation of the first Jewish Statute: "the first reactions of non-Jews are very favorable towards Israelites, in the occupied zone as in the free zone: if official antisemitism is growing, it is clearly diminishing in the people."[82] The Jewish children of the Refuge quickly became part of the Crocq community, inviting local residents to celebrate Hanukkah with them and participating fully in the town's fundraiser for local prisoners of war.[83] Such connections had lasting effects as the political situation for Jews worsened over the course of the war.

Economics provides another explanation beyond religiosity, politics, or personal relationships. Louis Aron noted that the positive reception of Jews in the Limousin often had more concrete financial reasons. After the initial expenditures for the repair of the homes in the Haute-Vienne and the Creuse, the Jewish organizations continued to provide a boost to the local economy. Providing food was, by far, the most expensive aspect of maintaining the homes. The public assistance inspector for the Creuse reported that the Refuge spent 265,223.70 francs on food in 1941, representing more than half of the organization's total budget.[84] At the end of 1943, Félix Chevrier owed the following for food purchased to supply the children at Chabannes: 6,663.90 francs to the pork butcher for six months' worth of meat; 23,075.30 to the beef butcher for meat purchased in October through December; 16,378.40 for wine and potatoes to the wine wholesaler; 6,750 francs to a local farmer for 2,250 kilograms of

---

[81] Alain Giévis, "Les réfugiés juifs et l'opinion publique en Limousin (1940-1943)" in *Le Sauvetage des enfants juifs de France.*
[82] *Journal de Louis Aron* (October 16, 1940), 36.
[83] Ibid. On Hanukkah, see the journal entry for December 10, 1939, p. 13. On participation in the POW fundraiser, see entries for July 19, 1941, p. 59 and July 27 and 28, 1941, p. 60.
[84] ADC 95 W – 18 – Etranger juif-dossier individuels. L'Inspecteur de l'Assistance Publique à Monsieur le Préfet de la Creuse. Objet: Enquête sur le Refuge Israélite de l'Enfance à Crocq. Ref: votre lettre du 8 Janvier 1942, p. 2.

carrots; a total of 8,021.95 francs to three different grocers for items like salt and sugar; and, 6,480 francs to the potato syndicate for 4,000 kilograms of potatoes delivered in April and June.[85] Local residents and businesses profited from the group homes' provisioning needs and their large budgets.

Relationships based upon material needs did not change significantly as a result of increased antisemitic persecution. In September 1940, Aron reported that the lack of surveillance of the Creuse in general and Crocq in particular meant that despite the introduction of ration cards for bread, meat, and cheese, local merchants sold these products to the Refuge until their supplies ran out.[86] Fearing requisitions that October, a grocer in Crocq offered to sell stockpiled items to Aron. The director thus acquired five hundred kilograms of pasta although ration cards only entitled him to thirty.[87] By frequenting the "usual farmers" and merchants, Aron procured milk, jams, and cheese without ration cards and in excess of the amounts allowed as the Refuge prepared for the first winter under the Vichy regime.[88] For the most part, merchants in Crocq ignored the ration cards throughout 1940 and until the summer of 1941, and the Refuge obtained amounts of food significantly greater than the official allotment. The girls shared forty-one kilograms of bread per day instead of thirty, twenty-five to thirty liters of milk each day instead of ten, and each person had six to seven hundred grams of meat per week instead of the allowed three hundred and fifty.[89] The timing of the changes is more closely related to changes in the supply situation – the first severe shortages, the proliferation of illegal family packages, the rash of denunciations – than to changes in Vichy's antisemitic policies. As the war progressed and shortages became more severe, sellers had to honor the rationing system, but Aron still reported unofficial sales in his journal. After the Refuge moved to the Château de Chaumont in 1942, the director purchased meat almost daily from peasants offering cuts from animals "accidentally" injured and therefore slaughtered.[90] Both the buyer and the sellers profited from these exchanges.

---

[85] CDCJ CCCLXXIV-1. Fonds Félix Chevrier – factures.
[86] *Journal de Louis Aron* (September 26, 1940), 34.
[87] Ibid. (October 22, 1940), 36. The same thing happened in January 1941. See journal entry for January 21, 1941, p. 45. In May, Aron also got 300 kilograms of pasta and 20 kilograms of semolina without ration tickets from a grocer fearing requisitions. See May 27, 1941, p. 55.
[88] Ibid. 37 and November 12, 1940, p. 38.
[89] Ibid. (February 9, 1941), 46, (March 12, 1941), 49, (March 25, 1941), 50.
[90] Ibid. (June 17, 1943), 136.

"The vast heart of mankind knows no boundaries"   181

Children at OSE homes also remember collecting provisions from local farmers. One of Stephan Lewy's duties at the Château de Chabannes was to pick up illegal food deliveries about once a week. Taking a team of oxen and a two-wheeled wagon, Stephan visited neighboring farms, filled the wagon with bags of potatoes, and covered the entire thing with hay to disguise the wagon's contents. Farmers soon visited the château about these clandestine shipments. They did not come to complain, but rather to warn the refugees to be careful because the wagon's squeaking wheels alerted everyone to the fact that Lewy was hauling something much heavier than hay.[91] Most of the urban children and staff members lacked this bit of rural knowledge.

Making purchases directly on the farm remained one of the most successful (and time-consuming) means of acquiring additional food, and each OSE home had a designated staff member whose duty was to supply the home. A Romanian refugee, Elysée Cogan, was the head of supplies for all the homes in the Creuse and the Haute-Vienne. His responsibilities included purchasing materials, placing orders, supplying the correct ration tickets for the purchases, and distributing the goods. Mia Kanner, the cook at Le Couret, remembers Monsieur Schlachter's "great powers of persuasion" in his role as the home's procurer. He "spent most of his time going to farms further afield begging for extra milk, eggs, and butter" and always returned with something to supplement the official rations.[92] Félix Chevrier kept detailed records of Chabannes' daily milk purchases from local farmwomen. The home got varying amounts of whole and skim milk from nine different farms in seven different communities.[93] At Louis Aron's Refuge, the duty for finding food fell to different members of the staff. In October 1940, Madame Kohn received special permission to travel the department by car two days a week in order to search for additional food.[94] As the war continued, Louis Aron often made trips to farms himself, once traveling eighteen kilometers to purchase 120 kilograms of potatoes and even promising to visit a farm at night for four dozen eggs. The peasants, "afraid of denunciations and surveillance" required such measures.[95] Before the Refuge's move to Chaumont, the director engaged Oscar Weisselberg – who had been working at the château since the spring of 1941 – to help with supplying because he "knows the region and the people."[96] After Weisselberg fled

[91] Stephan Lewy interview with the author (August 14, 2000).
[92] Kanner and Kugler, *Shattered Crystals*, p. 242.
[93] CDJC CCCLXXIV – 5. Fonds Félix Chevrier.
[94] *Journal de Louis Aron* (October 10, 1940), 36.
[95] Ibid. (May 20, 1941), 55 and (October 18 1941), 70. Quote from p. 70.
[96] Ibid. (July 22, 1942), 97.

possible arrest in March 1943, the position fell to various individuals, including girls housed at the Refuge and OSE employees using false identity cards.

The closing of the Refuge in 1942 emphasized money's effects in building relationships. The Refuge had to abandon its building in Crocq after the property's owner decided to rent Les Granges to the local gendarmerie brigade. Coming after the Refuge's incorporation into the Third Direction of the UGIF, the OSE decided to transfer the entire operation to the Château de Chaumont after dispersing Chaumont's children throughout the other OSE homes in the region. On July 1, Aron reported that the home's relocation was a popular topic of conversation in the village, especially among "the merchants, who are sorry to lose such clients." Beyond the economic impact, the director noted, "The population is in general kind towards us, and say that they will miss us."[97] Upon arriving at Chaumont, the Refuge's direction had to cultivate new relationships, but soon found suppliers willing to sell their items to the Jewish refugees. Despite the difficulties in provisioning, Monsieur and Madame Aron reported in their summary of the Refuge's operations throughout the war that the organization always maintained good relationships with the locals, due in part to its purchasing practices. The directors always paid for the purchased items upon their delivery, and even "if [the Refuge] never accepted to pay excessive prices, it was always a 'big client,' buying the totality of a farm's products" without subjecting the farmer to transportation or handling fees or government inspections and supervision.[98]

Thus sales and relationships between natives and refugee Jews that began during the Phony War continued under the Vichy regime, even after the promulgation of two Jewish statutes, hundreds of antisemitic laws, and the arrests of Jews. Such treatment contradicts previous findings that speculate that rural areas were more hostile to Jews than urban areas. Marrus and Paxton note "the Jews drew special ire in a time of economic crisis and national stress," especially in rural areas of France by the summer of 1941.[99] Marion A. Kaplan in her study of German Jewry under Nazism finds "[n]eighbors and acquaintances turned away most abruptly in small towns and villages" between 1933 and 1938.[100] The experiences of the Jewish group homes in the Limousin, however, appear to be an exception to these

---

[97] Ibid. (July 1, 1942), 96.
[98] Ibid. 194.
[99] Marrus and Paxton, *Vichy France and the Jews*, p. 169.
[100] Kaplan, *Between Dignity and Despair*, p. 37.

generalizations, complicating our understanding of public opinion during the Vichy years.

These homes remind us that official public opinion reports were not a direct predictor of local actions and that outward compliance with Vichy's laws does not always reflect real attitudes. During 1940 and 1941, the material and moral aid the people of the Creuse and Haute-Vienne provided to Jewish refugee children contributed to the erosion of Vichy's support and legitimacy. Just as they ignored the tenets of the National Revolution when it came to personal provisioning, native residents also disregarded antisemitism when it was to their economic advantage. We know that the French became increasingly adept at deceit and dissimulation, and these traits carried over into situations concerning Jews. This did not mean that antisemitism did not exist nor does it mean that public opinion reports did not mention antagonism toward Jews. In fact the assessments of public opinion reveal the contradictions and difficulties in determining local attitudes toward Jews. Creuse Prefect Jacques-Henry noted in October 1941 "an upsurge of antisemitism in the rural milieu, until now indifferent to racial questions."[101] Less than a year later, on the eve of the first roundups in the unoccupied zone, Gendarmerie Captain Chaumet reported that the refugee Jews in the area were "the object of a certain sympathy movement, due to their material and moral situation."[102] Once the roundups occurred on August 26, 1942, the prefect had a difficult time reconciling the population's reaction: "The population sharply disapproved of the measures taken. And yet they do not stop complaining about the presence of Jews and their practices!"[103] Material concerns, daily survival tactics, and deliberate silence all contributed to creating a confusing atmosphere. Attitudes toward Jews were often driven by economics rather than altruism, but ultimately both motivations contributed to the rescue of Jews after deportations began.

We cannot conclude, however, that all Jewish children received the same welcome in the region. The experiences of Jewish refugee children in the homes often differed significantly from those of children who spent the war with their families or in hiding. Liane Reif-Lehrer's most vivid memory of the years she spent as a refugee in Limoges contrasts sharply with accounts from children in the OSE homes. She remembers begging for additional bread from bakers to share with the other refugees who shared a room

---

[101] AN F ic III – 1150. Rapport Mensuel (October 2, 1941).
[102] SHGN Box 12557 – Grpt Creuse – Cie Guéret, R/4, Rapport du Capitaine Chaumet sur la physionomie de la Section, au cour du mois d'Août (August 24, 1942).
[103] AN F ic III – 1150. Rapport Mensuel d'Information du 1er août – 30 septembre 1942 (September 30, 1942).

with the family in an old bistro on the edge of town.[104] This is not to imply that the children in the Jewish homes did not suffer from hunger; most of the former residents do remember the period's extreme shortages. But without the aid of an organization that had access to funds from abroad and networks to supply food, material for clothing, or land for gardens, independent Jewish refugees faced greater challenges in negotiating the everyday.

Jewish children living with their families or in hiding with non-Jews often noted more antisemitism in their daily interactions. Stephan Lewy confidently stated that "I never encountered any antisemitism whatsoever" when he lived at the Château de Chabannes.[105] Marguerite Morris has different memories of the period. After police arrested her Polish father in Paris in May 1941, Marguerite and her mother continued to live in the city until the chief of police's wife warned them that they were on the list for the roundup of July 16, 1942. The pair illegally crossed into the unoccupied zone and went to live with an aunt in Limoges. Due to the city's overcrowding, Marguerite and her mother searched for an apartment in nearby towns and soon moved to Oradour-sur-Vayres. Marguerite attended school, but unlike the children at Chabannes, Chaumont, and Les Granges, she recalls: "I encountered more antisemitism in that little town than I had before because we were outsiders who had moved in after the war. When I was in Paris, even when I wore the yellow star, I was in a school where the kids knew me before and they – not all of them, but most of them – had some sort of empathy for me. In that little town we were like intruders." Mrs Morris goes on to explain that she was never physically injured, but she faced verbal assaults from children in Oradour-sur-Vayres and felt that the population in general resented the presence of Jews.[106]

Some children also remember less freedom and difficult living conditions with rural families that children in the homes did not face. The children in the homes swam in local ponds, hiked through the woods, participated in sporting competitions, and interacted with other children like themselves. Life outside the homes could be more isolated and restrictive. Hélène

---

[104] The story of the Reif family comes from many sources including Liane Reif-Lehrer, interview with the author (August 7, 2000); Liane Reif-Lehrer, videotaped testimony, Archives of the USHMM RG-50-030*186; Liane Reif-Lehrer, "Memory's Edge," *Boston* 80: 4 (April 1988); and Frederick Reif, interview with the author (August 1, 2000).

[105] Stephan Lewy interview with the author (August 14, 2000).

[106] Marguerite Morris, videotaped testimony, Archives of the USHMM, RG-50.091*35. National Council of Jewish Women, Cleveland Section collection (November 14, 1984).

Villeroy (née Kalina Grynsztein) hid her Jewish identity while living with two different families paid by the state in the Creuse town of Bourganeuf after her mother's arrest. At the first home, the girl's responsibilities included caring for the couple's four children while keeping up with her studies. With the next family, she taught the modest couple's children how to read. Hélène's sister spent her vacations with another rural family who "exploited her shamefully" as a domestic.[107] Marguerite Jeremias, after being liberated from the Gurs concentration camp by Jewish aid organizations, went to live with a family in Brive (Corrèze) where she worked as a maid and cared for the family's six children ranging from three months to 10 years old. Although the family was kind to her, Marguerite never left the house, even on her days off. The 16-year-old girl did not have anyone to share her experiences with, and the fear that her German accent would give her away isolated her even more.[108]

Although local authorities tolerated and even supported the presence of hundreds of Jewish children in the Creuse and Haute-Vienne, the children's parents presented another case entirely. At the beginning of January 1941, the prefect of the Creuse asked the local police to assess the implications of the OSE's eventual purchase of the châteaux it had rented in the department. The commissar acknowledged that such a request did not appear suspect; however, it was "inopportune." According to the report, numerous parents of the students had come to live in neighboring towns and "it could be feared, that if their installation became permanent, that the three communes in question would rapidly become rallying points for undesirable foreigners."[109] The children, and the organizations that supported them, were welcome, but individual Jewish families were not.

Although the commissar expressed common xenophobic sentiments, residents of the Creuse expressed similar opinions about the "undesirability" of *non-Jewish* parents in the region. Throughout the war, the Limoges region hosted various *colonies de vacances* for children, and by 1942 there were at least twenty *colonies* in the Creuse, Haute-Vienne, and the Corrèze. The Limoges Catholic diocese cared for 1,700 children that summer, the American Red Cross opened two *colonies* for needy children during the war, and in 1943 a train carried Jewish children from Marseille

---

[107] Hélène (Kalina Grynsztein) Villeroy questionnaire responses (August 2000).

[108] Marguerite Jeremias, interview with the author (August 29, 2000) and videotaped testimony, Archives of the USHMM, RG-50.002*119. Kean College of New Jersey collection (November 2, 1988).

[109] ADC 95 W – 18 – Etranger juif – dossier individuels. Le Commissaire de Police Spéciale à Monsieur le Préfet de la Creuse (January 10, 1941).

to Limoges for a *colonie*.¹¹⁰ Needy children also lived with individual families in rural areas, such as Jewish children sent from Limoges to Oradour-sur-Glane, or Parisian children sent to live with peasants in the Creuse.¹¹¹ Almost 5,000 children from the industrial suburbs of Paris arrived in the Creuse in April 1943 and lived with peasants throughout the department. The farmers did not complain about the 15 francs a day they received for housing the children or the labor the children could provide. They did, however, complain about the bad behavior of the children's parents who came to visit their children for the "sole purpose of supplying."¹¹² Local authorities worked to provide food, shoes, and shelter for children, but not for adults.

The choice of the Creuse as a place of refuge for Jewish children in 1939 proved to be propitious as the war continued for the next five years. Material considerations drove the decision to rent the châteaux in the region, but the attitude of local authorities and residents made the continuation of the homes possible under Vichy. Authorities did not unduly harass the inhabitants of the children's homes, students met very little antisemitism in schools or communities, and local farmers and merchants provided food to the refugees despite Vichy's growing anti-Jewish legislation. Eventually, the support of the community allowed hundreds of children to escape arrest as individuals alerted the homes' directors of impending arrests and even took in the boys and girls. Félix Chevrier summed up many non-Jews' attitudes toward the refugees: "When it has to do with children, the vast heart of mankind knows no boundaries."¹¹³ It is this attitude toward children that made Jewish children in institutions a special case within the Jewish community. Organizations and individuals committed resources, time, and energy to ensuring the survival of these children. Though priorities changed, the desire to protect the children remained constant and was reflected in their education, training, and material situation. At the height of its operation, the OSE cared for approximately 1,200 children, the

---

¹¹⁰ See ADHV 185 W 4-4 – Colonies de Vacances; ADHV 185 W 1-71 – Rapports mensuel du Délégué régional à la Famille. Rapport mensuel (September 12, 1942); and "Liste d'enfants devant partir en colonie de Vacances de Marseille à Limoges" YIVO UGIF records held by the USHMM, reel 74 section 98.4.

¹¹¹ On Oradour-sur-Glane see letter from Robert Pinède to André Baur, Vice-Président de l'UGIF (July 21, 1943) in YIVO UGIF records folder 31.9, p. 621 and Service Historique de la Gendarmerie Nationale (hereafter SHGN) Box 12708 – BT Limoges. Procès-verbal number 1516 (August 11, 1943). On the Creuse, see ADC 288 W – 42 – Oeuvre des petits réfugiés de la Creuse and ADC 288 W – 43/1 – Enfants evacués de la Seine.

¹¹² ADC 288 W – 43/1.

¹¹³ CDJC CCCLXXIV – 1. Fonds Félix Chevrier – album.

majority of whom resided in group homes in the Creuse and the Haute-Vienne. Despite being labeled undesirables, foreigners, and strangers, these children found material and moral support in the rural region of the Limousin. Even with the national government's best efforts, the definition of outsiders took place on a local level based upon stereotypes and daily interactions. Vichy's antisemitic agenda should have excluded Jewish children from local communities. Instead, the native population often welcomed the arrival of Jewish children's homes, and participated in the children's eventual rescue.

Conclusion

Between August 15 and 25, 1944, Resistance troops liberated the Limousin region, marking the end of five years of war, of restrictive laws, and of the authoritarian Vichy regime. Yet the war's last months following the Allied landings in Normandy on June 6, 1944, proved to be some of the most difficult, violent, and dramatic of the entire period. The hangings at Tulle on June 9 and the destruction of Oradour-sur-Glane on June 10 in reprisal for Resistance attacks continue to represent German brutality and are closely associated with public recollections of the Limousin at war. The proximity of Allied forces did not stop the deportation of Jews that summer either. At the end of July 1944, German troops arrested Jews living in the Creuse, many of whom arrived in Auschwitz-Birkenau in early September.[1]

As a result of these events, the history of the wartime Limousin has often been written as a story of heroic or dramatic events. Scholars, local historians, and museums have focused on the communist Resistance and the maquis, the events at Oradour, and the deportation of the Jews, but there is much to be learned from the everyday.[2] Most people were not active

---

[1] Ten Jews were arrested and imprisoned in Guéret on July 25. Others in the department had also been arrested. Archives Départementales de la Creuse (hereafter ADC) 1220 W – 16 – listes nominatives des Israélites à Guéret. Letter from le Commissaire de Police à Monsieur le Préfet de la Creuse (July 27, 1944). See also Hélène Villeroy questionnaire responses (August 2000).

[2] On the Resistance and maquis, see Georges Guinguoin, *Quatre ans de lutte sur le sol limousin* (Paris: Hachette, 1974); H. R. Kedward, *In Search of the Maquis: Rural Resistance in Southern France, 1942–1944* (Oxford: Clarendon Press, 1993); Sarah Farmer, "The Communist Resistance in the Haute-Vienne" *French Historical Studies* 14:1 (Spring 1985); Marc Parrotin, *La Résistance en Creuse* (Limoges: Verso, 1995); Parrotin, *Le Temps du Maquis: Histoire de la Résistance en Creuse* (Guéret: Verso, 1984); Parrotin, *Femmes de la*

members of the Resistance, nor did they have direct contact with the German occupiers. Likewise the majority of the French population never faced deportation for "racial" reasons. Instead, individuals recall extreme shortages of food, fuel, and housing and the ways sharing these limited resources with refugees shaped relationships. These everyday events cannot be removed from their political context nor should historians overlook the more dramatic episodes of the war years. But, for the majority of the population, life in wartime France revolved around daily struggles to find adequate food, clothing, and lodging. The history of the Resistance in the region was remarkable, the atrocities of the Liberation were striking, and the treatment of the Jews was deplorable; nevertheless, it is in the history of the quotidian where we can learn about the limits of ideology, the treatment of outsiders, and the strategies of survival.

Shortages must be central in any discussion of the everyday and of politics in France during the war. Almost every official document, memoir, videotaped testimony, or documentary remarks on the poor food or housing, yet most scholars have not focused on the politics of daily life. Rather than examining daily life from the perspective of national politics, this study has explored the period from the bottom up in order to understand what the Vichy government and its National Revolution meant for a variety of individuals as they navigated the quotidian. The ability to deal with shortages between 1939 and 1944 varied: wealthy men and women used their resources to purchase items on the black market, farmers kept a portion of their harvest and slaughter for their families, and transportation employees with the ability to travel bought items on their journeys. Socioeconomic factors certainly played a role in the ease of acquiring goods, but scholars have not fully explored another important determinant: one's status as a foreigner, undesirable, or stranger in a community. Under normal circumstances, buying food or finding a home often presented initial challenges for a new arrival in an unfamiliar town. One spent the first days or weeks trying

---

Résistance en Creuse (Ahun: Verso, 1997); and Parrotin, *Immigrés dans la Résistance en Creuse* (Ahun: Editions Verso, 1998). Museums in the Limousin dedicated to the Resistance include the Musée de la Résistance de Limoges and Le centre Michelet in Brive. On Oradour, see Sarah Farmer, *Martyred Village: Commemorating the 1944 Massacre at Oradour-sur-Glane* (Berkeley and Los Angeles: University of California Press, 1999) and the museum, Centre de la mémoire d'Oradour-sur-Glane. On Jews and internment, see Yves Soulignac, *Les Camps d'Internement en Limousin 1939–1945* (Saint-Paul: La Briderie, 1995); Gérard Gobitz, *Les Déportations de Réfugiés de Zone Libre en 1942. Récits et documents concernant les régions administratives de Toulouse, Nice, Lyon, Limoges, Clermont-Ferrand, Montpellier (Camp de Rivesaltes)* (Paris: L'Harmattan, 1996); and *Le Sauvetage des Enfants Juifs de France*. Actes de Colloque de Guéret – May 29 and 30, 1996.

to figure out when the local market was held, which shops had the best items at the lowest prices, how to use the public transportation system, where to find available housing, or looking for other forms of aid. During the shortage years of the Second World War, and especially after the establishment of the Vichy government, these problems took on immense proportions and even affected one's chance of survival. Thus, material issues and the politics of food were as important to French residents as the laws and decrees issued by the local and national government.

Politics in general lost importance as material concerns increasingly dominated day-to-day interactions. In most cases, political ideology was the background against which the quotidian played out and not vice versa. Even when the prefect of the Haute-Vienne outlawed provisioning trips to the countryside, urban residents set off on foot, on bicycles, or by tram and train to find additional milk, butter, vegetables, or meat. The ideal of a moral community in which sacrifices would be equally shared mattered less than finding enough to eat. Still others believed in profit more than strengthening families or celebrating rural life when they sent *colis familiaux* to urban residents. Examining the material situation also reveals the relationship between the treatment of outsiders in the community, political ideology, and the physical needs of French residents. Without approaching the period from the position of the everyday, these discoveries go unnoticed.

Individuals increasingly lost faith in the Vichy regime as the government failed to provide adequate food for its people. Local conditions did not match national rhetoric and residents began manipulating the system as early as the regime's first winter. As the government cracked down on material infractions, the French people formed relationships to ensure their own food supply. Such duplicitous relationships undermined the government's legitimacy, but shortages never resulted in a complete collapse of the regime. Limousin residents also remained complicit with the government and utilized certain tools – denunciations, anti-Jewish laws, the rhetoric of the National Revolution – when it created a material advantage.

Silence became a vital part of navigating the everyday, but it also complicated officials' ability to assess public opinion accurately. Such silence allowed the government to operate under the illusion that it had popular support, and has led scholars to assert that the French were largely indifferent to Vichy's antisemitic measures. But it is perhaps more accurate to state that the French proved willing to ignore official directives that compromised the possibility for material advantage. Local residents used silence to protect illegal provisioning practices and networks in the face of increasing shortages and regulations. Officials, however, often interpreted these actions differently. They noted, "Material worries prevented everyone from engaging in personal speculation on the big problems"[3] yet they insisted on the public's continued support. The prefect of the Haute-Vienne's report from April 3, 1941, displayed the determined optimism that characterized many official interpretations of silence:

> In the broad masses of the population, among the peasants and the workers most notably, people think more and more "French." It is fair to say that the politics of "collaboration" does not arouse any enthusiasm and that people accept it reluctantly, but it is equally true that the public understands better and better the tragic nature of our situation and the harsh necessity in which the government finds itself to determine its attitude towards the events and to consider nothing but the interests of France.
>
> It is in this spirit that the rationing measures and successive restrictions are received [*sont accueillies*] without too many recriminations. Supplying in March took place, by the way, in satisfactory conditions. The public understood the obligation to yield to the imposed disciplines in order to avoid famine in the months to come. The most noticeable restrictions are those that fall on bread and soap; people sometimes note it with bitterness, but in general, people do not question the appropriateness of the implemented measures.[4]

The prefect described the lack of expressed criticisms as evidence of quiet approval of both collaboration and rationing. But put within the broader context of individual activity taking place in 1941, such silence suggests that people often did not complain because it was to their advantage to remain silent and to continue to provision themselves illegally. The government had already proven its inability to supply adequately the nation or to successfully maintain total sovereignty. Keeping quiet meant individuals could avoid officials' scrutiny while they sent packages full of rationed foodstuffs, traveled into the countryside in search of rare products, and wrote anonymous denunciations. Individuals had a greater chance of improving their material situation if they avoided drawing attention to themselves.

Studying material shortages during the war also expands and complicates our understanding of what constituted an outsider during the Second World War in France. Tradition, history, and cultural assumptions have accorded Gypsies, Jews, and refugees a marginal place in French society for centuries. In some ways, they represent the quintessential outsiders, but this study shows that outsider status changed depending upon the circumstance.

---

[3] ADHV 185 W 1/45 – Rapports du préfet de la Haute-Vienne au ministère de l'Intérieur. Rapport mensuel (March 4, 1941).
[4] Ibid. Rapport mensuel (April 3, 1941), 5.

Identifying oneself as French certainly had advantages; however, French nationality did not guarantee acceptance and aid especially if one was Jewish, Alsatian, or Roma. People acted on their hunger more than on their national identity. Pragmatism and material concerns shaped how natives treated new arrivals and how outsiders responded to their environment.

Thus for the people of the Limousin, an outsider was more than just a foreigner or someone the government deemed an undesirable member of the French national community. The evacuees from Alsace-Lorraine constituted a distinct outsider group despite the fact that they were French. Cultural, linguistic, and religious differences made them unlike their hosts, but the material strains they placed upon the Limousin communities also made them outsiders. While officials in the Creuse accepted the presence of Jewish children in the department throughout the war and provided aid to Jewish-run institutions before their closings in 1943, the same authorities decried the presence of undesirable, foreign, adult Jews. One cannot conclude, therefore, at that particular moment, that solely being Jewish automatically made one an outsider. Prewar xenophobia and serious concerns about unwanted consumers also contributed to the differentiation. Furthermore, residents complained about the arrival of non-Jewish parents in search of food – they, too, must be considered unwanted outsiders. Urban residents who ventured into the countryside for food also represented a group of outsiders that were sometimes welcomed and sometimes turned away. The daily presence of consumers willing to purchase goods at high prices encouraged peasants to take advantage of the economic benefits of staying on their farms, but relentless consumers unwilling to take no for an answer and increased thefts also created tensions. Despite the national government's best efforts to shape popular perceptions, the definition of outsiders took place on a local level based upon stereotypes and daily interactions.

A comparison of Jewish and Gypsy experiences underlines the differences between national and local definitions of outsiders. On the surface, there appear to be many areas where the wartime experiences of these two groups overlapped. Before the war, French lawmakers did not view Gypsies and Jews as members of distinct races and considered the assimilation of both populations possible. Anti-Semites questioned Jewish patriotism because the Jews were seen as a nation within a nation. The Gypsies also raised concerns about loyalty because they regularly crossed country's borders and failed to display any national allegiances. During the war years, the Vichy government subjected Gypsies and Jews to restrictive laws and harsh punishments for infractions, and both groups faced internment.

Conclusion

In hindsight, the persecution of Gypsies and Jews allows historians to make connections and draw comparisons, but the French people living at the time did not associate the two groups. In fact, official policy toward these segments of the population varied considerably, and natives reacted differently toward each group. Authorities hoped that internment and regular work would turn the Gypsies into "French" people at the same time that French Jews faced accusations of being an inassimilable population forever outside the national community.[5] Although officials argued for the cultural assimilation of Gypsies, anti-Gypsyism (often based on racial stereotypes) pervaded society. The degree of local antisemitism proved much harder to determine, however. Gypsies, a considerably smaller population within French society, faced assigned residence and internment earlier than their Jewish counterparts, bore the brunt of accusations for stealing, and received no support from Limousin residents. Jews in the Limousin, however, received aid from neighbors and acquaintances as Vichy's policies became more sinister.

In many ways, the treatment of Gypsies by both the government and ordinary citizens was opposite to Jewish experiences in World War II France. While French officials fought against designating Gypsies as a race despite their visible ethnicity, Vichy law determined the biological basis of "Jewishness" for people who were more integrated into French society.[6] Despite the rise of xenophobia in the 1930s and the revocation of naturalizations of foreigners in general (and Jews specifically), the Third Republic and the Vichy regime continued to argue for Gypsy assimilability. The strength and tradition of French and international antisemitism contributed to Vichy's decision to pursue a racial definition of Jewishness while still advocating the assimilation of nomads. The size and importance of these two portions of the population may have also impacted official attitudes. Jews represented a larger proportion of the population, and through assimilation they had acquired powerful positions in business, politics, and society. This assimilation proved to be both an advantage and a disadvantage: It made Jews seem more powerful and threatening, leading to laws that excluded them from society, but at the same time, Vichy's laws differentiated between French and foreign Jews. Assimilation provided a degree of protection. During the war, the potential for assimilation also shielded

---

[5] François and Renée Bédarida, "La Persécution des Juifs," in *La France des années noires*, vol. 2, edited by Jean-Pierre Azéma and François Bédarida (Paris: Seuil, 1993), 134.

[6] For just one example of an explanation of French "racial" criteria in the Jewish Statutes, see Julian Jackson, *France: The Dark Years* (Oxford and New York: Oxford University Press, 2001), 359.

nomads from the worst of the Nazis' and Vichy's policies – deportation and extermination.

The questions of internment, race, and assimilation underline the differences between Jews and Gypsies. They were both undesirables in the French State, but the Vichy government maintained different legal stances toward each of them, did not associate them in its rhetoric, and treated them as separate entities. By conforming to accepted ideals, domiciled Gypsies avoided official persecution and internment, but the failure to conform eventually led to the incarceration of thousands in French concentration camps. Authorities hoped that by learning regular work habits and new ideas about family and community in these camps, nomads would turn into "French" men and women. Theoretically, these changes would allow nomads to reenter the French national community. The Gypsies' possibility of returning to society differed significantly from Jewish experiences during the war. For Jewish undesirables, camps were temporary only in that they housed Jews until they could be deported from France. There was no discussion of possible assimilation, especially in the case of foreign Jews, despite the integration of Jews into French society since their emancipation during the French Revolution. Ultimately 76,000 Jews were sent from France to death camps in Eastern Europe. Though the concentration of nomads in camps provided a large population that could have been used to meet deportation quotas imposed by Nazi officials, no Gypsies were deported from French camps. Despite Heinrich Himmler's order of December 16, 1942, demanding the deportation of all remaining Roma in Europe to Auschwitz-Birkenau, the 145 French Gypsies deported to Poland came from a camp in Belgium rather than one on French soil.

Material issues and the politics of food were as important to Limousin residents in their dealings with these outsiders as the laws and decrees issued by the government. By assigning nomadic Gypsies to certain areas, the Third Republic and Vichy regime hoped to rid the Gypsies of their wandering tendencies and to eventually integrate them into society. Deeply ingrained stereotypes of the dirty, stealing Gypsy, however, worked against these plans. Native residents wanted the process of assimilation to take place in internment camps removed from their daily view and away from their fields. The persecution of officially labeled undesirable Jews, rather than excluding these refugees from the local community, could inspire feelings of sympathy. The presence of Jewish refugees often also represented an economic boom for the community, which aided their integration in some circumstances. Though legal outsiders, some Jews found inclusion with families and organizations willing to make sacrifices (or to gain financially) to rescue the persecuted.

The malleability of the family as a political ideology – especially in relation to marginal members of society – is also revealed by examining shortages. Marshal Philippe Pétain called the family "the essential unit of society and of the homeland" and promised French men and women that "your family will have the nation's respect and protection."[7] But his statements applied only to specific families and only in certain circumstances. Although most black market activities committed in the name of family provisioning remained exempt from harsh punishment, Jewish families could not draw upon this justification to explain illegal purchases. But, the government had no trouble citing the preservation of the family unit when it demanded that Jewish children be deported with their parents. Gypsies often had large families, which fit with the government's fight against depopulation, but nomads did not display the proper familial characteristics. Unkempt, uneducated children needed protection from their exploitive parents and internment would provide this safety while changing the nomads into productive members of society. Even though it may not seem surprising that Vichy's conservative National Revolution excluded undesirables from its idea of the family, the extent of this exclusion reached unexpected degrees. The family, which was supposed to be benign and protective, could be wielded as a weapon that proved to be destructive for people on the margins.

Individual awareness of food and hunger during the war, however temporary or passing it may have been, had an enormous impact on the lives of those who suffered through it. For example, Frida Wattenberg's guilt over her access to food while other starved in concentration camps prevented her from speaking about the war for decades. As a Jewish social assistant during the war, Wattenberg traveled from town to town in the unoccupied zone, looking for additional ration cards at city halls and for non-Jewish individuals willing to hide people in danger. Her duties also included helping Jews escape to Spain or Switzerland, and her affiliation with a Jewish aid organization and participation in Resistance activities provided the young woman with access to precious ration cards, allowing daily servings of meat.[8] In spite of her involvement in rescue and resistance, Frida Wattenberg carried uneasy feelings for years because she ate everyday. For Hélène Villeroy, the disturbance of the daily lives of Limousin residents accounted for the

---

[7] Philippe Pétain, *Discours aux Français 17 juin 1940–20 août 1944* edited by Jean-Claude Barbas (Paris: Albin Michel, 1989), 71, 70.
[8] Frida Wattenberg, videotaped testimony, United States Holocaust Memorial Museum (USHMM) RG-50.146*04. Mémoire et Documents Collection.

population's varied political attitudes and helped explain one's wariness of strangers. Daily concerns also contributed to the natives' attitudes toward outsiders: "They were afraid, they were hungry, [and] propaganda influenced them. Their prisoner soldiers were suffering so 'Others' did not matter to them."[9]

But as the preceding pages have demonstrated, material concerns affected the integration of outsiders into their new communities, created deep tensions between urban and rural populations, justified the internment of Gypsies, provided reasons for the removal of Jews from cities, and created mutually beneficial relationships. Different religious, cultural, and social groups in the Limousin interacted, often for the first time, in unexpected and complex ways. It has been my intention to illuminate these complexities and to offer a new view of the Second World War that considers the importance of daily life and social interactions for individuals. Even though politics created a framework within which people could act, the material benefits of action or inaction weighed more heavily in people's decisions that any potential punishment. Some decisions undermined the Vichy regime and its National Revolution, while others upheld Vichy's ideological aims. One may see the areas in which individuals accepted and/or rejected the Vichy regime's laws only by examining their daily actions. The examination of the lives of foreigners, undesirables, and strangers in the Limousin in conjunction with the realities and pressures of daily life reveals much about the limits of political ideology, the ability of individuals to make accommodations in their thoughts and actions, the possibilities of simultaneously opposing and supporting a regime, and the definition of outsiders. There remains more to be explored about daily life in France during the Second World War, but we must not ignore the role shortages played in shaping individual experiences.

---

[9] Hélène Villeroy questionnaire responses (August 2000).

Bibliography

Archives

Archives Départementales de la Creuse – ADC (Guéret)

Series 2 W – Sous-Préfecture d'Aubusson
  16 – Crocq – Administration communale

Series 7 W – Sous-Préfecture d'Aubusson
  10 – Police
  12 – Police

Series 25 W – Préfecture – Bois et charbons
  44 – Réquisition de main d'œuvre agricole

Series 36 W – Centre d'internement administratif d'Evaux-les-Bains
  7 – Instructions et circulaires sur le fonctionnement des camps d'internement

Series 41 W – Direction départementale du service du travail obligatoire
  28 – Israélites: procès-verbaux de gendarmerie, dossiers médicaux, listes

Series 44 W – Cabinet du Préfet
  16 – Communications: interception de lettres, surveillance téléphonique
  17 – Communications
  18 – Communications
  20 – Contrôle postale
  21 – Etrangers
  22 – Etrangers
  31 – Etat d'esprit de la population

Series 95 W – Cabinet du Préfet
  18 – Guerre 1939–45, étranger, juif

Series 105 W – Cabinet du Préfet
  36 – Milice française
  65 – Etrangers

Series 287 W – Papiers de la guerre 1939–45
  3 – Statistiques mensuelles par commune et canton, janvier – décembre 1941

4 – Listes de Belges ne désirant pas rentrer dans leur pays; liste de réfugiés étrangers et israélites domicilés en Belgique avant le 9 mai 1940; listes de Français résidant en Belgique réfugiés dans le département; liste de réfugiés belges hospitalisés ou décédés
11 – Statistiques par communes
12 – Statistique mensuelle par communes et pour l'ensemble du département
13 – Réfugiés étrangers

Series 288 W – Service des réfugiés
2 – Alsaciens-Lorrains
33 – Etrangers, évacuation: demandes de rapatriement; allocataires israélites, statistiques; reclassement des réfugiés, réfugiés belges
34 – Etranger, allocataire
35 – Statistiques concernant les réfugiés alsaciens-lorrains et étrangers
36 – Listes des étrangers réfugiés de la zone occupée et des Alsaciens-Lorrains
42 – Œuvre des petits réfugiés de la Creuse
43/1 – Enfants évacués du département de la Seine
43/2 – Ibid.

Series 297 W – Papiers de la guerre 1939–45
1 – Guerre 1939–45, propagande, information

Series 976 W – Préfecture
65 – Etrangers
118 – Maisons israélites de refuge pour l'enfance: instructions, 1942
163 – Etrangers: statistiques communales, 1941
219 – Etrangers
221 – Etrangers: ramassage des étrangers et des israélites, 1943
237 – Recensement des israélites, 1942–4
239 – Reclassement des israélites dans l'économie nationale, 1943
259 – Coût de la vie: indices, rapports enquêtes, 1942–5
279 – Lettres anonymes, 1942
353 – Hébergement des israélites refoulés des frontières pyrénéennes et méditerranéennes
387 – Ravitaillement: colis postaux dits "familiaux," infractions, 1941

Series 1220 W – Commissariat de police de Guéret
16 – Guerre, bombardement, victimes de guerre

Archives Départementales de la Haute-Vienne – ADHV (Limoges)

Series 11 J – Fonds du comité d'histoire de la seconde guerre mondiale
2 – Internements politiques et raciaux
4 – Fiches individuelles de personnes (françaises ou étrangers) arrêtées sur le territoire du département de la Haute-Vienne (A–K)
5 – Ibid. (L–Z)
8 – Statistiques

Series 4 M – Police
269 – Espagnols – Emploi dans l'industrie et l'agriculture
274 – Espagnols – Enquête sur la situation sociale des réfugiés en vue de rapatrier ceux d'entre eux dont le chef de famille est sans emploi

275 – Espagnols – Rapports d'ensemble sur la situation des réfugiés dans le département et rapports divers

Series 10 M – Main d'œuvre étrangère
36 – Recensement des travailleurs étrangers en vue de leur intégration dans des professions présentant un intérêt pour la nation

Series 185 W 1 Fonds de la préfecture régionale de Limoges 1940–4 (Administration générale de la région)
44 – Rapports mensuels du préfet régional au chef du gouvernement
45 – Rapports du préfet de la Haute-Vienne au ministère de l'Intérieur
46 – Synthèses mensuelles des rapports des préfets et sous-préfets des circonscriptions administratives de la région de Limoges
49 – Rapports du préfet de la Corrèze
50 – Rapports du préfet de la Creuse
51 – Rapports du préfet de la Creuse
52 – Rapports du préfet de la Creuse
55 – Rapports du sous-préfet de Bellac
58 – Rapports du sous-préfet de Rochechouart
63 – Rapports mensuels du directeur régional du ravitaillement général
70 – Rapports mensuels du directeur régional de la santé et de l'assistance
71 – Rapports mensuels du délégué régional à la famille
73 – Rapports mensuels du chef de la police aux questions juives
74 – Rapports mensuels du directeur départemental du ravitaillement général
85 – Rapports mensuels de l'inspecteur départemental de la santé
86 – Rapports mensuels de l'inspecteur départemental des services d'assistance
147 – Union générale des Israélites de France
148 – Rapports du chef de la police aux questions juives pour la région de Limoges
149 – Instructions, réglementation à appliquer aux Israélites naturalisés et étrangers rentrés en France après le 1er janvier 1936
173 – *Valmy*
205 – Services des Contrôles techniques de Limoges
206 – Services des Contrôles techniques de Limoges
207 – Services des Contrôles techniques de Guéret
208 – Services des Contrôles techniques de Tulle
220 – Culte catholique
221 – Culte protestant
223 – Rapport du 3 février 1945 sur l'attitude des représentants de diverses confessions pendant l'Occupation et lors de la Libération

Series 185 W 3 – Police – Administration – Pénitentiaire – Justice
15 – Services départementaux des renseignements généraux – Haute-Vienne
18 – Services départementaux des renseignements généraux – Creuse
61 – Camp de Nexon
90 – Contrôle des étrangers et assimilés sur le territoire de la région de Limoges
107 – Surveillance de l'élément féminin français fréquentant les soldats de l'armée allemande

Series 185 W 4 – Santé, Famille, Population, Affaires Economiques
   4 – Commissariat général à la famille – Colonies de vacances
   5 – Démographie
Series 187 W – Fonds des réfugiés 1937–50
   4 – Réfugiés arrivés à Limoges en mai et juin 1940
   9 – Evacuation des communes situées dans la zone frontalière du Bas-Rhin
  10 – Evacuation des communes situées dans la zone frontalière du Bas-Rhin
  11 – Recensement des Alsaciens-Lorrains
  12 – Réfugiés du Bas-Rhin, Meurthe-et-Moselle, Moselle
  14 – Etats concernant les communes du Bas-Rhin repliées en Haute-Vienne
  17 – Administrations repliées en Haute-Vienne
  18 – Correspondance diverse relative aux réfugiés alsaciens
  81 – Instructions ministérielles (exode de mai–juin 1940)
 116 – Listes nominatives par commune des familles de réfugiés étrangers
 188 – Etats statistiques par commune des réfugiés hébergés, secourus et non secourus
 189 – Etats numériques par commune des réfugiés secourus
 190 – Etats numériques par commune des réfugiés israélites secourus et non secourus
Series 985 W – Fonds de la préfecture
  484 – Israélites français et étrangers
  485 – Israélites français et étrangers
 1632 – Israélites français et étrangers – Union OSE
 1633 – Apposition de la mention "Juif" sur les titres d'identité
 1634 – Listes nominatives diffusées par les préfets de la zone libre concernant des Israélites étrangers recherchés pour être arrêtés en application de la circulaire ministérielle du 5 août 1942
Series 993 W – Affaires militaires
  27 – Camps de séjour surveillé – Camp de Nexon
 113 – Presse – Information
 117 – Presse – Information
 221 – Mesures gouvernementales prises à l'encontre des Juifs
 222 – Recensement des Juifs (loi du 2 juin 1941)
 223 – Commissariat aux affaires juives (délégation de Limoges)
 224 – Commissariat aux affaires juives (délégation régionale de la section d'enquête et de contrôle de Limoges)
 225 – Commissariat aux affaires juives (délégation régionale de la section d'enquête et de contrôle de Limoges)
 608 – Recensement (par l'office du logement) des israélites réfugiés à Limoges (Israélites français)
 609 – Recensement (par l'office du logement) des israélites réfugiés à Limoges (Israélites étrangers)

Archives Nationales – AN (Paris)

Series AJ 38 – Commissariat Général aux Questions Juives (CGQJ) et Service de Restitution des Biens Spoliés
  5 – Correspondance – Intitulée "régional"
  6 – Dénonciations, plaints contre les Juifs; Lettres de Juifs au maréchal Pétain; Lettres en faveur de Juifs

7 – Tracts antisémites antérieurs à la guerre de 1939–40; Interceptions téléphoniques, rapports divers sur les Juifs, coupures de journaux, tracts.
52 – M 32 – Agriculture
  M 322 – Commerce agricole
61 – M 48 – Emigration juive
  M 60 – Trafic et marché noir juifs
65 – M 793A – Agriculture
66 – M 7991 – Santé publique
67 – M 8 – Dossier "psychologique" (dénonciations, protestations, rapports, tracts)
113 – Oeuvres juives d'assistance et de secours: documentation, correspondance
122
123 – 60 – Questions diverses
74 – Alsaciens-Lorrains
147 – Recensements des Juifs – Listes et statistiques de départements de la zone sud, 1944
230 – PQJ et SEC
242 – PQJ et SEC de Vichy
244 – Rapports d'activité des délégations régionales de la zone sud
253–280 – PQJ et SEC de Limoges

Aryanisation économique:
  539 – Juifs étrangers. Juifs alsaciens.

Other:
  608 – Statistiques diverses
  1141 – OSE et Oeuvre israélite de séjours à la campagne

UGIF:
  5770 – l'émigration, l'organisation des secours
  5771 – Association israélite pour la protection de la jeune fille
  5772 – Assistance aux Juifs
  5773 – Budgets, comptes rendus mensuels

Series AJ 43 – Organisation Internationale pour les Réfugiés (OIR)
  14 – Correspondance avec les organismes officiels et les organisations bénévoles
    113 – "Hias – JCA Emigration Association" (HICEM)
  15 – suite
    168 – "Central Council for Jewish Refugees"
    177 – "American Council for Judaism"
    189 – "American Jewish Conference"
  16 – suite
    307 – "Jewish Colonization Association"
  45
    96 – Enfants
      142 – Enfants emmenés de force hors de France
      216 – Enfants juifs en France occupée

46
     106 – Statistiques des réfugiés
     474 – Le problème des réfugiés juifs
  52
     112 – Assistance
     223 – Assistance aux Juifs par l'intermédiaire du Vatican
     226 – Juifs turcs en France
  84
     136 – Réfugiés espagnols
     584 – Réfugiés espagnols en France

Series F 1a – *Ministère de l'Intérieur – administration générale*
  3645 – Questions juives
  3660 – Réfugiés
  3661 – Secours National. Santé publique
  3706 – Ministère de l'Intérieur, sous-direction des cultes: statut des juifs
  3743 – Opinion publique
  3744 – Etat d'esprit (contrôle postal)
  3745 – Situation en France (en général et par régions). Réfugiés
  3784 – Lettres de condamnés à mort. L'Eglise et les Allemands. Alsace-Lorraine. Juifs
  4000 – Région de Limoges

Series F 1c III – *Rapports de Préfets, Ministère de l'Intérieur – Vichy 1940–4*
  1147 – Corrèze
  1150 – Creuse
  1197 – Vienne (Haute)
  1200 – Limoges – Rapports des Préfets Régionaux 1942–4

Series F 7 – *Police Générale*
  14926 – Inspection régionale de Limoges et commission de St. Amand
  14929 – Inspection régionale de Limoges
  Camps d'internement: classement par départements
    15096 – Calvados à Dordogne
    15110 – Vienne (Haute) à Yonne
    15310 – Juifs
    15347 – Questions juives
    16033 – Franchissement de la ligne de démarcation
    16044 – Etrangers exerçant une profession ambulante
    16113 – Tableaux de la population étrangère dans les départements

Series F 9 – *Affaires Militaires*
  5578 – Camps

Series F 23 – *Services Extraordinaires des Temps de Guerre*
  220–236 – Service Central des Réfugiés et des Alsaciens-Lorrains

Series F 60 – *Secrétariat Général du Gouvernement et Services du Premier Ministre*
  293 – Alsace-Lorraine
  294 – Alsace-Lorraine
  363 – Cultes

490 – Contrôle des Etrangers. Israélites.
491 – Israélites sous le Gouvernement de Vichy, correspondance
Series 72 AJ – Comité d'Histoire de la Deuxième Guerre Mondiale
5 – Enquête de la CHOLF dans la région de Limoges
71 – Service de protection des Juifs (devenu Mouvement national contre Racisme) et protection des étrangers (abbé Glasberg)
621 – Papiers Clément Vasserot – préfet de la Creuse pendant la guerre

Bibliothèque Marguerite Durand (Paris)
396 UNI – Union des femmes françaises 1939–1945
940.4 GUE – Guerre 1939–1945: Femmes dans la coupures
940.4 GUE – Guerre 1939–1945: Témoignages

Centre de Documentation Juive Contemporaine – CDJC (Paris)
LVII-6, 39, 73
CIX-14, 37, 43
CXCIII-83
CCCLXVI-1, 10, 16
CCCLXXIII-1
CCCLXXIV-1, 5, 10 and album
CDXI-61
CDXII-51
CDXIII-31, 37, 38, 39
CDXV-22, 34, 38, 53
CDXXX-15
DCLXIV-9

Oeuvre de Secours aux Enfants – OSE
(Library of the Alliance israélite universelle (AIU) Paris)
Boîte I – Histoire de l'OSE
Boîte III – Correspondance diverse
Boîte XXV – Rapports d'activité
Boîte XXVI – Rapports de Centres medico-sociaux Limoges-Paris-Toulouse
Boîte XXVIII – Listes d'enfants placés en maisons OSE 1940 à 1943
Boîte XXXIX – Témoignages professionnels OSE

Service Historique de la Gendarmerie Nationale – SHGN (Fort de Charenton)

	Creuse		
Carton Number	Corps or Unit	Type	Period
12536	Groupement Creuse	R/2	1939–41
12537	Grpt. Creuse	R/2	4/22/1941–2/18/1942
12538	Grpt. Creuse	R/2	2/18/1942–12/16/1942
12539	Grpt. Creuse	R/2	12/16/1942–9/20/1943
12540	Grpt. Creuse	R/2	9/2/1943–5/27/1944
12552	Compagnie Bourganeuf	R/4	1939–46
12557	Cie. Guéret	R/4	1939–44
12631	Battalion La Souterraine	R/2	1/18/1939–2/8/1945

	Haute-Vienne		
Carton Number	Corps or Unit	Type	Period
12639	Groupement Haute-Vienne	R/2	1/2/1939–7/26/1940
12640	Grpt. Haute-Vienne	R/2	7/26/1940–11/4/1941
12641	Grpt. Haute-Vienne	R/2	11/4/1941–12/1/1942
12642	Grpt. Haute-Vienne	R/2	1942–3
12643	Grpt. Haute-Vienne	R/2	11/4/1943–9/22/1944
12647	Grpt. Haute-Vienne	R/4	1938–46
12691	Battalion Limoges	R/4	1939–46
12701	BT. Limoges	CD	1944–5
12701	BT. Limoges	PV	1941
12702	BT. Limoges	PV	1941
12703	BT. Limoges	PV	1941
12704	BT. Limoges	PV	1941
12705	BT. Limoges	PV	1942
12706	BT. Limoges	PV	1942
12707	BT. Limoges	PV	1942–3
12708	BT. Limoges	PV	1943
12709	BT. Limoges	PV	1943
12710	BT. Limoges	PV	1943–4
12721	BT. Nexon	R/4	1942–6
12724	BT. Nexon	PV	1940–1
12725	BT. Nexon	PV	1942
12725 bis	BT. Nexon	PV	1943–4
12741	BT. St. Germain-les-Belles	R/4	1939–46
12750	BT. St. Léonard-de-Noblat	R/4	1939–42 and 1944–6
12753	BT. St. Léonard-de-Noblat	PV	1941
12754	BT. St. Léonard-de-Noblat	PV	1941–2
12755	BT. St. Léonard-de-Noblat	PV	1943
12756	BT. St. Léonard-de-Noblat	PV	1943–4
12768	BT. St. Yrieix-la-Perche	R/4	1939–46

U.S. Holocaust Memorial Museum Archives – USHMM (Washington, D.C.)

Microfilm Collections

RG-43.004 – Selected records from the Centre de Documentation Juive Contemporaine relating to the "Jewish Question" in France.

RG-43.005M – Union Générale des Israélites de France: Records, 1940–4 from YIVO Archives

RG-43.017M – Record Group F 9 (Affaires Militaires) from Archives Nationales de France

RG-43.024M – Commissariat Général aux Questions Juives from the Centre de Documentation Juive Contemporaine

1997.A.0197 – Selected Records from the Departmental Archives of Bas-Rhin, France

1997.A.0282 – Record Group AJ 38 (Commissariat Général aux Questions Juives) from Archives Nationales de France
1999.A.0004 – Record Group AJ 43 (Organisation Internationale pour les Réfugiés) from Archives Nationales de France

Memoirs and Personal Papers
RG-02.013 – Esther Bergman memoir
RG-02.114 – "A Memoir for Paul, David, and Adam" by Paulette Barrett
RG-02.138 – Childhood Memoirs of World War II by Eva Rappart Edmands
RG-02.141 – Nadia Gould collection
RG-02.195 – "Dear Kurt" by Ruth Ilan
RG-10.144 – Lucien Dreyfuss collection, 1903–43
RG-10.148 – Hans Behr letter and postcards, Feb.–Mar. 1943
RG-23.005 – Cecile Cerf papers, [1944] –61
RG-43.002 – "An Unpublished Chapter in the History of the Deportation of Foreign Jews from France in 1942" by Roswell McClelland

Oral Histories
RG-50.002*32 – David Dorfman (March 8, 1989). Kean College of New Jersey collection
RG-50.002*34 – Lilly Gottlieb (February 7, 1989). Kean College of New Jersey collection
RG-50.002*119 – Marguerite Jeremias (November 2, 1988). Kean College of New Jersey collection
RG-50.030*064 – Eva Edmands (October 18, 1990)
RG-50.030*136 – Simone Margaret Weil Lipman (July 3, 1990)
RG-50.030*186 – Liane Reif-Lehrer (October 24, 1989)
RG-50.030*194 – Alice Lang Rosen (March 6, 1990)
RG-50.030*230 – Hessy Levinson Taft (February 15, 1990)
RG-50.030*374 – Marthe Cohn (July 29, 1996)
RG-50.042*0011 – Paulette Fink (March 7, 1992)
RG-50.091*35 – Marguerite Morris (November 14, 1984). National Council of Jewish Women, Cleveland Section collection
RG-50.106*19 – Ernie Marx (July 26, 1995). Oral History Volunteer collection (audiotape)
RG-50.146*03 – Sophie Micnik. (April 11, 1990). Mémoire et Documents collection
RG-50.146*04 – Frida Wattenberg (no date). Mémoire et Documents collection
RG-50.146*09 – Leon Tsevery (1994). Mémoire et Documents collection
RG-50.146*15 – Cypora Gutnic (October 20, 1989). Mémoire et Documents collection
RG-50.146*19 – Frania Haverland (March 21, 1994). Mémoire et Documents collection
RG-50.146*27 – Jacques-Albert Zandkorn (May 10, 1993). Mémoire et Documents collection
RG-50.146*28 – Jacques Szmulewicz (January 30, 1994). Mémoire et Documents collection
RG-50.146*31 – Margareth Acher (1993). Mémoire et Documents collection

RG-50.146*32 – Francine Christophe (May 12, 1997). Mémoire et Documents collection
RG-50.393*0025 – Philip Vock (May 26, 1994)
RG-50.431*365 – Joseph Lerman (March 7, 1996). Oral History Collection of the Holocaust Documentation and Education Center, Inc.

Personal Interviews
Aimé Avniel (August 16, 2000)
Micheline Cohen (August 9, 2000)
Suzanne Dortort-Glantz (August 2, 2000)
Gerda Freund (August 15, 2000)
Marguerite Jeremias (August 29, 2000)
Eva Lang (August 10, 2000)
Joseph Lerman (July 27, 2000)
Stephan Lewy (August 14, 2000)
Liane Reif-Lehrer (August 7, 2000)
Frederick Reif (August 1, 2000)
Louis Scott (August 18, 2000)
Henry Wertheimer (August 7, 2000)

Questionnaire Responses
Marcel Baum
Fernande Bodner
Harry Herzel
Ida Kosiorowski
James P. Marcuse
Eric P. Thorn
Hélène Villeroy
George Zelik Zeff

Wished to remain anonymous:
Rodolphe E.
Leon B.
Lydia J.
Felix R.
Ruth R.

Newspapers
Le Courrier du Centre
Le Courrier de le Creuse
L'Echo des Réfugiés
L'Humanité
Le Journal Officiel
Je suis partout

Films
Une Affaire de femmes. Directed by Claude Chabrol. 1988.
Le Chagrin et la pitié. Directed by Marcel Ophuls. 1971.
The Children of Chabannes. Produced and directed by Lisa Gossells and Dean Weatherell. New York: Perennial Pictures, 2000.
Le Corbeau. Directed by Henri-Georges Clouzot. Paris: Continental Films, 1943.

Into the Arms of Strangers: Stories of the Kindertransport. Directed by Mark Jonathan Harris. 2000.
Uranus. Directed by Claude Berri. 1990.

Books and Articles

Accomando, Claire Hsu. *Love and Rutabaga: A Remembrance of the War Years*. New York: St. Martin's Press, 1993.

Adler, Jacques. *The Jews of Paris and the Final Solution: Communal Response and Internal Conflicts, 1940–1944*. New York and Oxford: Oxford University Press, 1987.

Les Affameurs. 1946.

Allen, Keith. "Sharing Scarcity: Bread Rationing and the First World War in Berlin, 1914–1923." *Journal of Social History* 32:2 (Winter 1998): 371–93.

Amouroux, Henri. *La grande histoire des Français après l'occupation*. Vol. 9: "*Les règlements de comptes, Septembre 1944–Janvier 1945*." Paris: Editions Robert Laffont, 1991

———. *La grande histoire des Français sous l'occupation*. 8 vols. Paris: Editions Robert Laffont, 1976.

———. *La vie des Français sous l'occupation*. Paris: Fayard, 1961.

Anderson, Benedict. *Imagined Communities: Reflections on the Origin and Spread of Nationalism*. London and New York: Verso, 1983, 1991.

Asséo, Henriette. *Les Tsiganes: une destinée européenne*. Paris: Gallimard, 1994.

Audoin-Rouzeau, Stéphane. *Men at War 1914–1918: National Sentiment and Trench Journalism in France during the First World War*, translated by Helen McPhail. Oxford and Washington, D.C.: Berg, 1992, 1995.

Avakoumovitch, Ivan. "Les manifestations de femmes 1940–1944." *Cahiers d'histoire de l'institute de recherches marxistes*. No. 45 (1991): 5–53.

L'Avant-Scène: Cinéma 186 (April 15, 1977).

Aymé, Marcel. *Uranus*. Paris: Gallimard, 1948.

———. "Traversée de Paris"in *Le Vin de Paris*. Paris: Gallimard, 1947.

Azéma, Jean-Pierre, and François Bédarida. *La France des années noires*. 2 vols. Paris: Seuil, 1993.

Balaire, Mireille. "La Haute-Vienne d'Août 1930 à Juillet 1940." Mémoire de Maîtrise en Histoire Contemporaine. 2 volumes. UER de Lettre et Sciences humaines de Limoges. Sous la direction de M.G. Le Beguec. 1988–1989.

Baumann, Denise. *Une Famille comme les autres*. Paris: Société d'Édition Droit & Liberté, 1973.

Becker, Jean-Jacques. *The Great War and the French People*, translated by Arnold Pomerans. Introduction by Jay Winter. Leamington Spa/Heidelberg/Dover, New Hampshire: Berg, 1995.

Bellanger, Claude. *Histoire Générale de la Presse Française Vol. 4 (1940–1958)*. Paris: Presses Universitaires de France, 1975.

Bellot-Antony, Christine. "La Vie quotidienne en Creuse durant la Seconde guerre mondiale (1939–1945)."Mémoire de Maîtrise d'histoire contemporaine. Sous la Direction de M le Professeur André Gueslin. Université Blaise Pascal(Clermont-Ferrand II), 1993.

Bensimon, Doris, and Sergio Della Pergola. *La Population Juive de France: Socio-Démographie et Identité*. Edition of *Jewish Population Studies* 17 (1986).

Bergerson, Andrew Stuart. *Ordinary Germans in Extraordinary Times: The Nazi Revolution in Hildesheim*. Bloomington and Indianapolis: Indiana University Press, 2004.

Bernadac, Christian. *L'Holocauste oublié: Le massacre des tsiganes*. Paris: Editions France-Empire, 1979.

Billig, Joseph. *Le Commissariat général aux questions juives (1941–1944)*. 2 vols. Paris: Editions du Centre, 1955.

Birnbaum, Pierre. "Between Social and Political Assimilation: Remarks on the History of Jews in France" translated by Jacqueline Kay, in *Paths of Emancipation: Jews, States, and Citizenship*, edited by Pierre Birnbaum and Ira Katznelson. Princeton, New Jersey: Princeton University Press, 1995.

———. *La France aux Français: Histoire des haines nationalistes*. Paris: Editions du Seuil, 1993.

Bonzon, Thierry, and Belinda Davis. "Feeding the Cities" in *Capital Cities at War: Paris, London, Berlin 1914–1918*, edited by Jay Winter and Jean-Louis Robert. Cambridge: Cambridge University Press, 1997: 305–41.

Boswell, Laird. "From Liberation to Purge Trials in the 'Mythic Provinces': Recasting French Identities in Alsace and Lorraine, 1918–1920." *French Historical Studies* 23:1 (Winter 2000): 129–62.

———. "Franco-Alsatian Conflict and the Crisis of National Sentiment during the Phoney War." *Journal of Modern History* 71 (September 1999): 552–84.

———. *Rural Communism in France, 1920–1939*. Ithaca, New York, and London: Cornell University Press, 1998.

Boulet, François. "Etrangers et Juifs en Haute-Loire de 1936 à 1944." *Cahiers de la Haute-Loire: Revue d'études locales* (1992): 301–50.

Bourdelle, Jean. *Limoges (1870–1919): la mémoire ouvrière*. Périgueux: Pierre Fanlac, 1984.

Bouton, Cynthia A. *The Flour War: Gender, Class, and Community in Late Ancien Régime French Society*. University Park: The Pennsylvania State University Press, 1993.

Brubaker, Rogers. *Citizenship and Nationhood in France and Germany*. Cambridge, Massachusetts: Harvard University Press, 1992.

Burrin, Philippe. *France under the Germans: Collaboration and Compromise*, translated by Janet Lloyd. New York: The New Press, 1996.

Caron, Vicki. "French Public Opinion and the 'Jewish Question,' 1930–1942: The Role of Middle-Class Professional Associations" in *Nazi Europe and the Final Solution*, edited by David Bankier and Israel Gutman. Jerusalem: Yad Vashem, 2003.

———. *Uneasy Asylum: France and the Jewish Refugee Crisis, 1933–1942*. Stanford, California: Stanford University Press, 1999.

———. "The Antisemitic Revival in France in the 1930s: The Socioeconomic Dimension Reconsidered." *The Journal of Modern History* 70:1 (March 1998): 24–73.

———. "The Politics of Frustration: French Jewry and the Refugee Crisis in the 1930s." *The Journal of Modern History* 65:2 (June 1993): 311–56.

———. *Between France and Germany: The Jews of Alsace-Lorraine, 1871–1918*. Stanford, California: Stanford University Press, 1988.

———. "Prelude to Vichy: France and the Jewish Refugees in the Era of Appeasement." *Journal of Contemporary History* 20:1 (January 1985): 157–76.

Cazals, Claude. *La Gendarmerie sous l'occupation*. Paris: Les Editions La Musse, 1994.

Cépède, Michel. *Agriculture et Alimentation en France durant la IIe Guerre Mondiale*. Paris: Editions M-Th. Génin, 1961.

Chateau, René. "*Le Corbeau* ridiculise la censure à Vichy" in *Le cinéma français sous l'Occupation. 1940–1944*. Courbevoie: Editions René Chateau, La Mémoire du cinéma, 1995.

Comité Français de Service Social. *Journées d'Études de Service Social. Paris, 24–25 Février 1940. Le Travail Social auprès des Évacués dans les Départements d'Accueil*. Paris: Édition Sociale Française.

"Convention on the Prevention and Punishment of the Crime of Genocide." *United Nations Treaty Series* 78 (1951).

Corbin, Alain. *Archaisme et modernité en Limousin au XIXe siècle 1845–1880*. 2 vols. Paris: Editions Marcel Rivière et Cie, 1975.

Cretzmeyer, Stacy. *Your Name is Renée: Ruth Kapp Hartz's Story as a Hidden Child in Nazi-occupied France*. New York and Oxford: Oxford University Press, 1999.

Daguin, Marcelle. *Recettes de cuisine et conseils ménagers en période de restriction*. Paris: A. Michel, 1940.

Darmon, Pierre. *Le monde du cinéma sous l'Occupation*. Paris: Stock, 1997.

Davis, Belinda J. *Home Fires Burning: Food, Politics, and Everyday Life in World War I Berlin*. Chapel Hill and London: The University of North Carolina Press, 2000.

Delclitte, Christophe. "La catégorie juridique 'nomade' dans la loi de 1912." *Hommes & Migrations* 1188–89 (Juin–Juillet 1995): 23–30.

De Grazia, Victoria with Ellen Furlough, eds. *The Sex of Things: Gender and Consumption in Historical Perspective*. Berkeley: University of California Press, 1996.

De Pomiane, Edouard. *Cuisine et restrictions*. Paris: Corrêa, 1940.

Diamond, Hanna. *Women and the Second World War in France, 1939–48: Choices and Constraints*. London: Longman, 1999.

Dietrich, Claire. "Les protestants d'Alsace du Nord durant l'évacuation en Haute-Vienne (1939–1940)." *Bulletin de la Société de l'Histoire du Protestantisme Français* 133 (October, November, December 1987): 579–601.

Dombrowski, Nicole Ann. "Beyond the Battlefield: The French Civilian Exodus of May–June 1940." Ph.D. Dissertation, New York University, 1995.

Downs, Laura Lee. *Childhood in the Promised Land: Working-Class Movements and the Colonies de Vacances in France, 1880–1960*. Durham, North Carolina and London: Duke University Press, 2002.

Dupeux, Georges. *Atlas Historique de l'urbanisation de la France (1811–1975)*. Paris: Editions du Centre National de la Recherche Scientifique, 1981.

Dutourd, Jean. *The Best Butter*, translated by Robin Chancellor. New York: Greenwood Press, 1969.

Du Plessis de Grénédan, "Le Marché Noir à la Campagne."Collection "mon Village." Paris: Foyer Rural, 1942?
Eggers, Christian. "L'internement sous toutes ses formes: approche d'une vue d'ensemble du système d'internement dans la zone de Vichy." *Le Monde juif* (January–April 1995): 7–75.
Ehrlich, Evelyn. *Cinema of Paradox: French Filmmaking Under the German Occupation*. New York: Columbia University Press, 1985.
Engel, Barbara Alpern. "Not by Bread Alone: Subsistence Riots in Russia during World War I." *Journal of Modern History* 69 (December 1997): 696–721.
Esquilat, Pierre. *Le Ravitaillement de la France en temps de guerre*. Paris: Librairie du Recueil Sirey, 1941.
Farge, Arlette. *Subversive Words: Public Opinion in Eighteenth-Century France*, translated by Rosemary Morris. University Park: The Pennsylvania State University Press, 1995.
Farge, Yves. *Le Pain de la Corruption*. Paris: Éditions du Chêne, 1947.
Farmer, Sarah. *Martyred Village: Commemorating the 1944 Massacre at Oradour-sur-Glane*. Berkeley and Los Angeles: University of California Press, 1999.
———. "The Communist Resistance in the Haute-Vienne." *French Historical Studies* 14:1 (Spring 1985): 89–116.
Filhol, Emmanuel. *Un camp de concentration français: Les Tsiganes alsaciens-lorrains à Crest 1915–1919*. Grenoble: Presses Universitaires de Grenoble, 2004.
———. "L'internement et la déportation de Tsiganes français sous l'Occupation: Mérignac-Poitiers-Sachsenhausen, 1940–1945." *Revue d'histoire de la Shoah: Le monde juif* 170 (September–December 2000): 136–82.
Fishman, Sarah. *The Battle for Children: World War II, Youth Crime, and Juvenile Justice in Twentieth-Century France*. Cambridge, Massachusetts and London: Harvard University Press, 2002.
———. *We Will Wait: Wives of French Prisoners of War, 1940–1945*. New Haven, Connecticut and London: Yale University Press, 1991.
———. "Waiting for the Captive Sons of France: Prisoner of War Wives, 1940–1945" in *Behind the Lines: Gender and the Two World Wars*, edited by Margaret Randolph Higoneet, Jane Jenson, Sonya Michel, and Margaret Collins Weitz. New Haven, Connecticut and London: Yale University Press, 1987.
Fishman, Sarah, Laura Lee Downs, Ioannis Sinanoglou, Leonard V. Smith, and Robert Zaretsky, eds. *France at War: Vichy and the Historians*. Oxford and New York: Berg, 2000.
Fitzpatrick, Sheila, and Robert Gellately, eds. *Accusatory Practices: Denunciation in Modern European History, 1789–1989*. Chicago and London: The University of Chicago Press, 1997.
Fitzpatrick, Sheila. *Everyday Stalinism: Ordinary Life in Extraordinary Times, Soviet Russia in the 1930s*. New York and Oxford: Oxford University Press, 2000.
———. *Stalin's Peasants: Resistance and Survival in the Russian Village after Collectivization*. New York and Oxford: Oxford University Press, 1994.
Fogg, Shannon L. "Denunciations, Community Outsiders, and Material Shortages in Vichy France." *Proceedings of the Western Society for French History* 31 (2003): 271–89.

Fonseca, Isabel. *Bury Me Standing: The Gypsies and Their Journey*. New York: Alfred A. Knopf, 1996.
Fontenelle, Sébastien. *La France des mouchards: Enquête sur la délation*. Paris: Belfond, 1997.
Forien de Rochesnard, Jean-Georges. *Histoire du Rationnement Alimentaire au cours des Ages*. Auxerre: Imprimerie Moderne, 1949.
France during the German Occupation 1940–1944: A Collection of 292 Statements on the Government of Maréchal Pétain and Pierre Laval, translated by Philip W. Whitcomb. 3 vols. Stanford. California: Stanford University Press for The Hoover Institution on War, Revolution, and Peace, 1958.
La France peut-elle se nourrir? Paris: Editions R.B. Textes et Dessins de Pélan, 1942.
Francos, Ania. *Il était des femmes dans la Résistance*. Paris: Stock, 1978.
Frankel, Johnathan, and Steven J. Zipperstein, eds. *Assimilation and Community: The Jews in Nineteenth-Century Europe*. Cambridge: Cambridge University Press, 1992.
Fraser, Angus. *The Gypsies*. Oxford and Cambridge: Blackwell, 1992, 1996.
Friedländer, Saul. *When Memory Comes*, translated by Helen R. Lane. New York: Farrar Straus Giroux, 1979.
Fulbrook, Mary. *The Divided Nation: A History of Germany 1918–1990*. New York and Oxford: Oxford University Press, 1992.
Gatard, Marie. *La guerre, mon père*. Poitiers: Mercure de France, 1978.
Gellately, Robert. "The Gestapo and German Society: Political Denunciation in the Gestapo Case Files." *Journal of Modern History* 60 (December 1988): 654–94.
Gellately, Robert, and Nathan Stoltzfus, eds. *Social Outsiders in Nazi Germany*. Princeton, New Jersey and Oxford: Princeton University Press, 2001.
Gildea, Robert. *Marianne in Chains: In Search of the German Occupation 1940–45*. London: Macmillan, 2002.
Gildea, Robert, Olivier Wieviorka, and Anette Warring, eds. *Surviving Hitler and Mussolini: Daily Life in Occupied Europe*. Oxford and New York: Berg, 2006.
Gobitz, Gérard. *Les Déportations de Réfugiés de Zone Libre en 1942. Récits et documents concernant les régions administratives de Toulouse, Nice, Lyon, Limoges, Clermont-Ferrand, Montpellier (Camp de Rivesaltes)*. Paris: L'Harmattan, 1996.
Guillaume, Pierre. "Du Bon usage des immigrés en temps de crise et de guerre, 1932–1940" *Vingtième Siècle: Revue d'histoire* 7 (July–September 1985): 117–26.
Guillon, Jean-Marie, and Pierre Laborie, eds. *Mémoire et Histoire: la Résistance*. Toulouse: Editions Privat, 1995.
Guingouin, Georges. *Quatre ans de lutte sur le sol limousin*. Paris: Hachette, 1974.
Halimi, André. *La Délation sous l'Occupation*. Paris: Editions Alain Moreau, 1983.
Hallie, Philip P. *Lest Innocent Blood be Shed: The Story of the Village of Le Chambon, and How Goodness Happened There*. New York: Harper & Row, 1979.
Halls, W. D. *The Youth of Vichy France*. Oxford: Clarendon Press, 1981.
Hantarrède, Guy. "Les Tsiganes au camp des Alliers (novembre 1940–mars 1946)." *Etudes Tsiganes* 13:1 (1999): 120–31.

Hazan, Kathy. *Les orphelins de la Shoah: les maisons de l'espoir (1944–1960)*. Paris: Belles Lettres, 2000.

Healy, Maureen. *Vienna and the Fall of the Habsburg Empire: Total War and Everyday Life in World War I*. Cambridge: Cambridge University Press, 2004.

Hirschfeld, Gerhard and Patrick Marsh, editors. *Collaboration in France: Politics and Culture during the Nazi Occupation, 1940–1944*. Oxford, New York, and Munich: Berg, 1989.

Hubert, Marie-Christine. "Les Réglementations anti-tsiganes en France et en Allemagne, avant et pendant l'Occupation." *Revue d'histoire de la Shoah: le monde juif* 167 (1999): 20–52.

———. "L'internement des Tsiganes en France 1940–1946." *Etudes Tsiganes* 13:1 (1999): 10–18.

Hyman, Paula E. *The Jews of Modern France*. Berkeley, Los Angeles, London: University of California Press, 1998.

———. *The Emancipation of the Jews of Alsace: Acculturation and Tradition in the Nineteenth Century*. New Haven, Connecticut and London: Yale University Press, 1991.

Jackson, Julian. *France: The Dark Years 1940–1944*. Oxford and New York: Oxford University Press, 2001.

Journal de Louis Aron, Directeur de la Maison Israélite de Refuge pour l'Enfance Neuilly-sur-Seine 1939 Crocq (Creuse) 1939–1942 Chaumont (Creuse) 1942–1944, edited by Serge Klarsfeld with Annette Zaidman. Paris: L'Association Les Fils et Filles des Déportés Juifs de France and the Beate Klarsfeld Foundation, 1998.

Les Juifs sous l'occupation: Recueil des textes officiels français et allemands 1940/1944. Paris: Centre de Documentation Juive Contemporaine and Association Les Fils et Filles des Déportés Juifs de France, 1982.

Kanner, Mia Amalia, and Eve Rosenzweig Kugler. *Shattered Crystals*. New York, London, Jerusalem: C.I.S Publishers, 1997.

Kaplan, Marion A. *Between Dignity and Despair: Jewish Life in Nazi Germany*. New York and Oxford: Oxford University Press, 1998.

Kaspi, André. *Les Juifs pendant l'Occupation*. Paris: Editions du Seuil, 1991, 1997.

Kedward, H. R. *In Search of the Maquis: Rural Resistance in Southern France 1942–1944*. Oxford and New York: Oxford University Press, 1993.

———. "The Maquis and the Culture of the Outlaw (With Particular Reference to the Cévennes)" in *Vichy France and the Resistance: Culture & Ideology*, edited by Roderick Kedward and Roger Austin. London and Sydney: Croom Helm, 1985.

Kenrick, Donald, and Grattan, Puxon. *Gypsies under the Swastika*. Hatfield, United Kingdom: Gypsy Research Centre, University of Hertfordshire Press, 1995.

———. *The Destiny of Europe's Gypsies*. New York: Basic Books, Inc., 1972.

Kieval, Hillel. "Legality and Resistance in Vichy France: The Rescue of Jewish Children." *Proceedings of the American Philosophical Society* 124:5 (October 1980): 339–66.

Kitson, Simon. *Vichy et la chasse aux espions nazis 1940–1942: complexités de la politique de collaboration*. Paris: Editions Autrement, 2005.

Kladstrup, Don, and Petie Kladstrup with J. Kim Munholland. *Wine and War: The French, the Nazis, and the Battle for France's Greatest Treasure*. New York: Broadway Books, 2001.

Klarsfeld, Serge. *French Children of the Holocaust: A Memorial*, edited by Susan Cohen, Howard M. Epstein, Serge Klarsfeld, translated by Glorianne Depondt and Howard M. Epstein. New York and London: New York University Press, 1996.

———. *Le Mémorial de la deportation des Juifs de France*. Paris: Beate et Serge Klarsfeld, 1978.

Kligman, Gail. *The Politics of Duplicity: Controlling Reproduction in Ceausescu's Romania*. Berkeley, Los Angeles, London: University of California Press, 1998.

Kofman, Sarah. *Rue Ordener, Rue Labat* translated by Ann Smock. Lincoln and London: University of Nebraska Press, 1996.

Koreman, Megan. *The Expectation of Justice: France 1944–1946*. Durham, North Carolina and London: Duke University Press, 1999.

Kustanowitz, Esther. *The Hidden Children of the Holocaust: Teens who Hid from the Nazis*. New York: The Rosen Publishing Group, Inc., 1999.

Laborie, Pierre. *Les Français des années troubles: De la guerre d'Espagne à la Libération*. Paris: Desclée de Brouwer, 2001.

———. *L'opinion française sous Vichy: Les Français et la crise d'identité nationale 1936–1944*. Paris: Editions du Seuil, 1990, 2001.

———. "L'idée de Résistance, entre définition et sens; retour sur un questionnement." *Les Cahiers de l'Institut d'histoire du temps présent* 37 (December 1997): 73–91.

Lacan, Claude, Georges-Marie Proux, and Roland du Chalard. *Le Limousin de la Défaite et de l'Occupation. Chronique des années 1940–1944*. Limoges: Editions René Dessagne, 1978.

Lebovics, Herman. *True France: The Wars over Cultural Identity, 1940–1945*. Ithaca, New York and London: Cornell University Press, 1992.

Lecornu, Bernard. *Un préfet sous l'occupation allemande*. Paris: Editions France-Empire, 1984.

"Leçons Pratiques d'Actualités Alimentaires." December 1940, Croix-Rouge Française (Service Social).

Lefébure, Antoine. *Les Conversations secrètes des Français sous l'Occupation*. Paris: Plon, 1993.

Lefebvre, Georges. *The Great Fear of 1789: Rural Panic in Revolutionary France*, translated by Joan White. London: NLB, 1973.

Lemalet, Martine, editor. *Au secours des enfants du siècle: Regards croisés sur l'OSE*. Paris: Nil Editions, 1993.

Levendel, Isaac. *Not the Germans Alone: A Son's Search for the Truth of Vichy*. Evanston, Illinois: Northwestern University Press, 1999.

Lévy, Gaston. *Souvenirs d'un médecin d'enfants à l'OSE en France occupée et en Suisse, 1940–1945*. Paris, Jerusalem: Editions Le Manuscrit, 1974.

Lewy, Guenter. *The Nazi Persecution of the Gypsies*. Oxford and New York: Oxford University Press, 2000.

———. "Gypsies and Jews Under the Nazis." *Holocaust and Genocide Studies* 13:3 (Winter 1999): 383–404.

Liégeois, Jean-Pierre. *Gypsies and Travellers*. Strasbourg: Council of Europe, 1987.

Limouzin, René. *Une adolescence paysanne pendant la Seconde Guerre Mondiale*. (Nouvelle édition du "Temps des J3.") Naves: Editions de La Veytizou, 1996.

Lubetzki, J. *La Condition des juifs en France sous l'occupation allemande 1940–1944: la législation raciale.* Paris: Centre de Documentation Juive Contemporaine, 1945.

Lüdtke, Alf, ed. *The History of Everyday Life: Reconstructing Historical Experiences and Ways of Life,* translated by William Templer. Princeton, New Jersey: Princeton University Press, 1995.

Lutz, Brenda Davis, and James M. Lutz. "Gypsies as Victims of the Holocaust." *Holocaust and Genocide Studies* 9:3 (Winter 1995): 346–59.

Mabon-Fall, Armelle. *Les assistantes sociales au temps de Vichy: Du silence à l'oubli.* Paris: Éditions L'Harmattan, 1995.

Maga, Timothy P. "Closing the Door: The French Government and Refugee Policy, 1933–1939." *French Historical Studies* 12:3 (Spring 1982): 424–42.

Mandel, Maud S. *In the Aftermath of Genocide: Armenians and Jews in Twentieth-Century France.* Durham, North Carolina, and London: Duke University Press, 2003.

Marrus, Michael R. and Robert O. Paxton. *Vichy France and the Jews.* New York: Basic Books, 1981.

Marrus, Michael R. "Coming to Terms with Vichy." *Holocaust and Genocide Studies* 9:1 (Spring 1995): 23–41.

Merriman, John M. *The Red City: Limoges and the French Nineteenth Century.* New York and Oxford: Oxford University Press, 1985.

Muel-Dreyfus, Francine. *Vichy et l'éternel féminin.* Paris: Seuil, 1996.

Noiriel, Gérard. *The French Melting Pot: Immigration, Citizenship, and National Identity,* translated by Geoffroy de Laforcade. Foreword by Charles Tilly. Minneapolis and London: University of Minnesota Press, 1996.

Nye, Robert A. *Crime, Madness, and Politics in Modern France: The Medical Concept of National Decline.* Princeton, New Jersey: Princeton University Press, 1984.

Ofer, Dalia. "Everyday Life of Jews under Nazi Occupation: Methodological Issues" translated by Naftali Greenwood. *Holocaust and Genocide Studies* 9:1 (Spring 1995): 42–69.

Oms, Marcel. "Le Corbeau et ses quatre vérités." *Les Cahiers de la cinémathèque* 8 (1973): 58–61.

Orieux, Jean. *Souvenirs de Campagnes.* Paris: Flammarion, 1978.

Parrotin, Marc. *Immigrés dans la Résistance en Creuse.* Ahun: Editions Verso, 1998.

———. *Femmes de la Résistance en Creuse.* Ahun: Verso, 1997.

———. *La Resistance en Creuse.* Limoges: Verso, 1995.

———. *Le Temps du Maquis: Histoire de la Résistance en Creuse.* Guéret: Verso, 1984.

Paxton, Robert O. *French Peasant Fascism: Henry Dorgères's Greenshirts and the Crises of French Agriculture, 1929–1939.* New York and Oxford: Oxford University Press, 1997.

———. *Vichy France: Old Guard and New Order 1940–1944.* New York: Columbia University Press, 1972.

Pernot, Mathieu, editor. *Un Camp pour les Bohémiens: Mémoires du camp d'internement pour nomades de Saliers.* Arles: Actes Sud, 1991.

Peschanski, Denis. *Vichy 1940–1944: Contrôle et exclusion*. Brussels: Editions Complexe, 1997.

———. "Control or Integration? Information and Propaganda under Vichy" in *War & Society in Twentieth-Century France*, edited by Michael Scriven and Peter Wagstaff. New York: Berg, 1991.

Peschanski, Denis with Marie-Christine Hubert and Emmanuel Philippon. *Les Tsiganes en France 1939–1946*. Paris: CNRS Editions, 1994.

Pétain, Philippe. *Discours aux Français, 17 juin 1940–20 août 1944*, edited by Jean-Claude Barbas. Paris: Albin Michel, 1989.

Peukert, Detlev J. K. *Inside Nazi Germany: Conformity, Opposition, and Racism in Everyday Life*, translated by Richard Deveson. New Haven, Connecticut, and London: Yale University Press, 1987.

Piazza, Pierre. *Histoire de la Carte nationale d'identité*. Paris: Odile Jacob, 2004.

Pilard, Philippe. *Henri-Georges Clouzot*. Paris: Editions Seghers, 1969.

Pollard, Miranda. *Reign of Virtue: Mobilizing Gender in Vichy France*. Chicago and London: The University of Chicago Press, 1998.

Pour vivre mieux en temps de guerre, guide pratique donnant des conseils pour la santé de l'enfant, des remèdes simples pour les premiers soins, des manières de s'installer à peu de frais, un petit manuel de défense passive et les recettes de cuisine économique de Tante Marcelle. Paris: Horizons de France, 1939.

Poznanski, Renée. "French Public Opinion and the Jews during World War II: Assumptions of the Clandestine Press" in *Facing the Nazi Genocide: Non-Jews and Jews in Europe*, edited by Beate Kosmala and Feliks Tych. Berlin: Metropol, 2004.

———. "The French Resistance: An Alternative Society for the Jews?" in *Nazi Europe and the Final Solution*, edited by David Bankier and Israel Gutman. Jerusalem: Yad Vashem, 2003.

———. *Jews in France during World War II*, translated by Nathan Bracher. Hanover and London: University Press of New England, Brandeis University Press in association with the United States Holocaust Memorial Museum, 2001.

Rajsfus, Maurice. *Des Juifs dans la collaboration: l'UGIF (1941–1944)*. Paris: Etudes et Documentation Internationales, 1980.

Raphaël, Freddy, and Robert Weyl. *Juifs en Alsace: Culture, société, histoire*. Toulouse: Privat, 1977.

Rémy, Dominique. *Les lois de Vichy: Actes dits "lois" de l'autorité de fait se prétendant "gouvernement" de l'État français*. Paris: Editions Romillat, 1992.

"Roma and Sinti: Under-Studied Victims of Nazism." Symposium Proceedings. Washington, D.C.: Center for Advanced Holocaust Studies, United States Holocaust Memorial Museum, 2002.

Rosenberg, Clifford. *Policing Paris: The Origins of Modern Immigration Control between the Wars*. Ithaca, New York and London: Cornell University Press, 2006.

Rousso, Henry. "L'Économie: Pénurie et Modernisation" in *La France des années noires* Vol. 1, edited by Jean-Pierre Azéma and François Bédarida. Paris: Seuil, 1993.

———. *The Vichy Syndrome: History and Memory in France since 1944*, translated by Arthur Goldhammer. Cambridge, Massachusetts: Harvard University Press, 1991.

Ryan, Donna F. *The Holocaust & the Jews of Marseille: The Enforcement of Anti-Semitic Policies in Vichy France*. Urbana and Chicago: University of Illinois Press, 1996.

———. "Ordinary Acts and Resistance: Women in Street Demonstrations and Food Riots in Vichy France." *Proceedings of the Annual Meeting of the Western Society for French History* 16 (1989): 400–7.

Sachar, Howard M. *The Course of Modern Jewish History*. New York: Vintage Books, 1958, 1977, 1990.

Samuel, Vivette. *Sauver les enfants*. Paris: Liana Levi, 1995.

Sanders, Paul. *Histoire du marché noir 1940–1946*. Paris: Perrin, 2001.

———. "Prélèvement économique: les activités allemandes de marché noir en France 1940–1943" in *L'Occupation, l'État français et les enterprises*, edited by Olivier Dard, Jean-Claude Daumas and François Marcot. Paris: ADHE, 2000.

Le Sauvetage des Enfants Juifs de France. Actes du Colloque de Guéret – 29 et 30 Mai 1996.

Sauvy, Alfred. *La vie économique des Français de 1939 à 1945*. Paris: Flammarion, 1978.

Schneider, William. "Toward the Improvement of the Human Race: The History of Eugenics in France." *The Journal of Modern History* 54:2 (June 1982): 268–91.

Schor, Ralph. "Le facteur religieux et l'intégration des étrangers en France (1919–1939)." *Vingtième Siècle: Revue d'histoire* 7 (July–September 1985): 103–15.

———. *L'Opinion française et les étrangers en France 1919–1939*. Paris: Publications de la Sorbonne, 1985.

Schwartz, Paula. "The politics of food and gender in occupied Paris." *Modern & Contemporary France* 7 (February 1999): 35–45.

———. "*Partisanes* and Gender Politics in Vichy France." *French Historical Studies* 16:1 (Spring 1989): 126–51.

———. "Redefining Resistance: Women's Activism in Wartime France" in *Behind the Lines: Gender and the Two World Wars*, edited by Margaret Randolph Higonnet et al. New Haven, Connecticut and London: Yale University Press, 1987.

Scott, James C. *Weapons of the Weak: Everyday Forms of Peasant Resistance*. New Haven, Connecticut: Yale University Press, 1985.

Sigot, Jacques. "La longue marche vers l'internement des Tsiganes en France pendant la seconde guerre mondiale." *Etudes Tsiganes* 3:1 (1999): 19–28.

———. *Ces barbelés oubliés par l'histoire. Un camp pour les Tsiganes...et les autres, Montreuil-Bellay 1940–1945*. Châteauneuf les Martigues: Wallâda, 1994.

Sims, Gregory. "Henri-Georges Clouzot's *Le Corbeau* (1943): The Work of Art as Will to Power." *Modern Language Notes* 114:4 (1999): 743–79.

Smith, Bonnie G. *Confessions of a Concierge: Madame Lucie's History of Twentieth-Century France*. New Haven, Connecticut and London: Yale University Press, 1985.

Soulignac, Yves. *Les Camps d'Internement en Limousin 1939–1945*. Saint-Paul: La Briderie, 1995.

Sweets, John F. "Jews and Non-Jews in France During the Second World War" in *Nazi Europe and the Final Solution*, edited by David Bankier and Israel Gutman. Jerusalem: Yad Vashem, 2003.

———. *Choices in Vichy France: The French under Nazi Occupation*. New York and Oxford: Oxford University Press, 1994.

———. "Hold that Pendulum! Redefining Fascism, Collaborationism and Resistance in France." *French Historical Studies* 15:4 (Fall 1988): 731–58.
Taylor, Lynne. *Between Resistance and Collaboration: Popular Protest in Northern France, 1940–45*. New York: St Martin's Press, 2000.
"Le temps des restrictions en France (1939–1949)." Special edition of *Les Cahiers de l'Institut d'Histoire du Temps Présent*, Vols. 32–33, edited by Dominique Veillon and Jean-Marie Flonneau. Paris: Institut d'Histoire du Temps Présent, 1996.
Trouillé, Pierre. *Journal d'un préfet pendant l'occupation (Corrèze 1944)*. Paris: Éditions J'ai lu, 1964.
Valet, Joseph. "Gitans et Voyageurs d'Auvergne durant la guerre 1939–45." *Etudes Tsiganes* 6:2 (1995): 211–19.
Vallotton, Benjamin. *Feuilles dans le vent*. Lausanne: Librairie F. Rouge & Cie, S.A., 1941.
Vallotton, Gritou, and Annie Vallotton. *C'était au jour le jour: Carnets (1939–1944)*. Paris: Editions Payot & Rivages, 1995.
Veillon, Dominique. *Vivre et Survivre en France 1939–1947*. Paris: Editions Payot & Rivages, 1995.
Vinen, Richard. *The Unfree French: Life under the Occupation*. New Haven, Connecticut, and London: Yale University Press, 2006.
Wahl, Alfred and Jean-Claude Richez. *La vie quotidienne en Alsace entre France et Allemagne 1850–1950*. Paris: Hachette, 1993.
Weber, Eugen. *The Hollow Years: France in the 1930s*. New York and London: W.W. Norton & Company, 1994.
———. *Peasants into Frenchmen: The Modernization of Rural France 1870–1914*. Stanford, California: Stanford University Press, 1976.
Williams, Patrick. *Gypsy World: The Silence of the Living and the Voices of the Dead*, translated by Catherine Tihanyi. Chicago and London: University of Chicago Press, 2003.
Yagil, Limore. "Typologie de la résistance sans armes et de l'aide aux juifs en Limousin." *Revue d'histoire de la Shoah: le monde juif* 172 (May–August 2001): 228–65.
Yale French Studies 73 (1987).
Yoors, Jan. *Crossing*. New York: Simon and Schuster, 1971.
———. *The Gypsies*. New York: Simon and Schuster, 1967.
Zaretsky, Robert. *Nîmes at War: Religion, Politics, and Public Opinion in the Gard, 1938–1944*. University Park: The Pennsylvania State University Press, 1995.
Zeitoun, Sabine. *L'Oeuvre de Secours aux enfants (O.S.E) sous l'Occupation en France, Du légalisme à la résistance 1940–1944*. Préface de Serge Klarsfeld. Paris: Éditions L'Harmattan, 1990.
———. *Ces enfants qu'il fallait sauver*. Paris: France Loisirs, 1989.
Zuccotti, Susan. *The Holocaust, the French, and the Jews*. Lincoln and London: University of Nebraska Press, 1993, 1999.

Index

agriculture
  in the Limousin 10–12
  Jews and 171–3
  labor shortages and 44, 69
  National Revolution and 33
Alliance Israélite Universelle 156
Allier 101
Allied landings
  in Normandy 1, 188
  in North Africa 6, 12, 50
allocations
  evacuees/refugees and 58, 67–70, 75–6, 78, 84, 118
  of material goods 48
Alsace-Lorraine
  evacuation of 11, 22, 56–8, 64, 154, 157
  German annexation of 76, 94
  Gypsies in 89, 94
  Jews in 81–3, 118
  religion in 59, 71
Ambazac (Haute-Vienne) 122, 130
American Friends' Service Committee (Quakers) 152
American Joint Distribution Committee 158
anthropometric cards 88, 90, 92, 101
Antignac, Joseph 117, 124, 127
antisemitism xv, 18, 59, 81, 84, 114, 142, 156, 193

economic 128, 143
Jewish children and 160, 177, 184–6
National Revolution and 111, 170, 171
public opinion and 16, 117, 127, 140, 155, 177–83
in rural areas 128, 176, 183
Appel, L' 134, 141
Appel du Centre, L' 11
armistice 4, 11, 12, 23, 24, 36, 76, 81, 93, 107
Aron, Louis 159–62, 168, 174–5, 179–82
Aron, Yvonne 159, 163, 182
assimilation
  of Alsatian evacuees 63, 70, 78, 84
  of Gypsies/Nomads 89, 93, 108–10, 192–4
  internment and 194
  of Jews 192–4
Aubusson (Creuse) 129, 158
August 26, 1942 roundup of Jews 81, 144
  consequences of 155, 174, 176
  public opinion after 143, 144, 183
Auschwitz-Birkenau 188, 194

bartering 6, 39, 40, 97
Bas-Rhin 58, 62

Bellac (Haute-Vienne) 25, 135, 138, 146
Bersac-sur-Rivalier (Haute-Vienne) 63
bicycle 20, 26, 100, 146, 190
black market 3, 6, 25, 29, 39, 189
  families and 34, 37, 195
  Germans and 46
  Gypsies and 97
  Jews and 111, 112, 114, 128–43, 150, 172
  Law of March 15, 1942, 25, 37
  lenience toward 38–9, 54, 131
  media and 134
  peasants and 31, 36, 139–41, 143, 150
  Pétain and 36
  prevention of 35–6
  Resistance and 54
black marketeers 6, 13, 30, 32, 116
Boches 62
Bouches-du-Rhône 93
Bourganeuf (Creuse) 129, 139, 185
Bousquet, René 43, 173
bread 2, 5, 8, 23, 24, 29, 36, 45, 48, 135, 180, 183, 191
Brive (Corrèze) 38, 185
Bussière, A. (general director for national security) 61, 92
Buxerolles (Haute-Vienne) 19

Catholic Church 178
  reaction to roundup of Jews 145
Catholics 59, 114, 157
censors and censorship 40
Chabannes (children's home) 43, 152, 158, 161, 163, 164, 166–8, 170, 175–7, 179, 181, 184
Chantiers de la Jeunesse 33
charity 82, 125, 145, 149, 168
Chaudier, Albert 145
Chaumont (children's home) 158, 160, 163, 168, 169, 175, 180, 181, 182, 184
Chautemps, Camille 65–6, 72
Châteauponsac (Haute-Vienne) 149
Chevrier, Félix 161, 170, 176, 179, 181, 186

children 2, 10, 22, 66, 123, 125, 126, 127, 135, 144, 153
  Alsatian 68, 71–4
  concentration camps and 175
  deportation of 154, 176, 195
  education and 71–2, 153, 159, 161, 163–4, 166
  Gypsy 96, 97, 102–8, 195
  in hiding 145, 175, 185
  internment of 104, 106, 107
  provisioning and 104–5, 168–9, 181
  rations and 5–6
  rescue of 153–4, 155, 156, 175–6, 186, 187
Clermont-Ferrand xv, 9, 15
Coal 4, 6, 23, 29, 44, 98
colis familiaux. See also family packages 25, 32–4, 36, 97, 130, 135, 190
collaboration xiii, xiv, 16, 17, 40, 46, 76, 176, 191
colonies de vacances See also vacation colonies 156–8, 164, 176, 185–6
Commissariat général aux questions juives (CGQJ) 117, 124, 125, 140, 148, 149
communism
  rural 49
communists 157, 178
  Feminine Committees 48
  propaganda and 178
  in Resistance 48, 50, 188
  as undesirables 13, 76
Communist Party (PCF) 47–9
Compulsory Labor Service. See also *Service du travail obligatoire* (STO) 15, 50, 55
concentration camps. See also internment camps 89, 92, 93, 95, 144, 151, 175, 185, 194, 195
Corrèze 10, 38, 103, 185
Courrier du Centre, Le 23, 60, 62, 65, 66, 69, 77
Couzeix (Haute-Vienne) 19
Creuse 23, 25, 30, 33, 34, 35, 91, 92, 95, 98, 101, 102, 103, 118, 129, 176
  antisemitism in 130, 134, 139, 142, 147, 177–80, 183

establishment of children's homes in 152, 154, 158, 159–64, 181, 186, 187, 192
  Jewish refugees in 13, 111, 185, 188
  labor shortage in 42, 44, 173
  politics of 49, 178
  religion in 177–8
  Resistance in 10, 53
crime 19, 51, 54, 153
  Gypsies and 96, 98, 99, 107
Crocq 129, 130, 159, 160, 162, 163, 168, 179, 180, 182

Daladier, Édouard 115
David, Robert 69
demarcation line 11, 50, 76, 116, 146
denunciation 31–2, 180, 181, 190, 191
  of Jews 138–9, 142, 179
  versus délation 138–9
deportation 189, 194
  for German labor 50
  of Jews 14, 16, 83, 116, 130, 143, 153, 171, 175–6, 188
  mass 112, 143–44, 174
  protection from 146, 183
  Vichy government cooperation with Nazis 144
Derys, Gaston 134, 141
Deutsch, Abraham 81, 121
displaced persons 65, 67, 70, 80
drôle de guerre, See also Phony War 60, 63, 74
Droux (Haute-Vienne) 61
Ducombeau, Amédée 71

Écho des Réfugiés, L' 78, 80, 82
Eclaireurs Israélites 157
economic aryanization 116, 132, 137
education 71, 81, 156, 157, 159, 166, 170, 175, 186
Eigen-Sinn 17
employment 52, 58
  foreigners and 121
  Jews and 132–3, 146
  Nomads and 100–3
  rural 43
espionage 89

evacuations 21, 22, 57, 60, 63, 64, 66, 68, 70, 71, 74, 78, 79, 121, 123, 154, 157, 159, 165
Evaux-les-Bains (Creuse) 118, 129
exodus/*exode* 21, 23, 94, 146
Eymoutiers (Haute-Vienne) 39

family packages. See also *colis familiaux* 25, 32–9, 52, 135–8, 180
families 3, 6, 12, 35, 37, 38, 44, 48, 55, 57, 58, 66, 68, 80, 113, 119, 127, 134, 137, 144, 145, 147, 148, 157, 159–60, 163, 175, 183, 184, 185, 186, 189, 190, 194, 195
  Gypsy 88, 100, 102–3, 103–8
  National Revolution and 18, 33–4, 93, 103–8, 109
farmers 11, 26, 30, 33, 39, 41, 43–5, 52, 69, 131, 132, 135, 136, 140, 141, 145, 146, 162, 180, 181, 186, 189
  POWs and 42
  requisitions and 45, 48
  theft and 19, 51, 96, 97, 100, 102
Felletin (Creuse) 103
Feuilles dans le vent 70
"Fifth Column" 61, 84
"Final Solution" xv, 170, 174
First World War. See also Great War 8, 41, 167
food riots 22, 30
forains 88, 91, 93, 95, 96, 97, 98, 99, 100, 102, 103, 106, 107, 110
  definition of 87
Forbidden Zone 76
Foreigners 3, 4, 13, 14, 20, 65, 76, 83, 90, 113, 114–5, 118, 119, 121, 127, 128, 138, 185, 187, 189, 192, 193, 196
foyers 74–5, 84
Franco, General Francisco 65
Franco-Prussian War 89, 91
free zone. See also unoccupied zone 11, 93, 119, 145, 146, 179
  occupation of 6, 130
French Army 4, 62, 125

French citizenship 129
French Revolution 194
French sovereignty 46, 76, 191
French State 14, 28, 33, 45, 46, 86, 110, 125, 194
Fusion Amicale des Réfugiés d'Alsace et Lorraine, La 73, 77

gardens 75, 78–9, 105, 168–70, 177, 184
Gaullist propaganda 178
gazogène 98, 103
Gendarmerie Nationale 19, 57, 99, 124
Gender roles 13
German troops 4, 10, 12, 50–1, 93, 103, 111, 165, 188
Germans 6, 10, 40, 45, 46, 48, 50–1, 53, 62, 76, 83, 84, 147, 151
Germany 4, 7, 9, 12, 15, 21, 23, 42, 50, 52, 55, 57, 59, 60, 61, 71, 76, 110, 114, 146, 151, 156, 165, 168
Grand-Bourg (Creuse) 158
gray market 6
Great Depression 44
Great War. See also First World War 7–8, 22, 41, 71, 89–90
Groupement de travailleurs étrangers (GTE) 116, 118
Guéret (Creuse) 25, 102, 129, 130, 153, 158, 159, 160, 161
Guingouin, Georges 49–50, 52–4
Gurs concentration camp 185
Gypsies. See also Nomads and Roma 3, 4, 13, 18, 45, 77, 85, 94, 101, 191
  assimilation of 89, 110, 192, 194
  attitudes towards 86, 103, 110, 131
  begging and 104–5
  children 104–8
  criminality and 88–9
  Franco-Prussian War and 91
  Great War and 89
  internment of 14, 89–90, 93, 103, 107–9, 196
  Jews and 192–4
  laws regarding 87–91
  theft and 95–100, 131

Habsburg Empire xv, 7
Haute-Vienne 154, 159, 164, 172–3, 175, 177, 179, 181, 183, 185, 187, 190, 191
Henriot, Philippe 134
Himmler, Heinrich 194
Hitler, Adolf 48, 52, 62, 76, 114, 151, 167
Hitler-Stalin Pact. See also Nazi-Soviet Pact 49
Humanité, L' (Communist newspaper) 48, 49

Internat 164
internment camps. See also concentration camps 135, 137
  for foreigners 115, 118
  for Gypsies 106, 108, 109, 110, 194
  for Jews 116, 174
Israelite Social Aid Agency 83, 121
Israelites. See also Jews 114, 148, 175, 179

Jacques-Henry (Prefect) 35–6, 111, 112, 128, 129, 147, 183
Janailhac (Haute-Vienne) 103, 106
Jewish Statutes 81, 114, 115–6, 132, 155, 165–6, 179, 182
Jewishness 193
Jews 3, 4, 13, 18, 113, 149
  Alsatian 59, 76–7, 80–3, 118, 121
  blamed for shortages 14, 40, 112
  foreign 11, 45, 81, 111, 114–6, 118
  housing 112, 119–28
  identity/ration cards and 14–5, 143, 148
  indifference and 14, 112, 113, 118, 124, 126, 128, 129, 145, 154, 190
  in Limoges 81, 86, 116, 120–5
  National Revolution and 115, 143
  in newspapers 82, 134
  public opinion 16, 117–8, 124
  rescue of 145–7, 171, 193, 195
  in rural areas 43, 128–43, 150, 155
  in Saint-Léonard-de-Noblat 128–31, 133, 136, 145, 147

September 27, 1940 law and 81, 118–9
versus Israelites 114
Jura 35

Koenig, Joseph 167
Kristallnacht pogroms 90, 115

La Serre-Bussière (Creuse) 158
La Souterraine (Creuse) 25, 99, 129, 153, 161
Le Couret (children's home) 164, 166, 168, 176, 181
Le Dorat (Haute-Vienne) 124, 138
Le Havre 9
Le Masgelier (children's home) 158, 162, 168, 169
Le Moustier (Haute-Vienne) 26, 84
League of Nations 5
Les Granges (children's home) 159–61, 182, 184
Liberation 189
Limoges 2, 19, 24, 25, 26, 28, 29, 30, 38, 40, 56, 63, 73, 75, 77, 78, 82, 85, 97, 100, 117, 120, 128, 135, 144–5, 186
  occupation of by Germans 51
  population of 116, 119
  porcelain and 10, 44, 59
Loinger, Georges 178
Loire Valley xv, 9, 15
Lyon 10, 12

Malnutrition 9
Maginot Line 57
Magnac-Laval (Haute-Vienne) 44, 68
Mainsat (Creuse) 158
maquis xiii, 10, 47, 48, 50, 52–4, 188
Marianne, as symbol 72
Markets 19, 20, 23, 25, 26, 27–9, 30, 32, 38, 87, 96, 101, 111, 130, 131, 147
Marseilles 10, 12, 32, 185
Massif Central 10, 47
Meyer, Camille 82
Mézières (Haute-Vienne) 136, 145–6
Moissannes (Haute-Vienne) 100, 102–3

Montintin (children's home) 164, 166, 167, 168, 176, 177
Montreuil-Bellay camp for nomads 107
morality 61, 142

Nantes 9
National Assembly 23
National Revolution 4, 8, 13, 14, 16, 21, 24, 25, 32, 33, 34, 38, 44, 45, 46, 47, 86, 93, 101, 103, 107, 110, 111, 115, 139, 141, 143, 150, 155, 164, 165, 166, 170, 171, 183, 189, 190, 195, 196
Nationality Code 90
Nazi(s) xiii, 4, 10, 11, 12, 21, 40, 48, 49, 57, 60, 67, 93, 94, 144, 151, 154, 156, 165, 170, 173, 174, 175, 194
Nazi-Soviet Pact. See also Hitler-Stalin Pact 48
Neuilly-sur-Seine 158–9
Neuvic-Entier (Haute-Vienne) 66, 131
New France 24, 106, 108, 170
Nexon
  camp 38, 118, 144, 146
  town 38, 137
Nice 12
Nîmes xv, 9
Noé internment camp 135
Nomads. See also Gypsies and Roma 85, 90, 95, 106–8
  definition of 87–8
  immobilization of 89, 91–2, 93–4, 95, 101, 110
  National Revolution and 86, 3, 109–10
  work and 100–3, 109
Nord 76
Normandy xiii, 1, 2, 9, 158, 188

occupation xv, 4, 6, 8, 19, 24, 42, 50, 51, 76, 77, 83, 111, 130, 143, 164, 165, 173
occupied zone 9, 11, 12, 24, 46, 67, 81, 107, 109, 116, 119, 134, 137, 144, 177, 179

Oeuvre de secours aux enfants (OSE) 152, 155–82, 185–6
Oradour-sur-Glane 118, 137, 186
  massacre 10, 188
Oradour-sur-Vayres 62, 68, 184
Orieux, Jean 26–8, 84
Organisation-reconstruction-travail (ORT) 166–7, 170, 171, 173, 174, 176
Orphanages 83, 151

Paillassou, Reine (Irène) 161, 163, 175
Paillassou, Renée 163
Palestine 171–2
Paris xv, 9–10, 12, 19, 32, 33, 48, 74, 121, 129, 135, 137–8, 143, 146, 151–2, 156–62, 165, 177, 179, 184, 186
Pas-de-Calais xv, 76
patriotism 61, 62, 109, 192
peasants 3, 25, 26, 27, 28, 30, 31, 32, 34, 35, 36, 40–1, 42, 49–50, 51, 53, 54, 55, 64, 80, 94, 96, 97, 103, 130, 133, 143, 145, 150, 170, 172, 173, 178, 180, 181, 186, 191, 192
  National Revolution and 20–1, 33, 44–5, 139–41
Pétain, Philippe 4, 8, 15, 16, 18, 23, 25, 29, 32, 33, 36, 42, 44, 49, 52, 58, 76, 86, 101, 132, 144, 178, 195
Phony War, See also *drôle de guerre* 13, 22, 26, 54, 60, 70, 75, 81, 83, 84, 152, 155, 156, 158, 162, 164, 182
Poland 57, 109
police 14, 29, 44, 51, 90, 91, 115, 116, 143, 146, 147, 149, 172, 176, 184, 185
Police aux questions juives (PQJ) 112, 113, 118, 123, 125, 126, 131
Popineau, (Delegate Prefect) 47
Popular Front 157, 178, 182
Postal Control 35, 39, 40, 50
Poulouzat (children's home) 164
Pouponnière (children's home) 164, 167, 176
prisoners of war 12, 42, 102, 122, 126, 127, 141, 168, 179, 196

propaganda 20, 43, 47, 49, 82, 86, 93, 94, 134, 139, 140, 143, 150, 178, 196
Protestants 59, 72, 83, 114, 144, 145, 151, 157, 177
public opinion xv, 4, 15–6, 22, 32, 67, 86, 190
  Jews and 124, 127, 128–9, 140, 143, 145, 176, 183
  shortages and 1, 7, 25, 29, 37, 46, 54

Quakers. See American Friends' Service Committee
queues 19, 28
Rastouil, Monsignor 145
ration cards 2, 3, 5–6, 8–9, 14, 22–3, 24, 25, 35, 39, 47, 50, 52, 80, 131, 147, 158, 175, 180, 181, 195
  stamped "JUIF" 14, 111, 133, 145, 148
  theft of 53–4
rationing 5, 7, 8, 21–2, 24, 25, 26, 29, 30, 31, 45, 46, 52, 80, 94, 135, 180, 191
Ravitaillement générale (General Supply Services) 49, 80
Red Cross 56, 185
refugees 11–12, 13, 18, 20, 21, 22–4, 45, 57, 58, 60, 76–7, 94, 112, 151, 158, 161–3, 189, 191, 194
  Alsatian 56, 59, 61, 62–4, 66–70, 72–3, 75, 77–84
  foreign 3, 90, 159, 164
  Jewish 12, 111, 113–28, 130–1, 133–9, 141–50, 152, 154, 155–6, 160, 167, 170, 175, 177, 178, 181, 182, 184, 186
  Spanish 64–5
statistics 114–5, 118
Renseignements généraux (General Bureau of Information) 79, 123, 178
repatriation 21, 24, 29, 64, 65, 67, 76, 81
requisitions 5, 8, 12, 40, 45, 47, 48, 49, 50, 51, 53, 63, 119, 130, 160, 170, 180

Resistance xiii, xiv, xv, 10, 16–7, 22, 38, 46–55, 112, 117, 148, 188, 189, 195
"return to the earth" campaign 33, 43–5, 141, 168, 169, 172
Ricol, Lise 48
Rivesaltes internment camp 176
Rochechouart (Haute-Vienne) 25, 55, 63–4, 173
Roma. See also Gypsies and Nomads 88, 89, 93, 192, 194
Rothschild, Baron Robert de 158
roundups 82, 146, 149, 183

sabotage. See also Resistance 50, 53
Saint-Alpinien (Creuse) 103
Saint Germain-les-Belles (Haute-Vienne) 38, 132, 140
Saint-Gilles-les-Forêts (Haute-Vienne) 49
Saint Laurent-sur-Gorre (Haute-Vienne) 26
Saint Léonard-de-Noblat (Haute-Vienne) 98, 106, 107, 128–31, 133, 135–6, 139, 145, 147
Saint-Nazaire 9
Saint Pierre-de-Fursac (Creuse) 152, 158
Saint-Yrieix (Haute-Vienne) 71
Sauviat-sur-Vige (Haute-Vienne) 97, 102–3, 106, 135, 139
Saliers camp 93, 109
schools 71–2, 83, 84, 157, 159
  Jewish children and 81, 145, 147, 163–4, 167, 170, 184, 186
  shortages of 58
Schwartz, Lotte 160, 163, 168
Seine
  Department of 157
  River 151
Service du travail obligatoire (STO). See also Compulsory Labor Service 15, 50, 51, 52, 53
shopkeepers 70, 131, 145
shortages xiv, 2–3, 4, 11–13, 16, 21–2, 25, 28, 31, 32, 33, 37, 40, 41, 46, 48, 53, 54, 59, 60, 64, 66, 70, 78, 86, 95, 96, 104, 108, 118, 135, 139, 141, 162, 168, 180, 184, 190–1, 195, 196
First World War and 7–8, 90
food xiii, 1, 5–6, 19–20, 24, 45, 47, 50–1, 58, 109, 130, 131, 134, 143, 153, 189
fuel 9, 23, 26, 29, 44, 98, 112, 189
housing 6, 23, 51, 58, 112, 119–29, 134, 143, 189
labor 8, 21, 42–3, 45, 69, 102, 103, 114, 170
outsiders and 14–5, 18, 20, 84, 110, 150, 153, 191–2
social service workers 74
socialists 151, 157, 178
Soviet Union 49, 156
Spain 64, 129, 175, 195
Spanish Civil War 64
Star of David 112
Statut des Juifs. See Jewish Statutes
surveillance 29, 44, 61, 70, 82, 89, 90, 91, 94, 98, 103, 110, 128, 136, 146, 172, 180, 181
Sussac (Haute-Vienne) 52
Switzerland 175, 195
système D 6

theft 19, 20, 21, 47, 51–3, 55, 85, 94, 95–100, 102, 112, 192
Third Republic 4, 7–8, 11, 13, 21, 22, 23, 44, 48, 57, 58, 60, 67, 76, 87, 90, 91, 92, 93, 110, 155, 171, 193, 194
Toute la Vie 107
Tulle (Corrèze) 10
Union générale des israélites de France (UGIF) 82, 169, 173–4, 177, 182
unoccupied zone. See also free zone 9, 10, 11, 12, 14, 43, 76–7, 78, 83, 103, 113, 134, 137, 143, 152, 166, 183, 184, 195

vacation colonies. See also *colonies de vacances* 64, 156
Vallat, Xavier 117
Vallotton, Annie 56, 62, 66–8, 75

Vallotton, Benjamin 70
Vallotton, Gritou 56
Vel d'hiv round-up 143
Veyrac (Haute-Vienne) 68
Vichy regime xiii, xv, 1, 3, 4, 7, 8, 13, 15, 16, 17, 18, 20, 21, 24, 25, 31, 37, 40, 42, 45, 46, 48, 49, 50, 53, 54, 76, 78, 82, 83, 90, 91, 93, 99, 101, 107, 109, 110, 112, 115, 117, 127, 139, 153, 154, 155, 162, 165, 171, 174, 176, 177, 178, 180, 182, 188, 190, 193, 194, 196

Walter, Michel 62, 66
women 3, 8, 10, 16, 20, 22, 26, 28, 42, 56, 60, 61, 71, 74, 75, 85, 94, 95, 96, 97, 98, 100, 107, 109, 114, 135, 139, 147, 150, 161, 189, 194, 195
  black market and 37, 140, 141
  deportation of 144, 171
  Resistance and xiii, 46–7, 48
  wives of interned men 137
workers 3, 5, 9, 42, 43, 44, 54, 119, 121, 131, 161, 162, 167, 171, 173
  conscription of 50, 52

xenophobia xv, 18, 59, 75, 84, 91, 106, 110, 114, 132, 160, 171, 185, 192–3

yellow stars. See also Star of David 112, 134, 184
Yoors, Jan 96
young people 71, 153

For EU product safety concerns, contact us at Calle de José Abascal, 56–1°, 28003 Madrid, Spain or eugpsr@cambridge.org.

www.ingramcontent.com/pod-product-compliance
Lightning Source LLC
La Vergne TN
LVHW040735250326
834688LV00031B/309